Further Education & Training

History

Politics

Practice

Edited by Michael Murray,

Bernie Grummell & Anne Ryan

MACE
PRESS

First published 2014
Copyright: Authors' and Editors' own

Published by MACE Press

MACE Press is the publishing division of Maynooth University Department of Adult and Community Education. It provides a forum for writers and researchers concerned with radical education, theory and practice, policy making and innovation.

MACE Press, Maynooth University Department of Adult and Community Education, Maynooth University, Maynooth, Co Kildare, Ireland.

ISBN 978-0-9568411-2-4

Cover Design: Siobhán Clancy

Logo Design: Siobhán Clancy

CONTENTS

LIST OF TEXT BOXES

LIST OF FIGURES AND TABLES

ACKNOWLEDGEMENTS

We are grateful to the present and past students and staff of the Department of Adult and Community Education whose experiences as learners and educators inform this book.

LIST OF CONTRIBUTORS

Bríd Connolly is a lecturer in the Department of Adult and Community Education, Maynooth University. Bríd started working in adult and community education in 1985 as a women's studies tutor. There she learned about feminist pedagogy and critical groupwork. Subsequently, she brought that experience into work with people with disabilities and community development and education, both in local communities in the hinterland and within Maynooth University. Her research interests centre on critical pedagogy, 'really useful practice' and praxis.

Camilla Fitzsimons is a lecturer in the Department of Adult and Community Education, Maynooth University. Camilla has worked in a number of community education initiatives since the 1990s including women's groups, vocational groups, resident groups and campaign groups. Her publications in recent years include consideration of the community education landscape in the face of neo-liberal incursion, professionalization of community work, and the impact of accreditation on all types of community education - vocational, personal and political.

Bernie Grummell is a lecturer and research manager with the Departments of Education and Adult and Community Education, Maynooth University. Bernie's inter-department role involves developing and supporting research pertinent to both departments. She also lectures in research methods, sociology and equality in education. She has been involved in European and international research projects to enhance gender equality in education, develop adult literacy and critical media programmes, support lifelong learning, and create transformative education networks.

Kevin Hurley is a former Director of Adult Education at UCD. In retirement, he has acted as volunteer tutor, coordinator of the Return to Learning Programme and Facilitator of the Quality Framework at the Adult Learning Centre, Dun Laoghaire VEC, and as a VSO Volunteer in the Higher Education Relevance and Quality Agency, Ethiopia. In 2012 he completed a PhD at the Equality Studies Centre, UCD having previously graduated with a Masters in Adult and Community Education at Maynooth University.

Michael Murray is a sociology lecturer in the Department of Adult and Community Education, Maynooth University. He is Co-Director of the MA Community Education Equality and Social Activism (CEESA) and his research interests include education for political citizenship, power and governance, Northern Ireland and Environmental Justice.

Luke Murtagh is an adjunct lecturer in the Department of Adult and Community Education, Maynooth University and the former CEO of County Tipperary (NR) VEC (now Tipperary ETB). Luke completed both a Masters and a PhD in adult education in Maynooth University in 2001 and 2009 respectively. Luke's primary research interest is in the history and politics of policymaking processes in Irish adult and further education. He is currently a member of the editorial board of the Adult Learner.

Jerry O'Neill graduated from university as a mature student in London and then Belfast. He worked for several years as an educator in various Further Education colleges in Scotland. Since returning to Ireland in 2010, he has worked as tutor within the VEC/ETB work-place and community education programmes. He has also been involved as tutor and supervisor in Higher Education adult educator programmes and is working on a doctoral thesis which explores the experiences of adult education tutors.

Niamh O'Reilly is Head of Membership Services in the National Adult Learning Organisation (AONTAS). She is national coordinator of the Community Education Network, and a member of the board of the European Association for the Education of Adults (EAEA). She is specifically interested in the influence of National and European policy on community education practice. Her current PhD research explores the value of non-formal adult education in offering a transformative approach to widening higher education participation.

Anne Ryan is Chair of the Department of Adult and Community Education since 2005. She is also a co-founder and academic co-director of the Edward M Kennedy Institute for Conflict Intervention and Principal Investigator for the Irish Aid/ HEA funded TEN (Transformative Engagement Network) Project involving universities and rural smallholders in Zambia and Malawi.

FORWARD

In the Irish economic crisis of the 1980s considerable emphasis was placed on the education and training as a way out of unemployment. And while there were those who argued that this investment did nothing to increase the pool of jobs, but simply made one unemployed person more employable than another, it certainly had the effect of propelling education and training centre stage in the public mind and national policy discourse in addressing unemployment.

Today's unemployment crisis is different in some significant ways to that of the 1980s.

Firstly education levels in the overall population are significantly higher than they were then. This means that not only is the education deficit much less than it was then, but that those today with lower levels of educational attainment may well be more disadvantaged now relative to the population as a whole than would have been the case in the 1980s. If the rising tide fails to lift all boats, those left behind are left further behind!

Secondly, the scale of the problem today is different. In the EU there are more than 25 million people unemployed. Of these well in excess of 5 million are under 25. The majority of these are urban, working class males. In the 1980s Ireland was something of a special case in Europe. Today it simply embodies a Union wide phenomenon.

And thirdly the Euro common currency means that national economies –never mind local ones-have no necessary direct relationship with the currency with which they must operate and no leverage over that currency in their economic decision making or management strategies. Political sovereignty and economic sovereignty have become detached.

For these reasons, then, there is a sense that whereas in the 1980's Europe was seen as our salvation, today it is experienced as part of the problem.

And this is why in the world of Adult Education there is always a concern to explicate the link between the personal and the political. It is concerned, for instance, not only to reduce unemployment and to equip learners to compete in the employment market but also that they should come to an analysis of the factors which mean that some groups are always more vulnerable to unemployment than others and, in periods of economic downturn, as in recent years, those categories will be hit first, hardest and longest. Or, to paraphrase Peadar O'Donnell's rejoinder to De Valera on the issue of emigration, 50,000 people might well continue to leave the country every year but if he was in power but it would be a different 50,000.

And in this way at least Adult Education is different from the other education sectors. While all education must be relevant, Adult Education must be relevant and radical. This is never easy. That which is relevant is sometimes not radical and that which is radical is sometimes not relevant.

The sector, therefore, even when it is not trying to manage an identity crisis is certainly managing multiple identities simultaneously, a dilemma illustrated-and dealt with in the book by the difficulties in the sector in settling on its own name.

There is a sense that Europe as it painfully emerges from the currency crisis must recognise the risks which structural marginalisation in a period of prolonged economic disarray present. An engaged, critical citizenry is central to maintaining democratic culture and institutions. History teaches us that a citizenry denied hope or opportunity within a democratic framework will ultimately look for solutions outside of that framework.

The European economic crisis is, therefore, presenting an existential challenge to the ideal of an engaged critical citizenry sharing a common conviction around secular, democratic institutions. Such a conviction is at the core of the radical tradition in Adult Education.

And considering this background, there has possibly never been a time in Adult Education where the radical has ever been more relevant!

Hence, the timeliness of this book.

Professor Tom Collins

Head, Department of Adult and Community Education, Maynooth University, 1994-2001

INTRODUCTION

FURTHER EDUCATION AND TRAINING: HISTORY, POLITICS AND PRACTICE

Anne Ryan, Michael Murray and Bernie Grummell

Further Education and Training (FET) is a relatively new term in the lexicon of Irish education. It typically refers to the organised provision of educational opportunities outside the formal primary, second level and higher education sectors. This book adopts a more substantive description of Further Education and Training as the organised provision of alternative educational opportunities outside the formal primary, second level and higher education sectors which prioritise the multifaceted needs of the learners and those sectors of the population who are otherwise poorly served by mainstream education. While the term FET is new, this type of provision has a long history. Of particular significance at this time in its history are the moves afoot to professionalise this sector. The idea for this book was to take stock of the events and circumstances that have to date contributed to this development, or are currently determining the future shape of the sector. In compiling the book we have drawn on many sources including: research conducted by the staff and students of the Department of Adult and Community Education over a period of forty years, the intimate knowledge of the sector gained from the many educators and policy-makers who have worked with or studied in the Department over those four decades and the particular experiences and insights of the individual contributors, all of whom are engaged in the FET sector.

The aim of this book is to provide an overview of the history, politics and practices that inform FET and to make that overview easily accessible particularly for new educators entering the FET sector. As the form and content of the book evolved a recurring theme emerged; a theme of competing values and perspectives that make for a philosophical tug-of-war as to the purpose of education in general and FET in particular. The following quote from Paulo Freire captures the different values and perspectives that inform education:

Education either functions as an instrument which is used to facilitate the integration of generations into the logic of the present system and bring about conformity to it, or it becomes 'the practice of freedom', the means by which men and women deal critically and creatively with reality and discover how to participate in the transformation of their world. (Freire, 1972, p. 56)

Within FET 'integration into the logic of the present system' is exemplified by those who argue that FET provision should primarily prioritise the labour needs of the economy. The authors in Chapters 4, 5 and 6 locate this perspective within a neo-liberal viewpoint which currently dominates mainstream FET thinking and is regularly presented as indisputable. Those who espouse what Freire terms the 'practice of freedom' argue that FET should have a substantially wider remit prioritising the multifaceted needs of the learners and those sectors of the population who are otherwise poorly served by mainstream education. They point out that a neo-liberal viewpoint is just that – a viewpoint that can be countered. Furthermore they claim that neo-liberal approaches to FET compound social and educational inequalities (see Chapter Four for detailed discussion on developments in our understanding of equality/inequality). What is clear from the discussions that surround FET is that there is no possibility of adopting a neutral position when it comes to the purpose of FET. Deciding not to take a position is to accept the 'status quo' or the dominant discourse.

This book is very clearly and unequivocally located within Freire's 'practice of freedom' perspective. It could be described as a book that favours a radical FET agenda; an agenda that favours education that promotes global citizenship and sustainable communities based on human rights, equality and social justice.

This book traces the significant historical events and policy milestones that led to the emergence of FET in its current form including the impact of the competing and oppositional values and perspectives. All chapters in this book to a greater or lesser extent explore how these competing values and perspectives have impacted on the development of FET to date and are likely to impact on the organisation and practice of FET in the future.

The following quote provides a good overview of the kind of thinking that informs neo-liberalism.

The timing of this book

This book is designed to chart the major changes underway in FET, to describe how they came to pass and to critique their impacts on the sector. Most notable among these changes are: (i) the creation of SOLAS (2013) – the Further Education and Training Authority with responsibility for the strategic planning, co-ordination and funding of the sector; (ii) the establishment of Quality and Qualifications Ireland (QQI) (2012) with responsibility for the external quality assurance of further and higher education and training; and (iii) the requirement that FET teachers acquire professional qualifications on programmes approved by the Teaching Council. These three developments capture the essence of the changes that will reform, streamline, co-ordinate and standardise a sector that was hitherto characterised by fragmentation and diversity. As this new era dawns the editors of this book want to ensure that newcomers to this sector can access readings that provide: (i) a concise history of the events that led to the changes that are now happening; (ii) a critical appraisal of the changes including an interrogation of the constellation of assumptions, values and beliefs regarding education that are embedded in the terminology and in practices relating to indicators of success; and (iii) an overview of FET within the broader context of the totality of educational provision.

'Name calling'

Over its long history what is now referred to as FET has had many names that include Further Education (FE), Further Education and Training (FET), Adult Education (AE), Continuing Education (CE), Lifelong Learning (LLL), and Community Education. These are all terms that have come to popularity at different times to describe educational provision outside the school and higher education sectors. At one level, the terms can be described as largely interchangeable although as each new name emerged it signalled a degree of 'repackaging' that reflects sometimes subtle and sometimes more overt shifts in emphasis relating to the conceptualisation of the sector. Chapters 1 and 2 chart the developments that have impacted on this sector and have often been accompanied by a name change. Chapter 5 looks at the often occluded philosophical repositioning that lies behind a name change. It also considers how a name change in this context is not arbitrary but rather signals an attempt to privilege a particular economic/ political perspective.

The emergence of the term FET is an interesting example of a name change. When the White Paper on Adult Education entitled *'Learning for Life'* was published in 2000, 'Adult Education' was used an inclusive or umbrella term to describe a sector that embraced particular initiatives such as community education, further education, Youthreach, VTOS and others. Since the white paper there have been an increasing number of instances where the terms 'Further Education' and 'Further Education and Training' were interchanged with Adult Education as a descriptor for the sector. As such, a term that was originally used to describe a specific type of provision within the broad sector is now being used to name the entire sector.

The transition in terminology is evident from the Department of Education and Skills website which describes the Irish education system as made up of:

- Early Childhood
- Primary
- Post Primary
- Further Education and Training
- Higher Education
- Qualifications Recognition[1]

It is clear from this listing that Further Education and Training is being used instead of adult education to describe the sector. Elsewhere on its website the Department of Education and

---

[1] http://www.education.ie/en/The-Education-System (accessed 12 May 2014)

Skills is not so clear. The quote that follows uses a variety of terms apparently interchangeably:

> Further Education covers education and training which occurs after second level schooling but which is not part of the third level system. There are a number of providers of Further and Adult Education and Training and a wide variety of schools, organisations and institutions, are involved in the delivery of continuing education and training for young school leavers and adults...[2]

Three different terms are used in these two sentences – Further Education, Further and Adult Education and Training, Continuing Education and Training. What is evident here is: (i) little if any concern with subtle or nuanced differences in terms of the meaning that may be embedded in these different terms; (ii) the use of Further Education in the definition implies a preference for it as an overarching term to encapsulate the entire sector; and (iii) a distinct emphasis on training as a key aim of non-formal provision. With regard to the importance afforded training, reskilling and upskilling are in keeping with developments in OECD and EU documents as discussed in Chapter 6.

The lack of any universally acknowledged terms or definition for activities associated with FET, adult learning, community education or Life Long Learning reflects the reality of this field of education – it is comprised of multiple histories, local specificities, contested political viewpoints and vastly differing pedagogical approaches. None of these terms are used to signify a particular theoretical perspective. In usage FET, adult learning, community education or Life Long Learning can and have all been used to describe approaches that range from the neo-liberal to the radical. While cognisant of the range of terms that are and have been in use and the potential for difference within all of them we have opted to use the term 'FET' in this book, where appropriate, particularly in describing current provision and policy discourses that are shaping this provision. In using FET, we are keen to signify that the name may be new but the sector it refers to is not new – it has a past, which means theoretical and practical expertise exists in this sector and the different opinions and philosophical positionings regarding the purpose of FET continue to be relevant. In some instances, terms such as 'adult education' or 'lifelong learning' are used in particular chapters in order to

---

[2] http://www.education.ie/en/The-Education-System (accessed 12 May 2014)

differentiate between different policy paradigms, historical perspectives and philosophical approaches towards adult learning.

Structure of the book

This book is divided into three sections – history, politics and practice. Each section and chapter is summarised below. There are 'text boxes' in some chapters. These are used to augment the main text and are intended to allow the reader to easily access supplementary information. Within these boxes the reader will find a brief introduction to a core concept or a specific term used in the main text. They are also used to summarise a key piece of legislation or policy initiative that is seminal to that chapter.

At the back of the book the reader will find a detailed timeline compiled by Luke Murtagh. It provides a comprehensive guide to the key events that have contributed to the development of FET.

There is a glossary of terms describing key organisations, legislation or policies that play or played significant roles in the FET sector (Appendix 2). In addition there is a list of the many acronyms in common usage across the FET sector in Ireland and in the EU (Appendix 1).

The editors have maintained individual author styles within each chapter whilst ensuring uniformity across the volume in line with MACE Press style guidelines.

Section 1: The History of Further Education and Training

Although the existence of educational provision outside the formal sectors in Ireland predates the foundation of the state it was not until the very end of the twentieth century that decisions were made to professionalise the sector. The history section considers the events and players that have shaped the development of FET and that ultimately led to the decision to professionalise. The section also reviews recent and current decisions that are influencing how that professionalization is being realised. The first two chapters in this section trace the history of FET from the late nineteenth century to 2014. The third chapter explores the thinking that influenced the development of community education since the 1980s. Although moves to professionalise FET have not to date addressed community education it is likely to be dealt with in the near future.

Chapter 1: Humble Beginnings: From the Recess Committee to the Murphy Report. (Luke Murtagh)

Chapter 1 examines the development of FET in Ireland from the Recess Committee in 1896 to membership of the European Economic Community (EEC) in 1973. Murtagh considers the developments that took place from a number of viewpoints including those of the State pre and post-independence, civil society including rural organisations and the newly established AONTAS, third level education providers including UCC and the RTCs, key individuals including Horace Plunkett and Alfred O'Rahilly, initial teacher training and the state qualifications' system including the competition between home grown qualifications and City and Guilds. In exploring the viewpoints of these different interest sectors or groups Murtagh illustrates how different beliefs and different concerns both stem from and influence how sectors and groups regard education's relationship with the economy, culture and society.

Chapter 2: From Murphy to SOLAS. (Luke Murtagh)

In Chapter 2, which examines FET from 1973 to 2014, Murtagh reveals how the key players such as the State, the European Union (EU) and civil society continue to influence developments. He notes the important roles played by Non-Governmental Organisations (NGOs) such as AONTAS, NALA and IITD, not only in implementing FET, but also in influencing policy development. Reflecting the increasing importance of globalisation and transnational political bodies such as the EU to Ireland's political and economic fortunes, Murtagh traces the influence of EU policy on the expansion of FET from 1997 onwards. He looks at the efforts made to counter the previously fragmented approach to FET whereby responsibility for FET was dispersed among different government departments and agencies. Murtagh details the key reports and legislation that enabled an integrated policy framework to be put in place by 2013. He notes the vital importance of key developments that made the professionalization of FET possible and without which it could not have happened. These include the establishment of the Teaching Council where FET teachers/tutors are registered, and the completion of the qualifications' system which determines the level of award to students in the FET system. The chapter concludes by looking at the on-going challenges for FET.

Chapter 3 - Community Education since 1980: Conflicting Social Forces. (Bríd Connolly)

In this chapter Connolly outlines origins of the current wave of community education as it developed in Ireland in the 1980s. She highlights the role played by adult learning, particularly women's studies, as a means of challenging structural inequalities and radicalising community development. Connolly explores the tensions between the emancipatory intentions of the grassroots community education and the social activists involved and the more conventional tendencies of mainstream society, and how these tensions play out in the practice on the ground. She appraises the potential of community education as a model of resilience, for the FET sector, in which it responds to the needs of FET students by developing distinctive curricula and pedagogies and support for the FET educators.

Section 2: The Politics of Further Education and Training

This section focuses on the beliefs embedded in the discourses that are shaping the development of FET. The key arguments raised in this section are that neo-liberal FET policy discourses are increasingly proffering the view that the main purpose of education is to service the needs of the economy. These discourses tend to be presented as a "self evident fact" or "common sense", rather than one of a possible range of perspectives. The section reviews how neo-liberal policies create conditions that increase societal inequalities and marginalisation.

Chapter 4 - Taking Shape, Shaping Up, Changing Shape: Equality and Human Capital. (Kevin Hurley)

This chapter identifies the dominant perspectives in Ireland and the EU that have shaped FET from the 1970s to the present. Hurley considers the perspectives on equality evident in the Murphy Report 1973 – the first government report on FET – to the Green and White Papers on Adult Education 1997 and 2000, which revealed low levels of adult literacy. Hurley reveals how these perspectives reflect different definitions of equality. He particularly points to the emphasis on 'human capital' development and the philosophy of neo-liberalism as key policy drivers at EU and Irish government levels and he argues that due to these influences mainstream discourses of equality in the FET sector assume that inequalities are inevitable.

The chapter also includes the views of adult learners and educators on equality in society and in their experience of FET.

Chapter 5 - What's in a Name? Terminology, Power and Contestation. (Michael Murray)

This chapter focuses on the use of terminology in FET. The key argument offered is that efforts at defining terms, either by policymakers or practitioners, constitutes an exercise in power by attempting to privilege a particular philosophical and political approach over another.

Murray argues that in the FET sector the approach readily associated with a neo-liberal/ managerial perspective (and linked to increasing societal inequalities) has consistently been in conflict with a perspective that is rooted in humanism and emanicpatory discourses. He explores this conflict in the context of four key terms – further education, learner centredness, the role of the teacher/ educator and critical reflection. He argues that attempts at domination by the policymaking/ managerial discourse remain unsuccessful and this can be at least partly explained by: a lack of understanding of the nature of FET – at local and national levels; a lack of coherent research available for policymakers on the nature of FET learning; and a growing opposition by FET practitioners to what is viewed as the attempted colonisation of their discipline by neo-liberal and market forces, ultimately leading to greater societal inequalities. Lastly, he argues, that practitioners must be made aware that there are no self evident 'truths', rather the purpose and meaning of FET is highly contested and that conflicting political and economic discourses reflect conflicting viewpoints.

Chapter 6 - FET: Responding to Community Needs or Shaping Communities to suit a Global Marketplace in Crisis? (Bernie Grummell)

This chapter, as the title suggests, explores the competition between labour market needs and learner needs. It argues that policy changes increasingly emphasise discourses of employability and professionalization and favour the former to the detriment of the latter.

Grummell argues that employability is increasingly promoted as the principal objective of further education, with success measured by the achievement of awards and progression to employment or higher education. She claims that such changes shift attention away from the learner and learning processes. The chapter explores the implications of such a shift in terms of (i) how FE is defined in the Irish context (ii) how FET performs in the context of a neo-liberal employability agenda, and (iii) the role of professionalism in the governance and organizational structure of FET. Grummell claims that changes in these areas have profound impacts on the learning and knowledge base of FE, restricting the social justice and transformative capacity of FE.

Section 3: The Practice of Further Education and Training

This section focuses on the practice of FET. The first chapter argues that it is crucial that FET educators and practitioners are aware that: (i) neo-liberal perspectives can be challenged; (ii) neo liberal perspectives can have significantly negative impacts within the learning spaces where educators and learners interact; and (iii) the worldviews or values of educators which are never neutral, impact on their practice. The second chapter offers reflections, insights and comments from three practitioners based on their experiences of teaching and learning within the FET sector.

Chapter 7: Philosophical Imperatives within FET. (Anne Ryan)

This chapter highlights the importance of creating positive learning opportunities that acknowledge, value and consciously seek to reaffirm the identity, lived experiences and ways of knowing of all involved. Ryan argues that to do so FET needs to maintain the kind of radical interrogatory stance that has characterised a great deal of the educational theory and practice in this sector to date. She reviews the powerful role of the teacher/ educator as an agent of change; and calls for pedagogical expertise on the part of the teacher/ educator that transcends that of the mainstream classroom teacher.

Chapter 8: Practitioner Reflections on FET (Jerry O'Neill, Camilla Fitzsimons and Niamh O'Reilly)

In this chapter three practitioners offer insights from their experiences. Jerry O'Neill reflects on his own journey as a learner and educator, with a specific focus on the potential of narrative reflections in nurturing critically-engaged and democratic modes of educator development and knowledge. Camilla Fitzsimons shares her experiences of working as community educator. She argues that community education concerned with social justice and FET from a neo-liberal perspective make uncomfortable bedfellows. In such an encounter she fears that the result will be the dismantling of community education autonomy and diversity, and the blunting of its political intent. Niamh O'Reilly explores the challenge of advocating for a radical social justice agenda that is contrary to the ideology of the dominant neo-liberal national policies. She explores the fundamental dilemma of holding onto one's principles, whilst essentially being part of the system she wishes to change.

Conclusion - Further Education and Training: The Trojan Horse (Anne Ryan)

The final chapter considers the challenges and opportunities inherent in the repositioning of FET as part of the State's overall educational provision. Utilising the analogy of the Trojan Horse, Ryan explores possibilities for those involved in shaping FET policy and practice to engage with and influence the State's overall education provision. To date the professionalization of FET in terms of the programmes for initial educator training and the terminology used in all aspects of this training are drawn directly from the formal education sector. This has many drawbacks especially in relation to pedagogical considerations; however, it also has advantages. As FET is professionalised it finds itself no longer positioned as marginal or peripheral to the wider education provision but instead it finds described as an integral part of that provision. This new positioning offers unprecedented opportunities for those involved in FET to interact with the formal sector on the big issues pertaining to the purpose of education in the twenty-first century. This chapter calls on FET to honour its radical agenda by responding to the challenges this poses for the sector and to do so in ways that draw on its preference for educational provision that promotes human rights, equality, and social justice and that favours dialogue, inclusiveness and collaboration.

SECTION 1: HISTORY

CHAPTER ONE

FROM HUMBLE BEGINNINGS TO THE DAWNING OF A NEW ERA

Luke Murtagh

Introduction

Further education and training (FET) in Ireland has its roots in the British administration. A growing demand for Home Rule at the end of the nineteenth century led to the British setting up a local government system here and establishing the first Irish department – the Department of Agriculture and Technical Instruction (DATI) in 1900. Technical Instruction Committees (TICs) and County Committees of Agriculture were set up in each local authority area by DATI laying the foundations of FET in Ireland. The Irish state built on these foundations but in a way that led to the fragmentation of the system.

Chapter 1 examines the evolution of FET from the establishment of the Recess Committee in 1896 by the British to the decision by Ireland to join the European Union following a Referendum in 1972. Chapter 2 examines FET from the publication of the Murphy Report in 1973 to the establishment of SOLAS and the Education and Training Boards in 2013.

The evolution of FET is viewed through the lens of the state (British and Irish), civil society, third level education, initial teacher training (ITE) and the evolution of a state qualifications' system. These lenses were chosen because of their influence on the development of FET in Ireland.

Chapters 1 and 2 are necessarily very brief and I have therefore provided some additional information for the reader in appendices to Chapter 2. A time line of the history of Irish education is provided in Appendix 3 to help the reader situate FET in its broader educational context. Appendix 2 provides some additional, detailed information on key civil society and state FET organisations.

The next section examines the impact the British and Irish states had on FET with an emphasis on the holistic view taken by the British and the approach of the Irish which led to the fragmentation of FET.

The British Administration

As the time line shows (Appendix 3), the British Administration was active in primary, secondary and higher education following the Act of Union in 1800. The national schools' system began in 1831. Universities were established in Cork, Galway and Belfast in 1849 and Queens University was set up in 1850. The Intermediate Education Act (1871) allowed the state to fund private secondary schools through payments based on the results of the Intermediate Certificate Examination (Byrne, 1999; Coolahan, 1981).

FET received limited attention from the British until 1895 when the Recess Committee (see Box1) was established to report 'on the present economic conditions in Ireland' (Report of Recess Committee, 1896). The Committee was set up on the initiative of Horace Plunkett, an MP, one of the founder members of the co-operative movement in Ireland.

Text Box 1.1: Recommendations of the Report of the Recess Committee 1896

1. Reform the education system.
2. Place renewed emphasis on industrially related education.
3. Create a Department of Agriculture and Industry for Ireland.
4. Transfer the functions of the Science and Art Department, South Kensington to the new Department. (Byrne, cited in Hyland & Milne, 1987, p.8)

The Committee recommended the establishment of a Department of Agriculture and Industries for Ireland; called for reform of the education system and requested a new emphasis on industrial related education. In the event, the British Administration adapted the recommendations of the Recess Committee and established DATI and TICs in 1900 following the passing of the Agriculture and Technical Instruction (Ireland) Act in 1899. The new department was significant for FET and was a step on the road to home rule, - a burning issue in Ireland at that time.

As well as providing technical education through the local technical schools the TICs supported technical education in primary and post primary schools (Coolahan, 1981) and provided adult education courses geared to needs of agriculture and industry in their local area.

The new system was democratic and gave considerable responsibility to local TICs, who prepared FET plans for their own area. Funding was through a contribution from the rates by the local authorities and a grant from DATI. However, as Coolahan (1981, p. 89) argues, 'a serious difficulty in the path of technical education was the inadequate finance made available for laying the foundations of a new system'. The development of the system was further constrained by the outbreak of the First World War in 1914, the Easter Rising in 1916, the War of Independence and the Civil War.

The Irish Free State

Following the establishment of the Irish Free State in 1922 responsibility for FET passed to the Department of Agriculture first and in 1924 to the Department of Education (DE) (Coolahan, 1981). Agricultural education and training was now separated from training in education and general training. During the early part of its existence the Irish Free State focused on developing curricula at both primary and post-primary level to firmly establish the place of the Irish language, history and culture in the curriculum. FET was left to its own devices because cultural nationalism was not seen as important in that sector.

As well as cultural nationalism the new state was conscious of the need to secure the support of the Catholic Church, which meant, as Coolahan (1981, p. 46) claims, 'Successive ministers for education [adopting] the view that the state had a subsidiary role, aiding agencies such as the churches in the provision of educational facilities'.

DE became responsible for technical education, which was administered by the Technical Instruction Branch, in 1924. In 1926 DE set up a committee to 'inquire into and advise upon the system of Technical Education in Saorstát Éireann in relation to the requirements of Trade and Industry' (Hyland & Milne, 1992). The Commission, chaired by John Ingram, Senior Inspector of Technical Instruction, led to the passing of the Vocational Education Act, (1930). The Act established 38 Vocational Education Committees (VECs) to replace the TICs, which had up to 70 members each. This was the first piece of educational legislation enacted by the Irish State.

15

The process of preparing and enacting the legislation demonstrated the power wielded by the Catholic Church. Because the Church was afraid of losing control of the primary and secondary education systems the Minister for Education and the Government were forced to circumscribe the role of VECs. In a letter to the bishops following a meeting with them on the legislation the Minister pointed out that:

> ...By their very nature and purpose the schools to be provided under this Act are distinctly not schools for general education. General education, after the age of fourteen years, as well as before the age of 14 years will continue to be given in Primary and Secondary Schools. (Hyland & Milne, 1992, p. 220)

In his letter to the bishops the Minister gave the Church an assurance that he would limit the scope of the legislation to such an extent that it had nothing to fear from the new system and schools.

The role of VECs' established under the 1930 Act was to provide continuation and technical education. Continuation education was for young people between 14 and 16 to help them bridge the gap between primary education and technical education. Technical education was for those between 16 and 18. There was a strong vocational emphasis in the continuation courses for 14 to 16 year olds. Technical education was education in trades, manufacturing, commerce and other industrial pursuits as well as occupations of girls and women connected with the household (Hyland & Milne, 1992). The legislation 'enabled the various vocational education committees to make a substantial impact on the national provision of adult education' (O Murchú, 1984, p. 64) and VECs to become the major statutory providers of education for adults (Department of Education and Science (DES), 1998, p. 37).

The Report also led to passing the Apprenticeship Act of (1931) which envisaged VECs playing an important part in apprenticeship education. The Act established apprenticeship committees for skilled tradesmen but these were largely ineffective. The weaknesses identified were not addressed until 1959 when new legislation was passed. The Apprenticeship Act (1959) led to the establishment of An Cheard Comhairle, an executive agency of the state, to manage, co-ordinate and develop the Irish training and apprenticeship system (Gunnigle, Heraty, & Morley, 2006).

The 1960s saw Ireland awakening from its slumber following the publication of the First Programme for Economic Expansion in 1958, the seminal OECD Report *Investment in*

Education (1965) and the application in the early 1960s to join the European Economic Community (EEC). The main focus in education was on providing free-education for all at second level, establishing a network of Regional Technical Colleges and setting up the Higher Education Authority to manage the University Sector at third level. It was 1969 before the DE eventually turned its attention to adult education when it established the Murphy Committee which reported in 1973.

While DE was neglecting FET, a separate training system was put in place by the Irish state. A new Department of Labour was established in 1966, while in 1967 the Industrial Training Act was passed. An Comhairle Oiliuna (ANCO) was constituted as an executive agency of the Department of Labour to provide apprenticeship training, training for individuals and a training advisory service (DES, 1998, p. 37; Gunnigle et al., 2006). In the meantime, CERT (the Council for Education, Training and Recruitment for the Hospitality Sector) was set up in 1964 'to provide a range of tourism related training' and the National Rehabilitation Board (NRB) came into existence in 1967 with responsibility for 'co-ordinating training and rehabilitation services for people with disabilities' (Stokes & Watters, 1997, pp. 21-31). The National Manpower service was put in place in 1971 to provide an employment service for employers and employees.

The separation of FET in agriculture from education started in 1924 with the transfer of responsibility for technical education from the DATI and was cemented with the passing of the Agricultural Act (1931), which abolished DATI and re-established County Committees of Agriculture on a statutory basis. The separation was completed by the establishment of the Farm Apprenticeship Board in 1963, the Trainee Farmer Scheme in 1971, ACOT (An Comhairle Oiliúna Talamhaíochta) in 1977 and Teagasc in 1988.

The net result was that FET in Ireland became fragmented. A host of state executive agencies were competing for learners and funding as well as duplicating service delivery, management and administration. Unfortunately, for its first fifty years of existence, the state simply expanded and developed each domain of FET separately and did not reform the institutional FET architecture it put in place. Having examined the role of the state in FET the next section considers the contribution of civil society.

Civil society

The role of civil society is examined through the contributions of cultural nationalist, rural and urban organisations as well as that of Aontas to FET. Alcock (2003) argues that civil society is located 'amidst a complex of relations between the state, the commercial market and the individual' (p. 162). Voluntary organisations, the focus of this section, are a major part of civil society.

Cultural and nationalist organisations

DES (1998) argues that the emergence of cultural nationalist voluntary organisations such as the GAA (1984) and Conradh na Gaeilge (1893) shaped the 'nature of the society which would emerge after the foundation of the State'(pp. 37-38). These two cultural nationalist voluntary organisations 'played an important part in revitalising the cultural and intellectual climate in Ireland'. In reality, both organisations provided adult education for a large section of the Irish population as key players in civil society.

Rural organisations

Training in agriculture was important in a country dependent on farming. Horace Plunkett, a pivotal player in developing Irish agriculture understood that. Consequently, he played a pivotal role in establishing DATI. He was also active in civil society and formed the Irish Agricultural Organisation Society (IAOS) in 1894, which among other things, promoted adult education and training as a way to revitalise rural Ireland. Plunkett was also instrumental in establishing the United Irishwomen (UI) in 1910, the forerunner of the Irish Country Women's Association (ICA), which was established in 1942. Both IAOS and UI, promoted the personal, social, educational and economic development of men and women living in rural Ireland.

These organisations, with their self-help, personal and community development philosophies, provided the blueprint for the growth of a significant number of other important rural organisations such as Muintir na Tíre, Macra na Feirme, the National Farmers' Association (now the IFA) and the Irish Creamery Milk Suppliers' Association (DES, 1998, p. 38).

The IU/ICA were unique among rural development organisations. They adopted a three pronged, strategic approach to FET. The first was to employ county based development officers, much like Adult Education Organisers (AEOs), the second was the organisation of summer schools from 1929 to 1945 and the third prong was to establish a dedicated adult education institution, An Grianán in 1954 (see Text Box 1.2). The organisation reaped the rewards for strategic planning by getting financial support from the Kellog Foundation for the establishment of An Grianán (Heverin, 2000).

Text Box 1.2: An Grianán

An Grianán was the first ever residential adult education college for women in Ireland. In 1954 adult education was simply a thought in the minds of forward looking people. An Grianán turned that dream into a reality

The establishment of An Grianán owes much to the summer schools which had been held throughout Ireland from 1929 to 1953. (Heverin, 2000, pp. 65-66 and 120-125)

Urban organisations

If national rural organisations were the driving force behind adult and FET in rural Ireland, the trade union movement, inspired by the Worker's Educational Associations in other countries, and the Catholic Church were instrumental in setting up the People's College (1948), the Dublin Institute of Adult Education (1950) and the College of Industrial Relations (later the National College of Ireland) in 1951. O Murchú (1984) argues that these initiatives 'broadened access to adult education for trade unionists and workers during a period when increasing industrialisation… was beginning to alter the pace, structure and texture of Irish society' (p. 45).

An initiative that had national ramifications for training in business was the establishment of the Irish Management Institute (IMI) in 1952 by a group of businessmen with the support of the state. The new organisation recognised that training for managers was at the core of its existence. Consequently, IMI established an education and training committee which published a report entitled *Education and Training for Management* in 1956. By 1957 IMI had appointed a full time director and in 1965 Ivor Kenny, who later chaired the Commission on Adult Education (1984), became Director. An indication of the scale of the IMI operation is that by 1967 2,600 people were attending IMI courses annually and in 1972 it took over responsibility for supervisory management training in Ireland (Cox, 2002).

Aontas

Nineteen sixty nine was a milestone in the development of FET in Ireland when Aontas, a voluntary representative body for organisations and individuals interested in promoting and developing adult education in Ireland, was founded by Fr Liam Carey, who later became head of the Adult and Community Education Centre at Maynooth University. Aontas has played a key role since in developing, researching and critiquing adult education in Ireland. Both the VECs (now the ETBs) and the higher education sector contributed in large measure to developing and strengthening Aontas (see Text Box 1.3). In pursuit of its objectives Aontas: (i) carries out research on aspects of adult education including FET; (ii) publishes the outcomes of research, policy and position papers, internal reports including an Annual Report and Financial Statements, Regional meetings, the Learners Forum and Strategic Plans as well as the Adult Learner Journal, Explore Magazine and a weekly e-bulletin; (iii) participates in transnational work in adult education and FET.

Text Box 1.3: Aontas

Aontas was established in 1969 to be the representative organisation for those interested in adult education.

Its budget in 2012 was €917,720 of which €887,000 is core funding from DES. It has a staff of 9 people. Its membership in 2012 was 474. 54% of which were organisations and the remaining 46% individual members.

Organisation Members Types
- Women's and Men's groups
- Family Resource Centres
- Partnership Companies
- Museums
- Libraries
- Education and Training Boards, Third Level and Further Education Providers

Individual Member Types
- Adult Learners
- Tutors
- Facilitators
- Organizers of Adult Education
- Those interested in Adult Education.

(Aontas, 2013)

The work of Aontas involves:

- Supporting and developing the membership
- Influencing policy
- Making representation
- Promoting adult education
- Operating an information and referral service

In the next section the role of third level institutions in the development of FET is reviewed through the work of the universities and the emergence of the institutes of technology (IOTs).

The role of the third level sector

Universities

While Horace Plunkett was promoting FET in the state sector and civil society, Alfred O' Rahilly took up the cudgel for the universities after joining the staff of UCC in 1914. Like Plunkett, he was to leave an indelible mark on FET in Ireland. With the support of James Connolly and senior staff in UCC, he developed the University Extension Movement with the aim of promoting higher education in the Munster region and for the working class. Throughout his career O'Rahilly maintained good relationships with the trade union movement (O'Sullivan, 1989).

The extension programme had limited success at first. However, when O'Rahilly was appointed President of UCC in 1943, he actively promoted extension education. O'Rahilly developed Diploma Courses in Social and Economic Science, Social and Rural Science, Social Study and Social and Domestic Science from 1946 onwards. The extension approach proved a useful vehicle for delivering exciting new programmes to adult learners throughout Munster by co-operating with the recently established VECs. Co-operation between UCC and the VECs was facilitated by the wide brief given to VECs by the 1930 VEC Act (Ó Murchú, 1984, p. 68-69).

University College Dublin was inspired by O'Rahilly to follow suit and establish an Extension Courses Department in 1948 (McCartney, 1999, p. 180), while extension courses in University College Galway started in 1969 and Maynooth University established the Centre for Adult and Community Education in 1975 (DE, 1970).

The emergence of Regional Technical Colleges (IOTs)

The monolith of the universities as sole providers of higher education was broken following the *Report to the Minister for Education on Regional Technical Colleges* (1969) (DE, 1969). RTCs (Regional Technical Colleges) enrolled their first students in 1969. The system developed from then to become IOTs. A key function of the RTCs was to promote both FET and adult education.

Teacher training is provided at third level in modern education and training systems. The next section explores the growth of initial teacher education (ITE) in FET from short summer courses in 1900 to fulltime courses in the intervening years up to 1972.

Teacher training

'Initial teacher education is probably the single most important factor in having a well-performing public education system' (DES, 2012a, pp. 5-6). This reality was recognised by both the British and Irish governments. For example, within two years of the establishment of the National School system in 1831, the National Board of Education began training primary teachers and by 1838 it had opened Marlborough Street College (now the headquarters of DES) for training national teachers (Durcan, 1972).

One of the challenges faced by DATI and TICs was the availability of properly qualified teachers. To achieve its objective DATI organized summer courses from 1901 onwards in science, drawing, manual instruction, domestic economy and art. The scale of the challenge in implementing its policy is illustrated by the fact that 737 trainee teachers attended teacher training courses organised by DATI in 1907 (DATI, 1908).

The Report of DE for 1924-25 provides a historical background to the development of the FET system. The report asserts that ' the majority of the staffs of our Technical Schools have been trained at (a) Summer courses, (b) special courses [Woodwork, Metalwork] (c) Schools of Art or (d) Schools of Domestic Economy' (DE, 1926, p. 66).

The training of teachers for technical subjects was a particular challenge for the new Irish State. The Irish State built on the model developed by DATI of providing short intensive teacher training courses (special courses) for each technical subject. In time these were replaced by fulltime courses based in Coláiste Carman Gorey, Bolton Street, Cathal Brugha Street, St. Catherine's Blackrock and St Angela's Sligo.

By 1970 the first step in co-ordinating and integrating FET ITE took place with the Government decision to establish Thomond College of Education on the grounds of NIHE Limerick (later UL) to train Physical Education teachers. We will discuss how Thomond College became the location for teacher training for all technical subjects except Art and Home Economics in Chapter 2.

A part of ITE and education and training is an effective state, quality assured qualifications' system. The early stage of developing such a system is discussed next and the final stages in the evolution of a fully integrated qualifications' system will be considered in Chapter 2.

State qualifications' system

The early part of Irish education was dominated by examinations under the payment by results system at both primary and second levels.

In FET, an important part of the work of DATI was to train teachers for technical schools and to decide on the nature of the qualification needed to become a recognised teacher. DATI therefore developed a qualifications' system for permanent posts as teachers of Woodwork and Metalwork for Technical Schools in 1905. However, DATI also continued to recognise the City and Guilds teacher's qualifications in both subjects.

The continued recognition of City and Guilds qualifications is interesting because qualifications offered by that body still form part of FET today. DE, in its first report of the Irish education system in 1926, gives a neat summary of the examination system introduced by DATI for learners. '...Until 1913 when the Department's own Technical School examinations system was established students sat examinations under the Science and Art Department South Kensington, the City and Guilds Institute, the Royal Society of Arts, and other examination bodies'.

A revised system of technical examinations in building, electrical engineering, motorcar engineering, commerce, applied chemistry, domestic economy and art was introduced in 1936 (DE, 1935, 1938), and the Group Certificate was introduced in 1948 for students

23

attending Vocational Schools. However, their existence was short lived when both the Group and Intermediate Certificates were replaced by the Common Intermediate Certificate in 1966. The Leaving Certificate was also reformed at that time and a broadened Leaving Certificate Course, which included technical subjects, was introduced. These decisions made a useful contribution to the development of a state qualifications' system for FET.

Another important step in the development of a state qualifications' system for FET came in 1971 when the National Council for Education Awards (NCEA) was established to provide a national awards system for the newly established RTCs and the NIHE in Limerick. The NCEA developed a system of National Certificates, Diplomas and Degrees. Its work was to have a profound effect on certification in higher education and in FET (White, 2001).

Conclusion

The state had an important, formative role in the development of FET in Ireland from 1896 when the Recess Committee reported until accession to the EU in 1973. The British built the foundations of the system when they established DATI and the TICs as well as County Committees of Agriculture. When the Irish state took responsibility for FET it embarked on an unwitting strategy of segregating technical from mainstream education and both from training. The state fragmented the training system into apprenticeship, general training and sectoral training through a series of piecemeal reforms.

The fragmented approach to FET meant that limited attention was paid to training FET teachers and tutors and to developing a comprehensive qualifications' framework for education and training. The net result was that a series of ad hoc arrangements were made to cater for sectoral teacher/tutor/instructor training, certification and qualifications' system.

Universities contributed to the growth of FET through Extension Courses pioneered by UCC and adopted by UCD, UCG and Maynooth University, while IOTs began to make their mark towards the end of the period under review.

Civil society organisations became active in adult education from the 1950s in rural and urban areas. The models of provision developed by IAOS, UI and the ICA earlier served as models for the future provision of FET in rural Ireland.

24

Perhaps the most significant development during this period in an emerging, urbanising Ireland was the establishment and growth of IMI. The birth of Aontas in 1969 was also important because it provided a forum for FET. From then on FET had a coherent voice which critiqued provision by the state and argued for an integrated and enhanced adult education service.

The foundations for a successful ITE system were laid by the development of fulltime courses and the establishment of Thomond College in 1970. A primitive state qualifications' system was also put in place from 1896 on with the foundation of a proper system being developed by the NCEA in the early 1970s.

Two people played a major role in the growth and development of FET in Ireland. Horace Plunkett founded the co-operative movement and established and chaired the Recess Committee. Alfred O' Rahilly at UCC, continually promoted adult education and the links between the University and the community it served. O'Rahilly developed a model of provision to serve the community and strengthen community links. That model was subsequently availed of by the other universities.

Text Box 1.4: Sir Horace Plunkett	Text Box 1.5: Sir Alfred O'Rahilly
Plunkett was born in Dunsany Co. Meath in 1854.He founded the Dunsany Co-operative society in 1874.	O' Rahilly was born in Listowel, Co Kerry in 1884 thirty years after Plunkett. .He was appointed a lecturer in UCC in 1914, Registrar in 1920 and President from 1943 to 1954. Unlike Plunkett, he was a nationalist and was elected to the first Dáil.
He was elected Unionist MP for South Dublin in 1892 and founded the Irish Agricultural Organisation Society in 1894.	Soon after being appointed lecturer in UCC, he joined with Professor Smiddy to start The University Extension Movement.
The Recess Committee, which he chaired, was established in 1896. The Department of Agriculture and Technical Instruction was set up in 1900 as a result. Plunkett was head of the DATI until 1907.	When he became President he initiated the process which established the Diploma Course in Social and Economic Science in 1946 taken by 105 students in Cork, Kerry and Waterford.
He died in 1932	After his retirement he became a priest in 1955 and he died in 1969.

CHAPTER TWO

1973-2013: FROM MEMBERSHIP OF THE EEC TO THE ESTABLISHMENT OF SOLAS AND THE ETBS

Luke Murtagh

Introduction

This chapter tells the story of Further Education and Training (FET) from Ireland's accession to the European Economic Community (EEC) in 1973 to the establishment of SOLAS and the Education and Training Boards (ETBs) in 2013. It should be read in conjunction with Chapters 1 and 3. The themes of the state, the European Union (EU) civil society, ITE, and the qualifications' system are explored. There will be a particular emphasis throughout on the evolving architecture of FET, the role of the EU and the rapid expansion of the system from 1997 to 2014.

FET will be divided into three domains to manage its complexity. These are the education domain, the training domain (divided into sectoral and general training) and community domain (Murtagh, 2009). Because the State embarked on a process of significant architectural (structural) reform in 2010 the period from 2010 to 2014 will be given a separate section which dispenses with domains.

First, the role of the state in the education domain from 1973 to 2010 is examined. That will be followed by an analysis of the role of the state in the training and community domains.

The role of the State in the education domain

The State continued the piecemeal approach to FET from 1973 to 2010 which had been developed between 1922 and 1972 as discussed in Chapter 1. The net effect was that FET in Ireland was left with the legacy of a flawed institutional architecture. This flawed architecture (Murtagh, 2009) cracked under the spotlight of the FÁS scandal in 2008/9 and become politically untenable by 2010. The process of devising a new architecture started in 2010 and was cemented in legislation in 2013.

The long journey to reform FET and provide the sector with a sound institutional architecture started with the publication of the Murphy and Kenny Reports discussed next.

The Murphy and Kenny Reports

The first sign of the State becoming active in the education domain was the appointment of two committees to report on adult education within fifteen years of each other. The first was the Murphy Committee which reported in 1973. The committee was appointed in 1969 by the Minister for Education to carry out a survey 'on the needs of the community in the matter of adult education and to indicate the type of permanent organisation to be set up, in order to serve those needs' (Department of Education, 1970).

The committee presented an Interim Report in 1970. The final Murphy Report is an important milestone in the history of adult education because it was the first time the Sate recognised the existence of a distinct adult education sector. The main recommendations, which set the agenda for the future organisation and development of FET are set out in Box 2.1.

Text Box 2.1: Recommendations of the Murphy Report 1973

- Provide a dedicated budget for adult education.
- Establish an interdepartmental committee to improve communication between government departments involved in adult education.
- Set up of an Adult Education Section in the Department.
- Establish County Education Committees with an adult education subcommittee.
- Appoint Adult Education Officers to develop adult education in each area.
- Provide grant aid to Aontas.
- Introduce legislation to give effect to the recommendations.

The Kenny Commission was established in 1983 and reported in 1984. Its recommendation are shown in Box 2.2

Both Reports recommended the establishment of an integrated local and national institutional architecture for FET including a National Council for Adult Education.

Recommendations of Murphy (1973) and Kenny (1984) contributed to the development of the education domain. However, the recommendations on structures were largely ignored though some changes did occur. Developments included the appointment of Adult Education Officers (AEOs) to each VEC in 1979; giving a specific remit for adult education to Community and Comprehensive schools; funding both Aontas and the National Adult Literacy Association (NALA) as well as establishing a section for FET, headed by an Assistant Principal Officer, in DES.

The response to the proposal for local adult education committees was to establish them on an ad hoc basis in each VEC (Department of Education and Science, 1998, p. 55). They didn't have responsibility for policy, staffing and financing as VEC sub-committees. That reality was underpinned by the fact that they were established in each VEC in 1984 through a circular letter rather than by statute.

The challenges to Murphy and Kenny are clearly devising structures for FET in the context of Irish education which evolved incrementally as a tripartite primary, post primary and third level system over a period of one hundred and fifty years. The tripartite nature of system was reflected in the way the Department of Education and Science (DES) was organised.

FET fared badly in an organizational model that hardly acknowledged its existence and grudgingly catered for it. The highest ranking official with direct responsibility for FET was an Assistant Principal Officer until 1998. A separate FET section, with its own Principal Officer, was not established until 1998-25 years after being first recommended in the Murphy Report (Department of Education, 1973; Murtagh, 2009).

The net effect of the low status of FET was that it was invisible to the rest of Irish education and the general public. In 1997 it represented just 0.016% of the total education budget (Hurley, 1998, p. 36). The low status was further demonstrated by the fact that most of the FET staff employed in 1997 were appointed on a part-time basis.

Nineteen ninety seven and 2000 are critical years for FET and reflect a growing commitment by the State. Nineteen ninety seven is critical because a centre-right Fianna Fáil/Progressive Democrat government was elected and remained in power for ten years. The general policies pursued by that government from the middle of its second term in office (2004-2006) coupled with a global financial crisis ultimately led to the collapse of state finances and the need for a bailout from the EU, the European Central Bank and the International Monetary Fund.

This new Fianna Fáil/Progressive Democrat government appointed was serious about FET. It appointed the first Minister for Adult Education in 1997, published a Green Paper in 1998 and a White Paper in 2000.

The year 2000 was also important because the first White Paper on Adult Education in the history of the State was published. While the White Paper failed to adequately address the issue of an integrated, effective, institutional architecture for FET it provided a roadmap for the development of other aspects of the system (Murtagh, 2009).

The Green Paper and White Paper on Adult Education

As we have seen FET moved from the periphery to the mainstream of education and public policy following the decision to appoint the first Minister of State for Adult Education in 1997, and publish Green and White Papers in 1998 and 2000.

The Green Paper (DES, 1998) was followed by a national public consultation process which fed into the White Paper. The publication of the White Paper generated great excitement and confidence in the future of FET. In broad terms, the recommendations (Department of Education and Science, 2000a) fell into three main categories - (i) FET programmes, (ii) structures and (iii) support services.

There is little doubt that the implementation of FET programmes proposed in the White Paper (DES, 2000a) led to the development of the sector by widening provision, increasing funding and the number of full-time FET staff. The programmes recommended and established included the National Adult Literacy Strategy, the Back to Education Initiative (BTEI) and Community Education.

Proposed supports for adult learners included teacher training for FET, a national qualifications' framework, improved access for marginalised groups and an adult guidance and counselling service. The adult guidance and counselling service was introduced on a phased basis. The other services proposed are discussed later in this chapter.

The proposals in the White Paper (DES, 2000a) on FET structures were deeply flawed. The government was unwilling or unable to reconcile the competing interests of the Department of Enterprise and Employment (DETE), its executive agency FÁS with those of DES (Murtagh, 2009). By way of compromise the government authorized DETE to establish a Task Force on Lifelong Learning. The White Paper also proposed an unwieldy National Adult Learning Education Council (NALC), with very little power to do anything (DES, 2004; Murtagh, 2009). The proposal to establish Local Adult Learning Boards (LALBs) was bitterly opposed by DETE and FÁS and was not implemented (Murtagh, 2009).

The Taskforce on Lifelong Learning reported in 2002 (DETE, 2002). As a result the government put an overarching structure (an Interdepartmental Committee) in place to oversee the work of NALC. NALC, set up in the same year, was suspended eighteen months later and eventually axed.

The flawed institutional architecture, developed on a piecemeal basis since the Murphy Report (1973), effectively remained in place until 2013. The White Paper (DES, 2000) did not contribute to improving the organization of FET in. the education domain.

The role of the state in the training domain of FET is considered next.

The role of the State in the training domain: 1973-2010

The training domain is discussed under the headings of general training, sectoral training, and training by private providers and businesses (Garavan, Costine & Heraty,1995). General training, is training provided by FÁS in its training centres and by private contractors, on behalf of FÁS, in the larger centres of population. It does not include apprenticeship training. Training for specific sectors of the economy is described as sectoral training and includes training in agriculture, horticulture, fishing, forestry, management, health sector etc.

General training

There was little development in general training until 1967, when the passing of the Industrial Training Act (1967) represented a policy sea change. The Act established An Chomhairle Oiliúna (ANCO) as an executive agency of the Department of Labour (Garavan et al., 1995, p. 67). The legislation re-enforced the state policy of separating the education and training domains as well as heralding a more active role by the state in FET.

The establishment of FÁS in 1987 marked a new phase in training with an element of greater co-ordination of state labour market services. Co-ordination was achieved by giving FÁS responsibility for training and retraining, for employment services, employment advisory services and employment schemes. The establishment of FÁS was achieved by amalgamating ANCO, the Youth Employment Agency and the National Manpower Service. The Minister for Labour was given an expanded role in labour market policy. The Department of Labour was later subsumed into the Department of Enterprise and Employment in 1993[1].

The process of reforming the training domain was taken a step further with the *Culliton Report* (1992), which recommended the "reorganisation of FÁS and the re-directing of resources to training for those at work and preparing for work" (Gunningle et al., 2006, p. 211). The Report led to an overhaul of FÁS and reform of the apprenticeship system.

---

1 The Department became the Department of Enterprise Trade and Employment in 1997 Administration, Vol. 55: No. 1.

There were other developments in training from 1973 to 2010. The *White Paper on Human Resource Development* was published in 1997 by the Department of Enterprise and Employment. The Qualifications (Education and Training) Act was passed in 1999 and the *Report of the Task Force on Lifelong Learning* was published in 2002.

The Expert Group on Future Skills Needs (EGFSN), recommended in the *White Paper: Human Resource Development* (DEE, 1997, p. 179) was established in 1997 as part of Ireland's response to globalisation. EGFSN published several reports. Its most important report, *Towards a National Skills Strategy* (2007), is now part of the Government's lifelong learning strategy (Department of Finance, 2006, p. 189) and has a major influence on FET policy. The terms of reference and the main recommendations are shown in Box 2.3.

A National Employment Action Plan (NEAP) was published annually by DETE from 1998 to 2004 and forwarded to the EU[2]. This plan was in effect the strategy for the training domain of FET. Since 2005, NEAP was replaced by the National Reform Programme, which has a section on labour market policy (Department of Enterprise, Trade and Employment, 2005, p. 36-50) and which also has to be forwarded to the EU.

The most significant development in the training domain and for all FET was the public scandal surrounding FÁS in the 2008/2010 period. The controversy will be discussed in the section on FET from 2010 to 2013.

---

[2] It became the National Reform Programme in 2005.

Text Box 2.3: Towards a National Skills Strategy

The Minister for Enterprise, Trade and Employment asked the EGFSN 'to identify the skills required for Ireland to become a competitive, innovation -driven, knowledge-based, participative and inclusive economy by 2020' (Expert Group on Future Skills Needs, 2007, p.5). The terms of reference were:

- To establish the impact of the level of skills on productivity growth in an Irish context
- To set out current supply and project future supply of skills and qualifications to 2020
- To identify key objectives for education and training based on likely supply and demand
- To identify the roles of key stakeholders in supporting education and training and
- To identify the features of a skills development system which will provide the required skills.

The report identified that there was a significant shortage in the labour force of those with qualifications at NFQ levels 5 and 6 and a surplus at levels 1-5, who would find it hard to get employment. The report set out the objectives for enhancing skill levels by improving the qualification level of those leaving education and training an in the workforce as follows:

- 48% of the workforce should be at levels 6-10 an increase of 16% from 2005
- 45% should be at levels 4-5 an increase of 5%
- The remaining 7% will be at levels 1-3 but should aspire to skills at a higher level.

The One-Step-Up approach will be used to encourage learners to improve their place on the NQF by one step.

Expert Group on Future Skills Needs (2005)

Sectoral training

As explained in the introduction, sectoral training is distinguished from general training because of the way the Irish training system developed in a piecemeal fashion.

The growth of sectoral training mirrored the development of general training and was the result of a "focus on occupational training" by the state. Occupational training was promoted in the tourism, agriculture, fishing, nursing and disability sectors. Selected occupations or category of worker were deemed by the state to have particular training needs provided within the occupation and by trainers drawn from the occupation (Garavan et al., 1995, p. 96).

The evolution of agricultural training over the last eighty years followed a different path from training in the education domain. In 1931 legislation established the County Committees for Agriculture with a training remit. A Farm Apprenticeship scheme was set up in 1964, just three years before the establishment of ANCO. County Committees were abolished in 1980 and replaced by ACOT and Teagasc in 1988 (Daly, 2002). Both ACOT and Teagasc were executive agencies of the Department of Agriculture with a network of local offices.

Similar structures were put place in the tourism, fishing, nursing and disability sectors. The net result was that sectors of the economy had state executive agencies responsible for training in their own particular sector. FET became fragmented as a result.

By 1997, the training domain as a whole had well developed programmes and executive state agencies like FÁS, CERT, Teagasc, BIM, Coillte etc to manage both sectoral and general training. FÁS was the most important and influential training agency with regional and local networks and a cohort of fulltime staff. FÁS had a budget of almost £480 million and just over 2000 staff in 1997 (FÁS, 1998, p. 48).

The relative maturity of the training domain by 1997 was the result of state intervention from 1960 through on-going policy evaluation, legislation and financial support. The ESF was an important policy and financial contributor to the development of the training domain of FET (Gunnigle et al., 2006, p. 227).

The next section discusses the role of the private sector in both the education and training domains from 1973 to 2010.

The role of private providers in the education and training domains

Private provision is limited in the education domain. The main providers are 18 private third level colleges (Institute of Public Administration, 2011, pp. 231-234). It can be argued that self-financing courses, catering for 156,768 adults, mainly in public schools and colleges, represent private rather than state funded provision (Department of Education and Science, 1998, p. 53)

Training is also provided by employers (in the training domain) to meet employee needs. It is delivered by specialist training companies, by employer and employee representative organisations, Skillnets and relevant professional bodies. The IALS Survey (Department of Education and Science, 1997, p. 89) shows that the Government funds 19.6 % of adult education courses. Therefore, it is reasonable to assume that private enterprise funded 80 % (circa) of provision in 1995 in particular in the training domain.

We have discussed FET in both the education and training domains. The Community education domain is reviewed next.

The role of the State in the community domain

Community education was the last domain recognised by the state because it emerged as a bottom-up, democratic and empowerment focussed movement. It developed as a distinct domain from the mid-1980s with the support of state and EU initiatives including:

- the Adult Literacy and Community Education Scheme by DE in 1985 (Murtagh, 2009)
- the Community Development Programme by the Department of Social Welfare in 1990 (DES,1998, p 90)
- the Poverty Three Programme (1989-1994) funded by the EU (Frazer, 2007, p 50)
- the LEADER Programme funded by the EU starting with a pilot programme in 1989 (Daly, 2002, pp. 530-1)
- other EU Community Initiatives including NOW, EMPLOYMENT, INTERREG
- the establishment of ADM (now Pobal) by the state in 1992, DES, 1998, pp. 89-90)

Community education contributes to countering social exclusion, poverty and inequality (*National Anti-Poverty Strategy*, Government of Ireland, 1997, p. 9) and is imbued with a self-help, can-do approach. Women's groups, in particular, have benefited from the emphasis on combating social exclusion and grew from strength to strength since 1980 through funding from both the EU NOW Initiative and by the state (see Chapter 3).

The community domain is fragmented because it is funded by multiple state and EU sources (DES, 1998, pp. 88-89). According to the *Green Paper on Supporting Voluntary Activity* (Department of Social Welfare, 1997, p. 84), twelve government departments were funding community organisations at that time.

EU Initiatives, including NOW, EMPLOYMENT, INTERREG, LEADER and URBAN, provided focus and direction as well as significant funding for the development of community education though they also contributed to the fragmentation of the sector. The history of community education is explored fully in the next chapter.

The next section discusses the role of the EU in FET.

The role of the EU in FET

EU funded FET programmes

The founder members the EEC made provision for FET in the Treaty of Rome even though, as Hantrais (2000, p. 41) argues 'education and training were only of indirect interest'. A key driver of FET policy in the EEC was the European Social Fund (ESF) established by the Treaty to 'improve employment and the geographical and occupational mobility of workers' (O'Connor, 1998, p. 57). Consequently, the ESF fund could finance FET and over 90% of the Fund was allocated to vocational training (O' Connor: 1998).

The approach of the European Commission to education and training policy was one of caution and of promoting cooperation between member states rather than through direct action. Cooperation was effected through significant funding for: (1) programmes to collect and disseminate information on the FET system throughout Europe; (2) encouraging mobility between institutions and states; (3) providing work experience and vocational training in another state; (4) programmes on adapting new technologies. Where there was a policy gap the EU directly funded innovative programmes in member states to bridge that gap (Hantrais, p. 2000).

EU policy was driven initially by a concern about unemployment, marginalisation of certain groups and regional imbalances. As we moved towards the end of the 20th century and during the first part of the 21st the emphasis shifted to growth and competitiveness with education and training seen as a key element to developing human capital (European Commission, 1993, 1995, 2000; Hantrais 2000; Nugent, 2003; O' Connor, 1998).

Since the Treaty of Maastricht in 1992 the EU has begun to take a more direct role in education and training policies and has insisted on Member States taking prescribed actions to improve education and training as they were seen as important in tackling unemployment and social exclusion and increasing growth and competitiveness. *The European Employment Guidelines* (1997) were an important step in that direction (European Commission, 1997).

EU initiatives and policy documents impacting on FET policy in Ireland, since 1973 include: (i) the *White Paper on Education, Training, Teaching and Learning – Towards the Learning Society* (1995); (ii) the *European Employment Guidelines* (1997); (iii) the *Lisbon Agenda* (2000); (iv) the *Memorandum on Lifelong Learning* (2000); (v) *A European Area of Lifelong Learning* (2001); (vi) the *National Reform Programme Strategic Guidelines for the 2005* (DETE, 2005), and (vii) the *Council Resolution on a renewed European Agenda for Adult Learning* (2011).

These are the key policy documents developed by the EU and they have set the agenda for Irish FET policy both during the period under review and for the future.

The approach FET in Ireland was heavily influenced by Membership of the EU which transformed every aspect of life in Ireland. The greatest impact of EU membership was achieved through European legislation, the European Social Fund (ESF), the Common Agriculture Policy and the European Structural Funds. European policies and funds had a very definite impact on FET in particular (O' Connor, 1998).

There were a number of important FET developments supported by the EU Social Fund and 'EU Initiatives' from 1973. EU funding supported the provision of second chance education for specific marginalised groups in Irish society as a response to unemployment and youth unemployment in particular (O'Connor, 1998) and as we have just seen contributed to the development of community education.

A significant beneficiary of ESF funding was the Vocational Preparation and Training Programme (VPTP), which evolved into the Post Leaving Certificate (PLC) programme. An indication of the importance of this development is that by 2011 PLCs had 32,688 places approved for learners (DES, 2012b). Other FET programmes receiving EU funding included Traveller Education Centres, Adult Literacy, Youthreach and the Vocational Training Opportunities Scheme (VTOS).

The EU is the most important external influence on Irish public policy (Laffan & Tonra, 2005, pp. 430-31). EU institutions that have impacted most on FET include the European Commission, the European Council, the Council of Ministers, the European Parliament and the European Court of Justice. Within the European Commission, the Directorate on

Education, Training Culture and Youth is important. Among the EU agencies the European Centre for the Development of Vocational Training (CEDEFOP) promotes vocational and continuing education and has contributed to policy development and policy analysis of the FET system. The role of the EU is also examined in Chapters 4 and 5.

Having already discussed the roles of the state, the private sector and the EU we now examine the role of civil society in FET.

Civil society

This section will consider the role of AONTAS, NALA and IITD, the three main advocacy organisations for FET, during the last 40 years. It will also examine the impact of community based providers in the past twenty years. The first civil society organisation considered is AONTAS is also discussed in Chapter 1. AONTAS grew from a volunteer led organisation with a small budget in 1969 to a professionally run outfit with a budget of €917,720 and nine staff in 2012.

The development of AONTAS was kick started in 1973 when it secured an annual grant of £15,000 for five years from PJ Carroll and Company. This money was used to establish a secretariat, undertake research and host an international conference on adult education. The position of AONTAS was further strengthened in 1976 when it received its first state funding of £10,000 following the publication of the Murphy Report (1973).

AONTAS puts the adult learner at the core of its work, has a commitment to high quality research and adult education publications including *The Adult Learner*, engages with adult education internationally, and is committed to timely and effective engagement with the FET policy process. In more recent years AONTAS engaged strategic planning (AONTAS, 2013; Ó Murchú, 1984).

Achievements include having a key role in the establishment of National Adult Literacy Agency (NALA) in 1977, successful lobbying with NALA to appoint a Minister for Adult Education (1997), support for women's groups from the 1980s on and contributing to the development and implementation of the White Paper in Adult Education. One of the tasks given by DES to AONTAS was to provide a training programme for the newly appointed Community Education Facilitators following the *White Paper on Adult Education* (2000).

The second civil society organisation is NALA, which is discussed next.

Text Box 2.4: NALA

- NALA was established in 1980 following an initiative by AONTAS arising out of the Murphy Report and holding of a conference on adult literacy in 1979.
- Its head office is based in Dublin, with a regional office in Cork.
- Its budget in 2012 was €2,068,133 of which €1,908,949 is from the Government. It has a staff of 34 people.
- Its membership numbers in 2012 was 514.

(NALA, 2013)

NALA, established in 1980 is an independent charity committed to making sure people with literacy and numeracy difficulties can fully take part in society and have access to learning opportunities that meet their needs. NALA, like Aontas, is a registered company with limited liability and charitable status. It receives a grant from DES that enables it to staff a national office in Dublin and a regional office in Cork. DES funds specific research and development work as do other government departments, state bodies, the EU and the private sector (NALA, 2013).

The publication of the IALS Report in 1997 put literacy firmly on the policy agenda. NALA seized the opportunity and actively engaged with the preparation and implementation of the *White Paper on Adult Education* (2000). Essentially, NALA prepared the first National Adult Literacy Strategy and became an executive agency of DES to oversee the implementation of the strategy (Murtagh, 2009).

NALA has engaged effectively with several government departments and agencies to promote adult literacy. Among its most exciting partnerships has been with RTÉ to provide nine TV series about adult literacy. Another is its 'Plain English' campaign to encourage state bodies and larger businesses to use simple English in all communications. NALA has grown to become a professionally run, well-funded FET advocacy organisation. Like Aontas, NALA has been strong on research, quality publications and strategic planning.

The third civic society organisation considered is the Irish Institute of Training and Development (IITD), which is very active in the training domain. The IITD was established in 1969 and has just over 2000 members. It is a 'professional body for personnel engaged in training and human resource development in the industrial, commercial and allied fields' (IPA, 2011). The organisation provides access, formal, accredited training and development programmes, short skills development courses and opportunities for continuous professional development for its members and customers (www.iitd.ie). IITD achievements include contributing to the professionalization of the training function in Irish business, developing graduate and post graduate qualifications with the university sector for trainers as well as providing a wide range of training courses for businesses.

Higher Education

The role of HE in FET has grown since 1973. Provision was expanded by the introduction of the Regional Technical Colleges (RTCs) in the 1970s and the National Institutes of Higher Education in Limerick (1970) and Dublin (1980). The government established the HEA in 1971 to oversee the university sector and the NCEA in 1979 to oversee the IOT sector.

During this period there were two other important developments in addition to those in teacher/tutor training discussed in the following section.

The first was the growth of adult education departments in HE institutions, which evolved over a thirty year period from adult education centres or units to academic departments. For example, Maynooth University formally established the Maynooth Centre for Adult and Community Education in 1975 and in the same year ran a Higher Diploma in Adult & Community Education course for FET practitioners (Corish, 1995). These initiatives in Maynooth University led to the appointment of the first professor of adult education there in 2005 and one of the first Postgraduate Diploma in FET recognised by the Teaching Council in 2012.

An example of the development of FET provision in the IOT sector happened in Waterford Institute of Technology (WIT), which in 2014 has a School of Education and a head of the Department of Adult and Continuing Education. One of WIT's initiatives was offering a degree level course for adult literacy tutors with NALA. The course arose directly out of the establishment of a Literacy Development Centre in 1997 to incorporate the NALA/WIT Accreditation Project (WIT, 2013).

The second HE development, which contributes to FET, is the increase in the number of adults attending HE. This increase was influenced by the state embracing the concept of lifelong learning in the 1990s and affirming the concept in *Learning for Life: White Paper on Adult Education* (DES, 2000). The White Paper made a number of recommendations to improve participation rates by adults and to achieve a target of 15% representation by 2005.

The higher education sector and DES responded positively. Following the *Report of the Action Group on Access to Third Level Education* (DES, 2001) the National Office for Equity of Access to Higher Education was established in 2003 to facilitate educational access and opportunity for groups under-represented in HE. The National Office published national plans in 2005 to cover the 2005 to 2007 period and in 2008 to cover the period from 2008-2013. The target set in the latest plan is to achieve a 20% enrolment by 2013.

A recent development from the perspective of FET is the strategy published by the HEA *Part-time and Flexible Higher Education in Ireland: Policy, Practice and Recommendations for the Future* (HEA, 2012). Included in its recommendations are equal treatment for part-time learners, the abolition of the distinction between full-time and part-time including financial supports by 2016 and an accessible co-ordinated applications system for all applicants to HE. While mature students still face severe barriers (HEA, 2012, pp. 28-31) and the experience of learners in individual HE institutions is far removed from the targets in the 2012 plan much has been achieved since the Murphy Report in 1973.

FET teachers/trainers/tutors

The requirement for a proper system of initial education (ITE) for FET practitioners was recognised in the Murphy Report (1973), the Kenny Report (1984), the Green Paper (1998) and the White Paper (2000). It is now also widely accepted that all educators should engage in continuous professional development (CPD) throughout their career (Department of Education, 1994; Teaching Council, 2011).

In this section we will consider ITE for those engaged in FET in the three domains, starting with education.

Teacher training in the education domain

Initial teacher education for the FET sector was largely ignored by the state until the growth of PLCs in the 1980s and the introduction of the National Adult Literacy Strategy in 2000. The growth of the PLC sector, nested in the second level system, meant the Department of Education and Skills (DES) had to develop mechanisms to facilitate teachers of specialist subjects such as hairdressing, beauty therapy and media studies becoming recognised teachers. DES was faced with a similar dilemma when it wanted to offer permanent posts to literacy tutors as part of the National Adult Literacy Strategy.

At a broader policy level the state set up the Teaching Council (TC) in 2006 to regulate the teaching profession. Its functions include approving teacher training courses for all levels of education except HE. Historically, there were was no requirements by the state for a formal teacher training system for adult educators outside of PLCs and adult literacy. However, in 2009, the TC announced that from April 2013 all FET teachers will have to register. To register, teachers will require a postgraduate qualification in FET recognised by the Council.

From November 2013 all teaching staff, including those in FET, will be required to register with the TC in order to be paid out of state funds. As a result of these requirements Maynooth University, NUIG, WIT, Mary Immaculate, Limerick and the National College of Ireland are offering the first recognised ITE Courses in 2012/2013 for those wishing to become recognised FET teachers.

These developments contribute to the professionalization of FET and enhance its status in the education sector and in society. The sector will also benefit from the radical reform of teacher education introduced by DES in 2013, which integrates primary, post primary and FET provision.

Even though there was no state requirement to have a specific FET initial teacher qualification, except in the PLC sector, many working in FET recognised the importance of a professional qualification and participated in post graduate adult education courses in HE institutions from the mid-1980s on.

Continuous professional development (CPD) is also important for FET teachers. The main providers of CPD were VECs, DES, the Qualifications' Authorities (particularly FETAC), adult education advocacy bodies and HE institutions. Provision has been uneven and not adequate to meet the needs of a sector that was constantly growing and diversifying from 1997 on.

Next we examine ITE in the training domain.

Tutors/Trainers training of in the training domain

The glass ceiling between the education and training domains of FET is never more evident than in the provision of ITE. CEDEFOP argues that

> There is no requirement for appointment as a trainer to these agencies [FÁS, Coillte, Bord Iascaigh Mhara etc] to have a prior qualification in training. All of these state-funded organisations operate a system whereby newly appointed trainers undergo skills and pedagogic training programmes suited to their industry. (CEDEFOP, 1995, pp. 76-77)

In the case of private training providers 'there are no legally binding standards which can be imposed on persons who call themselves an *"Instructor"* or a *"Trainer"* outside of state run bodies such as FÁS' (CEDEFOP, 1995, p. 81).

Employers and HE institutions combined to provide a range of both initial training and CPD opportunities for trainers. FÁS led the way by combining with HE institutions to provide courses from level 6 to degree and post graduate level courses with Maynooth University, NUIG and UL. The courses could be undertaken voluntarily by individual trainers and FÁS actively encouraged and facilitated staff to attend these courses.

Two interesting developments in the private training sector have been the work of the IITD and Skillnets. IITD offers a suite of courses for trainers including short five day and ten day courses as well as level 8 and level 9 courses. The level 8 and level 9 courses are provided in co-operation with UCC.

Skillnets was established in 1999 and is funded by the state. It has facilitated almost 70,000 Irish enterprises, in over 400 networks to improve the range, scope and quality of training and allowed over 300,000 employees to up-skill and meet their work related training needs. The basic idea is that networks of like-minded companies come together to form training networks and receive funding for CPD, which is recognised as important in the training domain.

A *Trainers' Learning Skillnets*, managed by IITD, was established in 2008 with the aim of providing:

> Relevant training and opportunities to HR, Training and Development professionals for their Continuing Professional Development (CPD) and to ensure that all members are provided with the opportunity to keep a pace with the ever-changing world of learning and development. (www.skillnets.ie)

The majority of the IITD *Trainers' Learning Skillnets* courses are at level 6 but it also offers a level 9 course in co-operation with UCC.

Training in the community domain

There are no specific requirements for tutors/teachers/trainers working in the community domain to have initial teacher training for any programme which does not lead to certification at level 4 or higher on the NQF or where the educator is employed by an ETB. However, similar to the education and training domains many tutors in community education have availed of courses in third level institutions to up skill themselves, often with support from their community-based provider.

Qualifications

Historically, assessment and certification in FET has been provided by the Technical Instruction Branch of the Department of Education in craft, apprenticeship and business examinations at intermediate and advanced levels and by British qualification bodies such City and Guilds Institute in London, the Royal Society of Arts, Pitman's and the London Chamber of Commerce.

An important step in the development of a modern Irish certification system was the decision by the National Council for Education Awards (NCEA) to quantify learning in terms of credits, develop single subject awards and provide for the accumulation of credits leading to an NCEA award (NCEA, 1985). This decision led to the establishment of the NCEA Accumulation of Credits and Certification of Subjects (ACCS) and to the provision of an NCEA Foundation Certificate (DES, 1998).

The next step was setting up the National Council for Vocational Awards (NCVA) in 1991 'to structure courses in vocational/technical education and training as provided in the education system, on a modular basis and to develop an appropriate framework of levels of qualification for these courses' (Hyland & Milne, 1992, p. 323). Though this development was limited in scope and confined to the education domain it provided further state certification opportunities for adult learners and started the process of weaning FET away from UK certification bodies.

State certification was tackled in earnest by the 1995 decision to establish TEASTAS, the National Certification Authority, on a non- statutory basis. One of its key functions was

> To advise the Minister for Education and Science on actions to be undertaken in putting in place a single, nationally and internationally accepted certification structure covering all extra-university third level and further and continuing education and training [FET] programmes. (DES, 1998, p. 101)

The fact that TEASTAS was established on a non-statutory basis meant that statutory bodies like FÁS were able to ignore TEASTAS and continue with the City and Guilds certification.

The state finally took control of certification through the Qualifications (Education and Training) Act 1999. The Act provided for the establishment of a National Qualifications Authority of Ireland, the Higher Education and Training Awards Council (HETAC) and the Further Education and Training Awards Council (FETAC). FETAC took over the role of the NCVA but in addition was given statutory responsibility for certification in the training domain. The impact of this legislation was that there was now a fully integrated qualifications' system, which provided FET learners with clear progression paths and state recognition underpinned by international currency.

The most recent step in the qualification's saga was passing the Qualifications and Quality Assurance (Education and Training) Act 2012. This was inspired by government policy to reduce the number of state bodies. The new Authority, Quality and Qualifications Ireland (QQI), is created by amalgamating three awarding bodies and a quality assurance body. The awarding bodies are the Further Education and Training Awards Council (FETAC), the Higher Education and Training Awards Council (HETAC), the National Qualifications Authority of Ireland (NQAI) and the quality assurance body is the Irish Universities Quality Board (IUQB). The new Authority assumes all the functions of the four legacy bodies (QQI, www.qqi.ie).

Developments in FET since 2010

The three years from 2010 to 2013 were momentous for FET. The fragmented system, developed over ninety years, was transformed in three short years. While full integration of FET was not achieved, significant progress was made.

At the end of 2009 FÁS became involved in a public controversy over lavish expenditure on travel to the US. The Director General resigned after a disastrous interview about the controversy on the *Today with Pat Kenny* programme on RTÉ Radio 1. Further controversy developed about the size of the severance package for the Director General, the Annual FÁS Jobs Opportunity Fairs and issues over examination results in FÁS computer courses in the North-East (Ross & Webb, 2010).

The situation of FÁS became politically untenable. The Board of FÁS was replaced and a new Director General appointed. The Government also transferred control of FÁS from DETE to DES. This decision was important because for the first time in the history of the State DES had overall responsibility for most FET.

A number of other far reaching changes took place in FET as part of the fallout from the controversy as well as from government policy to reduce the number of state agencies. Sixteen Education and Training Boards were established in 2013 to replace the thirty three VECs and carry out the training functions of FÁS at local level. The government also established SOLAS to carry out the national training functions of FÁS and Intreo to take over the employment related services of FÁS.

Conclusion

The period from 1973 to 2010 witnessed the piecemeal expansion, and ultimate transformation of FET in Ireland. The year 2010 saw the start of a three year process which led to the transformation of FET's institutional architecture and began sweeping away the shambolic structures that held back the development of FET up to then. The strengthening of the role of DES, the establishment of SOLAS and the ETBs should facilitate the development of a largely integrated FET system in Ireland.

The EU has played a major role in FET policy since we became members in 1973. It is going to play an increasingly stronger role in the future as it drives the Lisbon Agenda, shapes labour market policy, promotes the lifelong learning ideal, supports equality and implements the Council Resolution on a renewed European agenda for adult learning (European Commission, 2011).

Perhaps the most striking outcome for adult learners since the Murphy Report (1973) is the rapid expansion and diversification of provision and supports for learners in basic adult education, training, community education, second chance education and higher education. The development of the system is supported by an effective, internationally recognised Qualifications' Framework and more recently a professional ITE system for FET professionals.

Now that the state has put a sounder institutional architecture in place, overseen by the DES where FET now has status, the system should continue to improve with the weaknesses in community and higher education, in particular being addressed.

The challenge is to ensure that the system is not dominated by the needs of the economy and that there is a definite place for personal empowerment, community building and cultural development.

Figure 2.1 is the organisational map of SOLAS shown in their own Action Plan. Figure 2.2 is the author's analysis of the proposals revealed in the SOLAS Consultation Paper, 2011, while Figure 2.3 is taken from the author's submission to DES on the Consultative Document (Murtagh, 2012).

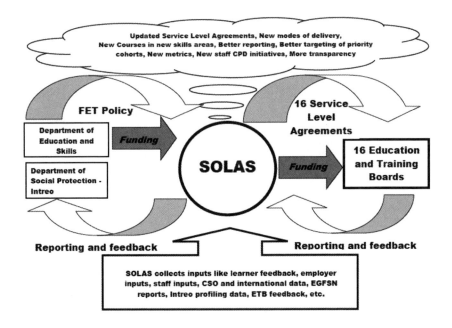

Figure 2.1: 2013 Organisational Map of SOLAS (Source: Action Plan for SOLAS, DES (2012b), Section 41)

SOLAS is shown in Figure 2.1 as the link between policy making by DES/ DSP and policy delivery by 16 ETBs. However, the diagram slightly misrepresents the Department of Social Protection's (DSP) role as it is purely consultative and not a policy role (Further Education and Training Act, 2013). The location of Intreo in the policy making box with DSP is inappropriate and confusing.

Policy delivery, shown on the right of the Figure is regulated by service level agreements with ETBs. Policy development and service effectiveness are managed through a reporting and feedback loop shown at the bottom of the figure linking the ETBs to SOLAS and SOLAS to the two government departments with responsibility for policy.

SOLAS is at the core of funding FET. It receives its annual funding from DES to finance its own operations and the delivery of FET through the ETBs.

The Figure ignores what happens at the point of delivery. This is unfortunate because most of the FET sites and players are operating at the point of service delivery.

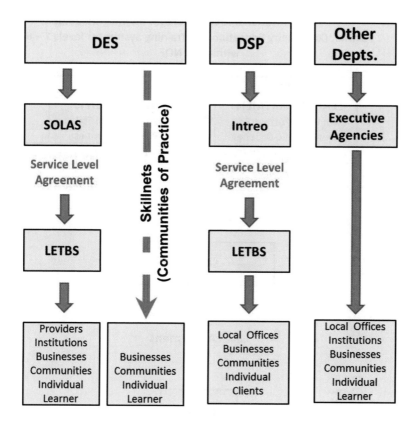

Figure 2.2: The Organisation of SOLAS in the Consultative Document

Figure 2.2 shows the architecture of FET proposed in the Consultative Document. While SOLAS, as envisioned in the document, integrates most FET, it excludes training under DSP and other government departments including Agriculture, Food and the Marine as well as Transport and Tourism. SOLAS will become the main state executive agency for FET. Other executive agencies such as Intreo, Teagasc and Fáilte Ireland will also be responsible for funding and managing parts of FET. FET will have a four-level delivery model: (1)The policy level involving government departments; (2) The executive agency level involving SOLAS, Intreo, Teagasc, Failte Ireland etc.; (3) The regional level (LETBs, now known as

ETBs) excluding provision by the 'other government departments'; and (4) The delivery level.

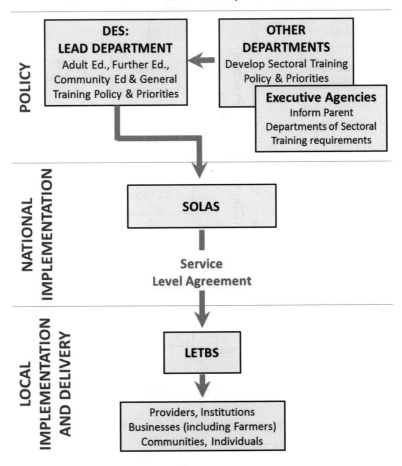

Figure 2.3: Proposed organisation of SOLAS in Author's submission (Source: Response to SOLAS Consultation Paper Luke Murtagh 2012)

The recommendation in Figure 2.3 is that all FET will fall within the ambit of DES and SOLAS. At policy level DES has total responsibility for FET policy but must consult with the other government departments before decisions are made. SOLAS is to be the sole FET executive agency. The executive agencies of other government departments, currently with a training role, will inform their parent department of training needs, and communicate with DES. At the regional level the (L)ETBs will be responsible to SOLAS for all FET in their region. Finally, at delivery level all FETs will relate directly to the ETBs.

Figure 2.2 shows that the full integration of the FET service has not been achieved through the legislation. While SOLAS will be responsible for most FET some sectoral provision will remain outside its remit.

CHAPTER THREE

COMMUNITY EDUCATION: EXPLORING FORMATIVE INFLUENCES WITHIN THE MAELSTROM OF CONFLICTING SOCIAL FORCES

Bríd Connolly

Introduction

When I started in community education in 1985, I was immersed in a new world that immediately felt welcoming and authentic. I had gone through formal education with a certain sense of unease, although my experience in Higher Education was generally more positive, mainly because I was involved in student politics and social activism, rather than the formal processes of learning. In addition, I had attended adult education classes, including arts and crafts, touch typing, yoga, and the like. However, community education was very different from my other experiences. This chapter will explore these differences, endeavouring to understand the context for the emergence of community education and its impact on educational and social policy, particularly on the development of Further Education and Training, FET.

Camilla Fitzsimons has provided the definitive analysis of the trajectory of community education, as it emerged from this chrysalis, and the ways in which it has been co-opted to the neo-liberal project of the individualist, market-led national skills strategy (Fitzsimons, 2012). However, this chapter will supplement this, with the focus on the analysis of the formation of the field, and how that impacted on the social policy particularly relating to the feminist and equality agendas. It will also explore the tensions within and without the field, which both strengthened and undermined it in different ways. Finally, I will appraise the potential of community education as a model of resilience, which the FET sector could develop by theorising the practice: responding authentically to the needs of students, developing creative curricula and pedagogies, keeping the wider project of education at the forefront, and supporting adult educators in their own reflexivity and development.

I want to start with the story of community education and explore the differences in the vision of the founding education activists. This vision was formed in at least three spheres, adult basic education, the women's movement, the fledging radical community development movement as well as some influence from returning development workers, the labour movement, and newly emerging liberation theology. I will then look at the impact of community education on policy, particularly the report of the Second Commission on the Status of Women, which, ultimately, was lost in the struggle between traditional and emancipatory perspectives of women's lives. This was taken up again in the National Women's Council's position paper for the millennium when community educators became more influential in the organisation, with the attendant shift from formal political parties. Community education was also under the spotlight in the research community, including research undertaken by AONTAS, on both gender and social action in the context of community education. Moreover, the struggles between the contrasting perspectives emerged when the Department of Education and Science produced the *White Paper on Adult Education* (2000) and the Department of Enterprise, Trade and Employment produced the *Report of the Taskforce on Lifelong Learning* (2002). Finally, I will look at the implications for the FET field arising from this maelstrom of conflicting social forces.

Formative influences

My engagement with community education started in 1985, when I started facilitating an Extra Mural Certificate in Women's Studies, from the St Patrick's College, Maynooth, as it was at that time, in Lucan, Tallaght, Clondalkin and Newbridge, centres which organised adult education in the morning to facilitate women in particular. These centres, as well as many others, including Kilbarrack and Leixlip, were already established or in the process of being established, by local activists not necessarily from educational backgrounds. These activists organised the venues, worked with providers such as Maynooth University, and VEC Adult Education Organisers, connected with funders such as the Allen Lane Foundation and Joseph Rowntree Foundation, and later with the Combat Poverty Agency, and the Department of Social, Community and Family Affairs, as it was named at the time. It was recognised that community education had the power to address profound social issues, through community development (Powell & Geoghegan, 2004). The activists also developed local links with libraries, schools, community centres, churches and so on, to launch, advertise and recruit for the programmes, as well as all the other aspects of putting on new educational initiatives. Above all, these projects had qualities in common, including that welcome I recognised when I started; hospitality, with a tea and coffee as part of the provision, with the underlying acknowledgment that the informal learning of the tea-break was as vital as the formal learning; care, especially childcare; commitment strategic thinking, equality and justice and many other dimensions and elements, identified by research undertaken over the past few years (AONTAS, 2009a).

Mary Foley, one of the founder members of Leixlip Women's Studies, recalls this trend. The group was established with two key aims: to provide daytime classes for women, with crèche facilitates, and to use their own resources as far as possible. They held that women had enormous resources that could be shared, and that they could direct the project in their own way, if they relied on their own resources as much as possible. The group had been meeting informally in each others' homes, from 1981, according to Foley, but others may have met earlier, and the first organised classes were launched in September 1984. They were, according to Foley, the first self-funded, independent women's education group with a crèche in Ireland (Foley, 2011). Leixlip Women's Studies was responding to a felt need in the community for a social and cultural space for women who were interested in learning, but, also, arguably interested in expanding their identities in line with the changes brought about by feminism, a transformation from the traditional perspectives, while acknowledging the reality of women's lives.

Simultaneously, in the early 1980s, a group of local women founded KLEAR, Kilbarrack Local Education for Adult Renewal, with the support of a local community worker. Gradually, like Leixlip Women's Studies, they began to offer a range of classes, with a crèche for the children, with the support of the AEO, the VEC Adult Education Officer (www.kleared.ie). One of the founder members of KLEAR, Cathleen O'Neill recounts the impact of feminism and the women's movement on the participants in the KLEAR programme, and further, how the principles of community education were applied and adapted to other contexts, including the profound problems emanating from the illegal drug industry and the devastating impact it has on the lives of addicts and their families (O'Neill, 2014). Concurrently, the Tallaght learners taking the Maynooth Extra-mural certificate, linked up with Anne Louise Gilligan and Katherine Zappone, which led to the founding of

The Shanty, which in turn, evolved into An Cosán, an educational and entrepreneurial project in Jobstown, which uses the power of transformative education to address poverty and injustice (www.ancosan.ie). These were exemplary of the sources of community education: outside of the formal channels of adult education, the emphasis on the resources of the group, and support for the learners, especially with regards to childcare and the impact of social issues on their lives.

At this time, it is vital to understand that the learners took the learning out of the classroom and into the wider community, to address profound social issues, particularly related to gender and class. Empowerment was a key outcome of these projects, and the activists were fundamentally involved in local issues. This empowerment was expressed in local politics, in community-based responses to local issues, such as unemployment, drug misuse, community safety, and so on. For others, it emerged in community development projects. For example, activists in the Women's Studies project in Leixlip were very active in the Town Council (Foley, 2012), particularly Mary Foley who gave many years of service, before it was abolished within the past few years. Women were closely involved in fighting, not only the heroin addiction of their children, but also the oppression of the illegal drug industry, and shamefully, the violent responses orchestrated for diverse political and social agendas. These women built their own capacity and collective identity through community education, referred to as self-development, literacy and second chance in Murphy-Lawless, (2002, p 129-140), but including programmes familiar in the field, such as Counselling and groupwork, which, arguably were spearheaded by the extra-mural provision in Maynooth University.

Further, KLEAR established a very vibrant and essential Community Development project which was ultimately drained of funding in the late 2000s. Fitzsimons (2012) discusses the impact on community education with the spread of statutory provision, especially the VECs/ETBs. The melding of adult and community education and community development has been discussed, for example, by Connolly (1996) but the links between community education and empowerment, and the emergence of community development projects, the aspirations for the Community Development Programme on the part of the state and the communities, in addition to the orientations that those projects adopted is indisputable (Powell & Geoghegan, 2002, pp. 146-150). However, the seeds of their own corrosion were contained in those aspirations: they had the potential to bring about significant social change, but this was channelled into local partnerships, which submerged the community education and development projects in favour of enterprise and employment. This exemplifies the tensions between education and development per se, but also between the government departments responsible for these areas. I will return to this, later in the chapter, but firstly, I want to look at the initial impact on educational practice and policy, before the submergence of the field in the milieu of the changes of the more recent years.

Community education projects were in dialogue with the accrediting bodies, such as Maynooth University, as FETAC was yet to be established, at that time. This process of consultation between the learning and organising groups and institutions was already established by 1985, but it characterised another fundamental difference to most models of education: dialogue as a key principle of the process. This principle essentially interrogated the fundamental relationship between learners, teachers and organisers. Traditionally, teachers are deemed to be expert, not just in their discipline or subject, but also expert on what learners needed to know. Thus, in practice, the social activists who organised these programmes were clear that the adult educators were responsive, person-centred and facilitative, rather than the experts who controlled the entire process.

Curriculum development in community education

Another key difference centred on the curricula on offer in women's daytime education. I was facilitating Women's Studies, and this was almost unique in Ireland at the time, when it was just beginning to make an inroad into Universities. Even today, it is not available at second level, and is ultimately, at the present time, controversial in Further Education and Training (Connolly & Hussey, 2013). The other completely new topics/subjects included assertive communication, an approach to interpersonal relationships based on equality; personal development, based on deepening reflection and self-awareness, in order to build authentic self-esteem and confidence; creative writing, again very unusual in Ireland, where there was, and perhaps, still is, a belief that creative writing cannot be taught, unlike visual art, music, or any other the other arts; social analysis, based on a development education approach to uncovering the root causes of social issues, such as poverty, inequality and deprivation; counselling skills, perhaps best described as a first-aid approach to distress and concern; community development and leadership, for community activists; complementary therapies, such as aromatherapy, reflexology, and holistic living; and many others. This curriculum developed alongside more traditional curricula, English literature, art, cookery, and languages, without dissonance. This curriculum was the key conduit for bringing new ideas and perspectives into the lives of ordinary people. In particular, women's studies and counselling skills focused attention on the social issues that impacted disastrously on the private lives of many women, such as sexual abuse, domestic violence, rape and oppression, turning them from private concerns to deeply concerning public issues. In my experience, community education revealed incidences of rape, rape within relationships, incest, child abuse, violence, oppression, cruelty, and many, many other examples of the dark underbelly of social life (Connolly & Hussey, 2013). This exemplifies the process of consciousness raising, a pivotal process in both the feminist movement, and in adult and community education. Feminist education formulated the pivotal precept, the personal is political, Freire (1972) framed it as the process of conscientization, and Mills (1959) proposed the development of the sociological imagination, the transformation of private troubles into social issues. Thus, the curriculum developed in those early days of community education echoed emancipatory trends in other spheres: social liberation movements, such as the civil rights movement, the Black liberation movement and so on; the development of the sociological imagination; as well as adult education for redressing oppression and exclusion. When we interrogate the role of education in society, the answer is much closer to the work towards critical citizenship and democracy, regardless of the national strategy, rather than a sterile acquisition of skills.

These innovations around curriculum development probably could not have taken place in any other educational sphere. Sugrue and Gleeson identify the significant silences around education in Ireland, with their origins in political power struggles, particularly around the public good: the common good is in jeopardy when governments promote the market and the privatisation of the public interests (2004, pp. 269-273). As Fitzsimons points out, the current trends around community education includes the considerable shift towards the market economy (Fitzsimons, 2012). These trends are articulated as the essential structure of the knowledge economy, which had taken a back seat somewhat since the collapse of the monetarist economy in 2007-2008, but it revives when the discussion turns to education. However, this default setting of equating education with the knowledge economy misses a vital element. Chang argues that education is valuable, but its main value lies not in raising productivity, but enabling us to lead a more independent and fulfilling life, as the link between education and national wealth is tenuous and complicated (Chang, 2010, p. 189). The focus on skills and the needs of the economy has the effect of individualising and personalising clear social trends such as depressed wages and unemployment. This has had the effect of reining-in the curriculum, and draining potentially emancipatory programmes of their consciousness raising capacity, which are the elements that enable us to leading fulfilling lives, a factor recognised in social as well as educational policy, which I will address later in the chapter, but first I want to look at the practices developed in community education.

Emancipatory practices in community education

Another key area of innovation and creativity, along with curriculum development, is the scope of the practices developed in community education. Adult educators had adopted participatory methods of working with adults prior to the emergence of community education. This was especially the case with the adult basic education and literacy education from the 1970s, particularly arising from the publication of what become known as the Murphy Report (1973). And, additionally, the practice developed with the subsequent establishment of literacy education and advocacy agencies, such as NALA and the Dublin Adult Learning Centre (Carey, 1979). Further, the response within the VECs with the employment of Adult Literacy Officers and Adult Education (Organisers) Officers in 1979 supported participatory methods too. However, with the development of community education, an additional focus on groupwork, person-centred approaches emerged, adding a significant dimension to the existing processes. KLEAR identify that their approaches stem from the thinking of both Carl Rogers and Paulo Freire, and this is echoed in many other centres of community education. I wrote about the links between Freud and Freire, identifying feminist groupwork as an important aspect of this practice, (Connolly, 1999) and developed this further in Adult Learning in Groups (Connolly, 2008). Still, this was not without debate.

The story of community education is inextricably linked to empowerment and emancipation, and a key focus is on the status of women. However, this has been subject to profound tensions, some of which played out in community education. The public, 'common sense' (Gramsci, 1971, pp. 630-640), negative perception of feminism and feminists was the

58

fundamental obstacle to acknowledging the inequality around the status of women. There was, and perhaps still is, a profoundly damaging connotation around feminism. The Irish State was very slow to address women's inequality. In 1945, the UN established the first Commission on the Status of Women, urging governments to take up the issue of the status of women, and to address the obstacles that women experience, to full participation in society (UN/CSW, 2014). This was due to many reasons, but particularly the struggles between the traditional role of women, as articulated in the Irish Constitution and espoused in the main by the more powerful in society, and the emerging feminist movement, with the demands for personal and social emancipation. This negativity has emerged in many arenas. When the Council for the Status of Women was founded by a group of feminists, in 1973, through the Irish Housewives Association, the perception emerged very quickly that these women had very little in common with other women, on various grounds, and especially on the ground of class. The vernacular name was the Council for Women of Status, which prevailed prior to the change of name to The National Women's Council, under the leadership of Noreen Byrne, feminist activist from the community education and development field. This marked the beginning of the era when the community and adult education practitioners became more influential. These women marked the shift in the leadership from mainly political activists, such as Frances Fitzgerald, Monica Barnes, Nuala Fennell, to encompass the wider community, with Joanna McMinn, Noreen Byrne, Gráinne Healy, Katherine Zappone, Valerie O'Carroll, and Elva O'Callaghan. This shift was reflected in the *Report on Women and Education*, which identified three key areas for attention: the development of women's community education, especially including core funding; the recognition of women's ways of learning, with feminist pedagogies and curricula; and finally, attractive and welcoming learning environments, located particularly in the heart of the community (NWCI, 1999). This was a dramatic shunt from mainly direct political representation of a smaller number of possible candidates in to empowerment and capacitation of a very large population of women. This illustrates the scope of democracy, from aggregative democracy to inclusive deliberative democracy (Young, 2000, pp 19-22), and participative democracy, which marked significant progress in the status of women.

However, these changes were embedded within the backdrop of competing discourses around the underpinning ideology of women's community education: feminist or women-centred? Zappone (1991) argues that the use of the word feminism continues to be distracting even within participative practice examining gender inequality. Ryan takes up the reins, asserting her feminist stance, in the gaps between the liberal humanistic thinking of Rogers and Maslow, radical humanistic thinking of Freire, Marxian theory and the radical agendas of feminisms for personal development (Ryan, 2001). Thus, early tensions emerged around class and feminist thought, yet these discussions enriched the underlying philosophy, acknowledging the diversity of the field, rather than reinforcing a false homogeneity. Indeed, the transformation of the negative associations with feminism is part of the power of community education with women participants moving from antipathy towards feminisms to recognising the value, in the process of participation. In her study, O'Grady charts the foundations of the feminist grassroots movement in the Waterford Women's Centre towards a fully fledged community education project (O'Grady, 2012, p. 4). On the other hand, Longford Women's Link developed from a guild of The Irish Country Women's Association, which, by their own admission, is traditionalist, rather than feminist, and LWL is now a project characterised by the social advocacy and supportive practices that underpin women's community education. They now see their work as increasing the participation of women in Longford in the economic, social and cultural life of their community (LWL, www.longfordwomenslink.org).

Thus, these processes were adopted and adapted, in some cases, on an intuitive level, rather than an intellectual commitment, to shape the practices in community education. Nevertheless, a number of key terms surfaced at this time, terms such as empowerment, facilitation, holistic (adult education), pro-action, and groupwork, among many others, that have become quite commonplace. These concepts and many others like them ushered in an innovative way of speaking about education, a complete volte-face from traditional education which is focused on maintaining the power of the teacher, imparting specialised knowledge, to classes of individual students.

These ways of working with adults underpin much of the practice currently, even if they have been deprived of some of their emancipatory potential. The debate on the 'methods fetish' is on-going, and I have discussed it in some detail in Connolly (2008), but the dissociation of facilitative practice from participation and democracy is detrimental, and the response of the Community Education Network, with the facilitator's guide, forms part of the bulwark against empty methods (O'Reilly, 2013). When we look at the impact of community education on social and educational policy, it ought to restore faith in the processes, and re-ignite the emancipatory intentions. I will now look at exemplary policy, and argue that the power of the community education in the nineties in particular, held the possibility of social transformation.

In the firing line: The status of women

As I discussed above, the potential for community education to have a positive and material impact on social life was promising in the early 1990s, until the empowerment demonstrated by the activism was gradually eroded by the partial takeover of community education by the statutory providers, discussed at length by Fitzsimons (2012), but also the stalemate in the status of women, particularly working class women, who were taking control over their own lives, and the lives of their children and communities, through cutbacks, abolition, cooption by partnerships, and re-framing of community development from advocacy to active citizenship. This erosion seems haphazard, but there are significant milestones on the trajectory.

Perhaps it would be too harsh to name the *Report of the Taskforce on Lifelong Learning* (DETE, 2002) as part of the backlash, but it certainly shifted the orientation of community education away from its emancipatory potential, towards the role of serving the economy. Murtagh has provided the authoritative analysis of the course of actions that prevailed at that time, highlighting the rivalry between the Departments of Education and Science, on the one hand, and the Department of Enterprise, Trade and Employment on the other. This rivalry centred on the control of adult education policy, and illuminates the strong emergence of neo-liberal visions for the future, not just of education but of the nation (Murtagh, 2009). I want to stress here that the Report was published a mere two years after the publication of *Learning for Life: White Paper on Adult Education* (2000), which was widely welcomed in the sector. The title of the two documents contains the first clue to the regression: following an extensive consultation with the key participants and stakeholders, *Learning for Life* was the first Irish White Paper on Adult Education, marking the adoption of lifelong learning as the governing principle of educational policy. In addition, the White Paper identified six priority areas, some of which were very familiar to community educators and learners: Consciousness Raising, Citizenship, Cohesion, Competitiveness, Cultural Development and Community Building. In Chapter 5, on community education, the White Paper recognised the inherent innovation of the project, and the ways in which it differed fundamentally from all other forms of education, not merely in terms of the curriculum, but also in terms of the relationship between the participants and educators, and learning and the assessment processes (DES, 2000).

Yet, within two years, the Taskforce on Lifelong Learning developed another document, completely incongruent with Learning for Life. The Report of the taskforce stated its vision that the state and the population would work together to achieve the skills, motivation, supports and resources to engage in lifelong learning to enrich lives and develop a more prosperous and inclusive society. However, the onus for achieving the vision was placed on individuals and enterprises to make the learning and the potential benefits that it could deliver a reality (DETE, 2002, p. 7). The work that was accomplished in community education and the contribution that the sector made to Learning for Life was completely undermined and the hopes and dreams of the activists were dashed. However, it wasn't the first time that another agenda colonised social policy that would have materially improved the status of marginal and disadvantaged groups. The Second Commission on the Status of Women (1993) was another area that recognised the intrinsic value of community education, yet it was ultimately silenced by a conservative stance, ten years prior to the publication of the two adult learning policy papers.

The Second Commission for the Status of Women in Irish society, chaired by Justice Mella Carroll, was established in order to address the areas omitted from the first commission in 1972, which brought a raft of legal and attitudinal changes, particularly in employment, pay and social welfare, but remained quite silent on childcare, re-productive health, marriage and education. With regards to education, the second commission was very ambitious. It had taken cognisance of the women's community education movement, and made critical recommendations with regards to women's access to education. For example, paragraphs 9.6.2, states:

> The commission recommends that the Government should develop a coherent strategy of adult education that responds to the actual and diverse needs of adult women returning to education, i.e., by providing opportunities for self-development, preparing women for returning to or establishing a career and enable women to assist in their children's education. (Department of Equality and Law Reform, 1993)

62

Further, in 9.6.4, the commission recommended that a supportive adult education officer be appointed in each region; that women's community education groups have guaranteed premises; and child-care facilities provided. Significantly, it also recommends that women's groups be enabled to access financial support on an informed basis. This would be the ambition of many centres and projects, and would fundamentally change the status of the provision from peripheral to core activity.

Finnegan and Wiles highlight the significance of this report in the development of policy on the equality of women, while acknowledging the limitations of the effects (2005, p 317). Moreover, the disagreement between the authors of the report, and in particular the publication of the Minority Report by Dr Finola Kennedy, rendered the work of the commission mute. Dr Kennedy's contention was that women's traditional role in the home was undermined by the report, and she published a minority report, which was acknowledged in the Dáil debates at the time, but it spelled the end of the aspirations of the second commission, combining with other traditional and conservative forces at work at the time, including the X-Case, the discussions around divorce and access to contraception, to undo the progress made by the feminist movement in the theocratic and conservative Ireland. And ultimately, there was no pressure on the state to implement progressive policy. Indeed, the opposite was more like the case. This was particularly striking in the case of the continuity between community education and community development, in the projects specifically set up to address fundamental social issues.

In the firing line: Social purpose community development

The development of community education projects was diverse and quite varied. Some projects developed into more fully fledged adult education providers, with the support of the statutory agencies, for example, Dundrum Adult Training and Education, DATE. This project provides a programme for the local community, through the work of a voluntary committee, with the support of the local ETB and Dundrum Shopping Centre (www.ddletb.ie). However, many community development programmes were underpinned by the learning from community education, and this gradually become a key instrument for enabling communities to identify their needs and to work together to meet those needs. Community Action Network, CAN, developed the discussion on this radical iteration of community development, which aims to enable people to take control of their lives, to fulfil their human potential, and to promote community empowerment. The ultimate aim was to bring about fundamental policy and social change, highlighting the need to redistribute society's resources (Kelleher & Whelan, 1992, p. 1). This model was very influential with the Combat Poverty Agency, which published jointly the Kelleher and Whelan volume. The CPA was established in 1986, and it helped to set up the infrastructure of community development as a key strategy for tackling poverty in the twenty years between its foundation and its eventual shift into various government departments in 2009 (www.combatpoverty.ie). This model was also influential with the Department of Social, Community and Family Affairs, as it was at the time. Around 1994, though there is no date included, the Department of Social, Community and Family Affairs published a handbook for the emerging Community Development Programme, in which it proposed that community development had an important role in encouraging participation, in addressing community needs, in seeking the equitable distribution of power and resources, and in challenging discrimination, prejudice and racism (Department of Social, Community and Family Affairs, n.d.). That is, the policy and practice in the Department was quite radical, in the otherwise conservative Ireland.

However, that agenda was challenged fundamentally when the department was dismantled, and the community section was transferred to the Department of Community, Rural and Gaeltacht Affairs, in 2002. This move marked the end of the support for the empowering models of community development, and led to a series of actions in which the field was reined-in, nominally, to re-assert the position of elected representatives. This move was heralded in 2000, when Noel Ahern famously identified The National Adult Literacy Agency, Community Workers' Co-op, Conference of Religious of Ireland, European Anti-Poverty Network, Focus Ireland, Gay and Lesbian Network and Community Action Network, among others, as a 'motley crew' undermining the role of the elected politicians (Ahern, 2000). These organisations have one thing in common: they have worked relentlessly, and at great cost to themselves at times, for people who are not served by the current construction of representative democracy, either then or now. The focus on such groups is telling, rather than, for example, CIF, (Construction Industry Federation), IBEC, Alcohol Beverage Federation of Ireland, and so on, which also advocate on behalf of their members, and are extremely influential in that role. With the removal of community affairs from the Department of Social, Community and Family Affairs to Community, Rural and Gaeltacht Affairs, came the concerted onslaught on the sector. The Community Development Programme was dismantled, with the final blow emanating from the research conducted by the Centre for Effective Services (Bamber, 2010), which led to the withdrawal of statutory funding for many of the community development projects remaining in the programme.

However, the environment for community education was and remains less vulnerable, due to the funding mechanism, through the ETBs, the support of the Community Education Facilitators, successful projects that have withstood the maelstrom of the conflicting forces, such as An Cosán, Longford Women's Link, Waterford Women's Centre, and many others, in addition to research and other publications undertaken by national agencies, such as AONTAS and NALA.

Withstanding the maelstrom

One of ways in which community education builds resilience include the formation of the Community Education Network, CEN, which has developed the discussion on the nature of the practice in Ireland, with the following paragraph:

> Community Education is a process of personal and community transformation, empowerment, challenge, social change and collective responsiveness. It is community-led, reflecting and valuing the lived experiences of individuals and their community. Through its ethos and holistic approach, community education builds the capacity of groups to engage in developing a social teaching and learning process that is creative, participative and needs-based. Community Education is grounded on principles of justice, equality and inclusiveness. It differs from general adult education provision due to its political and radical methodologies. (CEN, 2014)

It is heartening to see the connections between this discussion and the discussion initiated by CAN, which was immeasurably significant in the development of social purpose community development (Kelleher & Whelan, 1992). These connections focus on the principles of justice, equality and inclusion, as the foundation stones of their philosophy. That is, an unequivocal statement of the ultimate purpose of community education. But it is also heartening to understand that the statutory response may be interpreted as supportive, in contrast with the responses discussed throughout this chapter. Ciaran Cannon, the Minister for Training and Skills, endorses community education, acknowledging the purpose of community education outside of the classroom and employment.

Community education is one means of providing opportunities for learners who need help in improving personal development and building self-confidence. These are fundamental strengths in returning to learning and also in participation in community (Cannon, 2013, p. 4).

A further dimension of this resilience is the way in which the work of community education is carried out, the social action model. The social action model of community education is, fundamentally, conveyed through educators, and the Facilitator's Guide endeavours to equip educators with the resources, and the reflexivity to maintain the ethos, (O'Reilly, 2013). NALA also recognises the centrality of practice and the ethos of the practitioners and looks to research to strengthen literacy education. But a key principle is the social action model, as a critical response to the deficits in literacy levels currently prevailing in Ireland (NALA, 2014). Currently, a number of PhD research students in Maynooth University are conducting research focused on the development of educators, in both the community education and the further education field. While the research is not completed, it illuminates the interest in the ways in which educators practice and how their ethos is influential in their environments. While we await the completion of these studies, it is heartening to review the ethos of one of the key community education projects that has withstood the vicissitudes of the backlash in education, community development and the status of women (An Cosán, 2014)

> It is the ideals, beliefs, values and principles that underpin all our work, our culture and our philosophy. We often state that it is not so much what we do but how we do things that makes the difference that supports individuals and communities to change and develop. (An Cosán, 2014)

And in many ways, these are the key lessons for the FET sector. FET educators and researchers need to examine their ideals, beliefs, values and principles, in order to strengthen the field, and to build the confidence and capacity of practitioners to meet the needs of FET students, to enable them to take their place in the wider society.

SECTION TWO: POLITICS

CHAPTER FOUR

TAKING SHAPE, SHAPING UP, CHANGING SHAPE: EQUALITY AND HUMAN CAPITAL

Kevin Hurley

Introduction

In the previous section the development of adult education to contemporary times was outlined. This chapter is concerned with the condition of equality as a motive force within adult education, in particular within that sector of adult education which is most subject to the conditionality accompanying state policy. The sector in question resides primarily in one of the four pillars identified in the foregoing White Paper (Department of Education and Science, 2000, pp. 85-86) as constituting a framework of second-chance and Further Education provision, namely the Back to Education Initiative (BTEI) entailing VTOS, PLC, Youthreach/ Senior Traveller education. This is not to diminish the other three pillars - a National Adult Literacy Programme, an ICT Basic Skills programme, that dimension of community education which is state-funded, and self-funded part-time Adult Education in schools - but the dependency of the providers on funding from the exchequer and the EU is all-determinant with regard to the function of the BTEI pillar.

The Irish state professes that it is interested in contributing to equality through adult education. It makes this claim in *Learning for Life*, the White Paper on adult education published in 2000. This is an issue of profound public interest if only given one dimension alone, the very unequal distribution of wealth in Irish society as revealed periodically by the Central Statistics Office (CSO) in its SILC surveys and the consequences flowing from that as revealed in the growth of deprivation rates in recent years.

Table 4.1: Changes in Deprivation Rate 2007 - 2011[1] (Source: CSO, 2011, p. 1)

2007	2008	2009	2010	2011
11.8%	13.8%	17.1%	22.6%	24.5%

Social justice demands that this condition be addressed at all relevant levels and much of the theory informing adult education places an onus on the field to contribute to this by the fostering of critical consciousness.

The emergence into explicit consciousness of equality as a normative dimension of adult education in Ireland can be traced to a period in the late 20th century. Paradoxically, during that same period, neo-liberalism also grew significantly in Ireland with the full complicity of the State apparatus.

As shown in the previous section, much of the surge of interest in adult education in the last quarter of the 20th century was due to internal factors, as Ireland gradually awoke to the importance of providing access to learning for adults. However, external factors increasingly came into play as Ireland began to encounter ideas from abroad. Much of this influence came from the OECD and UNESCO but more sustained prompting followed Ireland's entry to membership of what was then known as the European Economic Community (EEC) in 1973. The latter developments in particular had an important bearing on the shape of adult education in Ireland and its orientation with regard to the conceptualization of equality. What follows is a brief exploration of the application of the idea of equality, especially in the light of developments in equality theory, within the adult education narrative. The chapter also sets out to reveal the impact on the equality function of adult education of its conflation with lifelong learning in the light of the latter's increasing colonization by human capital theory, a distinct hallmark of the onward march of neo-liberalism. This requires taking account of the

---

[1] Experienced two or more types of the following enforced deprivation: Without heating at some stage in the last year; Unable to afford a morning, afternoon or evening out in the last fortnight; Unable to afford two pairs of strong shoes; Unable to afford a roast once a week; Unable to afford a meal with meat, chicken or fish every second day; Unable to afford new (not second-hand) clothes; Unable to afford a warm waterproof coat; Unable to afford to keep the home adequately warm; Unable to afford to replace any worn out furniture; Unable to afford to have family or friends for a drink or meal once a month; Unable to afford to buy presents for family or friends at least once a year.

impact of policy development in the European Union and other bodies to which Ireland subscribes. It also includes some segments from research I completed as part of a PhD thesis which were informed by fieldwork.

Inequality Uncovered: Equality Re-Discovered

Adult Education in Ireland: A Report of a Committee appointed by the Minister for Education, popularly known as the Murphy Report, was published in 1973. In advance of the report, research had been commissioned by the committee. This revealed an Ireland with deep-seated fault-lines as far as equality in access to learning was concerned and from which widespread inequality in society can be inferred. Among many findings, data showed that, generally speaking, those participating in adult education had completed at least two years of post-primary education and were drawn from higher socio-economic groups. This left the field largely to a privileged minority, since only some 11% of the relevant age cohort transferred to higher education at the time (Coolahan, 1981, p. 266). Unsurprisingly, perhaps, the motivation for participation in adult education was dominated by personal needs ranging from 'personal enrichment and satisfaction' to 'loneliness' (Department of Education (DE), 1973, p. 16). Wider societal issues only registered marginally: 'commitment to a group, community, society etc' and 'to study the methods and techniques of scientific research and thus help them to assess, and perhaps remedy, social problems' (DE, 1973, p. 16).

The committee's report was compiled during a period when a transformation in Irish thinking about the role of education had been effected by the OECD-sponsored report *Investment in Education* in 1966 (DE, 1966). Following lengthy negotiation on entry into the (then) European Economic Community, which was accessed by Ireland on 1 January, 1973, continental perspectives also began to impact. Quite divergent influences were therefore beginning to play out, culminating in a meshing of the traditional and the progressive in the three-fold agenda set out for adult education in Murphy, namely to 'interpret, analyse and cope with change...preserve basic cultural and Christian principles in this storm of human, social and technological change...[and] remedy human and technological obsolescence which is an outcome of such rapid change' (DE, 1973, p. 25).

Among what were designated as major recommendations no reference was made to equality. Ten of these were concerned with structure. The others related to developmental issues – the training of tutors, research, grant-in-aid for AONTAS, and correspondence courses. Instead of equality, the reference to remedying 'human and technological obsolescence' might be seen as laying the seedbed for the neo-liberal orientation which is discussed in later chapters.

Yet, if the report can be seen as unpropitious from an egalitarian perspective, it would be unfair to dismiss it as irrelevant to the historiography of equality in Ireland. It was a product of its time during which a transition from a theocratic to a mercantile paradigm in education was occurring (O'Sullivan, 2005, pp. 106–111). While, in Ireland, the concept of equality is traceable at least to the Proclamation of 1916, it suffered a stifling eclipse thereafter, being subordinated to preoccupations with nationalistic constructs. Social justice in theory and practice was deemed to be more appropriately the domain of the churches and was to remain largely so for decades, as indicated by the sociologist Nic Ghiolla Phádraig (1995, p. 612) 'the former emphasis on Christian charity has given way to a highlighting of justice and equality'. The historian, Ferriter (2004, p. 702), following earlier remarks on the state's abdication from the equality aspirations of the 1916 Proclamation, makes the observation 'In a sense, poverty had been "discovered" only in the 1970s'. Indeed, Ferriter records that: 'An EEC study of 1977 revealed that there was a low awareness in Ireland regarding the structural causes of poverty' (2004, p. 703). He acquiesces in the suggestion that the catalyst for modest change was external, following the accession of Ireland into the EEC (2004, p. 684).

The Kenny Report was published over a decade after the Murphy Report. The Kenny Report was a considerable advance on its predecessor, both in terms of theory and the emergence of egalitarian considerations, notwithstanding it introduced into adult education discourse the kind of duality - justification on both social and economic grounds - that has been equivocally present in all of the subsequent policy documents bearing on the field. The recommendations of the Commission were quite visionary and many of these remain unfulfilled. Equality makes its appearance among these, in the assertion that provision must go beyond existing demand and extend 'educational opportunity' in response to the real, if 'unexpressed' needs of different sections of society. Other recommendations which had a bearing on equality issues, if less explicitly so, were the need for enhancement of urban and rural community education, political education, women's education and an exhortation to third-level institutions to develop more flexible approaches to access and participation for mature students. These lacked force however, as a result of being presented merely in list form among the 'Detailed Recommendations' (DE, 1984, pp. 143-150). While the

Commission was strikingly alert to the general dereliction applying to adult education, its concept of equality did not extend beyond the need to provide for the development of greater educational opportunity for those hitherto excluded, placing it, accordingly, in the category of liberal equality, discussed below.

The *Report of the National Education Convention*, published in 1994, unquestionably provided the most significant boost for adult education as a field within the wider education fold. The convention was an event without precedent and provided a forum for a critique of the entire spectrum of issues relating to education. Equality issues were given a thorough airing as was adult and community education. In the discussion on equality, the concept of equality of condition was invoked in references to measures that were necessary to counter the entrenched inequalities still being experienced by women (DE, 1994, p. 116). Furthermore, a chapter on 'Adult, Community and Continuing Education' constituted an acknowledgement of adult education's potential to tackle educational disadvantage. This concluded with a strong argument '...for prioritising the needs of socio-economically disadvantaged groups, communities and of low-income women' (DE, 1994, p 106). Significantly, the Freirian-like rider was also added that this should be accompanied by the development of adult education's potential for critical reflection, emancipation and empowerment.

Enter the State

Adult Education in an Era of Lifelong Learning (1998), the first ever Green Paper on Adult Education duly saw the light of day as a direct response to the low levels of literacy among Ireland's adult population revealed in the OECD study, *Literacy Skills for the Knowledge Society* of 1997. The Paper constituted a thorough review of Irish adult education both in theory and practice. It adopted the definition coined by the Commission on Adult Education of 1984, which, however, only hints at its potential for equality:

Adult Education includes all systematic learning by adults which contributes to their development as individuals and as members of the community and of society, apart from full-time instruction received by persons as part of their uninterrupted initial education and training. It may be formal education which takes place in institutions e.g. training centres, schools, colleges, institutes and universities, or non-formal education which is any other systematic form of learning including self-directed learning. (Department of Education and Science, 1998, p.16)

Notwithstanding this, the Green Paper is informed by an equality standpoint throughout and this breaks through explicitly from time to time. Indeed, it first surfaces among the nomenclature of one of the grounds on which the case for investment and development is based: 'Promoting equality, competitiveness and employment' (DES, 1998, p.12).

Community education was recognised as presenting a profile that set it apart and initiatives in this sector were appraised as holding 'great promise in relation to social change and in their success in engaging disadvantaged communities' (DES, 1998, p.88). Indeed, an entire chapter of this Paper was devoted to community education which emerged as the sector most identifiable with the pursuit of social justice. Among other hallmarks, community education was depicted as 'a process built on models of active participation, and inclusive discourse and decision-making' (DES, 1998, p. 89).

The White Paper, to which this Green Paper was 'to provide the consultative background' (DES, 1998, p. 6), had a surfeit of challenges to address, if it was to be convincing. From an equality perspective, the issue was whether its horizon would be confined to that of the Green Paper, which was clearly anchored in the notion of equality of opportunity, or would extend beyond that to addressing the condition of society.

Learning for Life: White Paper on Adult Education, 2000, proved to be a thorough document although largely addressing the issues through the realpolitik lens which constrain the official gaze. At the outset this Paper sets out nine aims: 'to provide a template for the development of the Adult Education sector' (DES, 2000, p. 26-27)[2]. These can be seen as evocative of themes repeatedly surfacing since the *Programme of National Recovery* of 1987 (Department of An Taoiseach, 1987). While they contain no explicit reference to equality, it is possible to detect implications in one or two. For instance, the 'development of this society' can only imply some basic concern for equality given its unequal condition and the connotation attaching to 'development' in contemporary times.

The definition of adult education used appears uncontroversial: 'systematic learning undertaken by adults who return to learning having concluded initial education or training' (DES, 2000, p. 27). However, it becomes problematic when qualified 'to encapsulate: continuing education and training i.e. professional or vocational development of people in the workforce or re-entering the workforce regardless of the level' (DES, 2000, p. 28) as one of five categories. To admit training as one of the defining categories of adult education is to forsake the principles upon which the latter is traditionally based. Regrettably, the Paper is committed to an ostensible agenda of facilitating crossover between education and training and, in doing so, can be said to have departed from its remit to be a White Paper on Adult Education, per se. Equally, the apparent ceding in the paper of responsibility for lifelong learning to a taskforce under the aegis of the Department of Enterprise and Employment is very revealing of the Government's perspective.

The section on 'vision' restores some confidence in the unfolding of policy on adult education's role in fostering equality. Six priority areas are identified (DES, 2000, p. 28).

---

[2] These aims are to - reflect on the role of Adult Education in the context of an overall vision for the development of this society; - build on the consultation process surrounding the Green Paper ... - set out Government priorities and ... framework for the future development of the sector ... - identify the priority areas for public investment in Adult Education, in the light of a rapidly changing societal and cultural context and in the context of an overall commitment to lifelong learning; - identify priority groups and programme areas ... - elaborate upon the roles of various providers in the field ... - provide for a learner-centred framework incorporating infrastructural elements such as guidance and counselling, quality assurance and the training of trainers, and ... a coherent range of pathways for adults between education and training and other relevant supports; - propose a comprehensive structural framework at national and local level - set adult education as an integral element of a framework for lifelong learning.

Text Box 4.2: Adult Education within an Overall Vision for the Society

1. consciousness raising - to enable people realise their full human potential in a way that draws on the links between their individual personal experiences and wider structural factors

2. citizenship - enabling individual members of the society to grow in self-confidence, social awareness and social responsibility and to take an active role in shaping the overall direction of society ... and to engage proactively in community and societal decision-making.

3. cohesion -the empowerment of those experiencing significant disadvantage so that they may play a full and active part in all areas of the social and economic life

4. competitiveness - providing a skilled workforce to meet the needs of a knowledge society and in promoting prosperity, employment and growth supporting adaptability and change

5. cultural development – enriching the cultural fabric of society

6. community building – the development of a structural analysis and a collective sense of purpose among marginalised people who share common problems

(DES, 2000, p. 28).

These are proposed as constituting an overall framework of lifelong learning and could be regarded as a charter for emancipatory adult education, were it not for the inclusion of 'competitiveness'. The conflict at the heart of the Paper is laid bare in its assignation to adult education of the role of:

> providing a skilled workforce to meet the needs of a knowledge society, and in promoting prosperity, employment and growth. The skill levels and quality of the workforce are increasingly viewed as providing the cutting edge in competing in the global economy. (DES, 2000, p. 29)

This exposition accords with classical human capital theory which is explored below and the inclusion of 'competitiveness' is justified with the contention that 'All industrialised countries now recognise the validity of a broadly-based, investigative, learning model focused not only on specific task-related skills but on personal development and interpersonal issues' (DES, 2000, p. 29). The absence here of a socially-centred focus is noteworthy. Following this, the assertion is then made that: 'This White Paper is underpinned by three core principles namely: (a) Lifelong Learning as a Systemic Approach; (b) Equality; (c) Inter-culturalism (DES, 2000, p. 30).

The principle of equality is duly rehearsed as follows in Text Box 4.3:

Text Box 4.3: The Principle of Equality as Expounded in the White Paper (2000. p. 33)

The Government recognises that barriers arising from differences of socioeconomic status, ethnicity, disability and gender continue to hinder the emergence of a fully inclusive and cohesive society. Considering the significance of educational attainment in a society where qualifications are becoming ever more important, inequalities in educational opportunities and attainments arising from such barriers are a major concern.

Inequalities in education due to socio-economic differences have been well documented and this Chapter presents an overview of current educational attainment levels of Irish adults. Clearly, if Adult Education is to counteract the impact of disadvantage in early school participation and achievement, there must be careful targeting of initiatives on those most in need. Such targeting is a central pillar of the National Anti-Poverty Strategy, and is reflected also in the key principles underpinning the £194m package of measures to address educational disadvantage published by Government in December 1999. These measures address every level of education from early childhood to adult literacy and third- level education.

Stripped of circumlocution, this outline of the equality principle amounts to little more than a policy statement to the effect that 'there must be a careful targeting of initiatives on those most in need.'

Following upon this perspective on equality, four 'Pillars' are projected. One, a National Adult Literacy Programme, is acknowledged as a response to "the International Literacy Survey (1997) [which] elevated concerns about the adult literacy problem to centre stage in educational policy" (DES, 2000, p. 86). Another, the Back to Education Initiative (BTEI), is designed to provide 'opportunities to return to learning for adults and ... a re-entry route for those in the workplace who wish to upgrade their skills in line with emerging needs' (DES, 2000, p. 93). An ICT (sic) Basic Skills programme is a third pillar. The fourth is 'Self-funded part-time Adult Education' which was to be facilitated by a variety of modest measures such as the abolition of 'the self-financing principle for *certain categories of students'* (emphasis in the original) (DES, 2000, p. 103). In its entirety, therefore, equality was to be advanced by a combination of opportunities residing in:

(i) the extension of the existing literacy provision,

(ii) a widening of access opportunities for those within and without the workplace,

(iii) the development of an ICT programme in basic skills and

(iv) some infrastructural support for school-based self-funded activity, historically designated liberal adult education.

Unfortunately, there is no indication as to how these programmes were to be articulated with the aforementioned priority areas which were deemed to reflect 'an overall vision for the society' (DES, 2000, p. 28) namely: consciousness raising; citizenship; cohesion; cultural development; and community building. Instead, the section elaborating on the 'Four Pillars' is replete with references to training, jobskilling and accreditation with, in the case of BTEI, the following outcomes specified: 'ICT, electronic, engineering and e-commerce training, the development of foreign language proficiency, and the provision of childcare training' (DES, 2000, p. 95). This was clearly focussing on the labour market rather than the needs of the community.

It is in the chapter on community education that prospects of a significant emancipatory standpoint emerge. Community education is seen:

> ...in a more ideological sense as a process of communal education towards empowerment, both at an individual and a collective level. Such an approach to community education sees it as an interactive, challenging process, not only in terms of its content but also in terms of its methodologies and decision-making processes. (DES, 2000, p. 110)

A commitment to provide the community education sector with: 'the recognition and the resources that reflect its importance and which can release further potential' (DES, 2000, p. 114) is made in the Paper. This would appear to be corroborated by the appointment, as promised, of Community Education Facilitators (CEFs) nationwide in 2003. While the appointment of CEFs brought a welcome dynamic to the field and led to an increase in participation because of the increased reach it conferred on VECs/ETBs, their activities are determined by Circular letter 45/02 from which any consideration of the principle of equality is absent.

Much was promised in this White Paper. White Papers are noted for their promise but fulfilment is another matter. At least equality was afforded centrality in the White Paper, in the sense that it was designated as one of the three underlying principles. Additionally, a particular strategy in keeping with the prevailing standpoint on measures that would lead to a 'fully inclusive and cohesive society' emanated from that. While there was no attempt to define what was meant by a society so designated, this strategy reflected the narrative that had been in the ascendant throughout the later decades of the 20th century, namely that inequality could be countered by the provision of educational opportunity. Given that the expansion of such opportunity has led instead to a society which is among the most unequal in terms of income distribution, a data-driven strategy is clearly ineffectual from an equality perspective. Instead, the narrative and the perspective represented could only be adjudged as commensurate with what has been designated liberal egalitarianism which 'is based on the assumption that many major inequalities are inevitable' (Baker et al, 2009, p.33).

While the resultant strategy has its merits as far as individual empowerment is concerned, it fails to incorporate any rationale for its impact on society at large. It is of interest to adult educators to reflect on what the correlation is between individual empowerment through educational opportunity and the well-being of society. Inglis (1997, p. 4) contrasts individual empowerment with emancipation and his comments bear more consideration than has been the case. In essence, he argues that:

> ...empowerment involves people developing capacities to act successfully within the existing system and structures of power, while emancipation concerns critically analyzing, resisting and challenging structures of power.

It is indeed likely that access to educational opportunity tends to lead more directly to social mobility for the individual than to a concern with the issues confronting society. After all, access to education in Ireland has increased exponentially in recent decades. Notwithstanding this, during much of this period income inequality fluctuated in a pattern whereby the average income of those on the highest income quintile remained unchanged at around five times that of those on the lowest quintile (CSO/SILC, 2011, p. 2). If anything, extending access to education as it is constituted would seem to contribute to the maintenance if not to the exacerbation of income inequality with all that flows from that, rather than eliminating inequality as an outcome.

From the perspective of developments since 2000, it is judicious to ask - how does the Paper's equality perspective resonate with theories of equality that have recently been injected into the narrative of human science?

Equality: From shadow to substance

The following table summarises equality of condition as expounded by Baker et al. (2009, p. 43), and shows how it compares with basic equality and liberal egalitarianism.

Table 4.2: Basic Equality, Liberal Egalitarianism and Equality of Condition

Dimensions of equality	Basic equality	Liberal egalitarianism	Equality of condition
Respect and recognition	Basic respect	Universal citizenship Toleration of difference Public/private distinction	Universal citizenship 'Critical interculturalism': - acceptance of diversity - redefined public/private distinction - critical dialogue over cultural differences Limits to unequal esteem
Resources	Subsistence needs	Anti-poverty focus Rawls's difference principle (maximise the prospects of the worst off)	Substantial equality of resources broadly defined, aimed at satisfying needs and enabling roughly equal prospects of well-being
Love, care and solidarity		A private matter? Adequate care?	Ample prospects for relations of love, care and solidarity
Power relations	Protection against human and degrading treatment	Classic civil and personal rights Liberal democracy	Liberal rights but - limited property rights; - group-related rights Stronger, more participatory politics Extension of democracy to other areas of life
Working and learning		Occupational and educational equal opportunity Decent work? Basic education	Educational and occupational options that give everyone the prospect of self-development and satisfying work.

The concept of equality as featured in the White Paper fails to incorporate any vision of the need for adult education to work towards a society characterised by features such as:

- mutuality of well-being and respect for, and appreciation of, diversity including ethical and cultural diversity
- substantive solidarity that would address class-based inequalities
- a fair and equal distribution of resources
- active, participative democracy
- equality in access and participation as applying to education and employment.

The foregoing features of equality of condition, listed as characteristic of an equal society, are merely summative, of course. Whereas other forms of egalitarianism are aimed at intervening in inequalities that are viewed as inevitable, the aim of equality of condition is 'to eliminate major inequalities altogether, or at least massively to reduce the current scale of inequality' (Baker et al, 2009, p, 33).

While, in the section on community education, some consideration is given to more emancipatory functions, the White Paper's outline of the principle of equality, as reproduced above, can be said to hinge solely on the provision of opportunities for 'attainment'. In the prevailing educational order this largely converts into the acquisition of qualifications. *Learning for Life* can be seen, therefore, as informed by liberal egalitarianism which is a set of principles guiding much of the mores and legislation operating throughout most of the so-called developed world. A leading tenet of liberal egalitarianism is that equality of opportunity should obtain in all matters. Unfortunately, that ignores the fact that in the competitive world that is a product of neo-liberal doctrine, people start out from unequal backgrounds and while measures are often introduced in attempts to compensate for this, the essentially unequal nature of society remains unchanged. Targeting resources on individuals is unlikely to bring about societal change. It is the structure of society that needs to be addressed and all the discriminatory measures that help sustain its inequality that need to be targeted.

Equality of condition is about seeking the emergence of a society in which individuals and their communities relate to each other through a distribution of power which is based on: mutual respect and recognition; a culture which is founded on such principles as love, care and solidarity; a distribution of resources that extends the prospect of well-being to all; and the provision of options for entry into learning and work which are based on fairness and justice rather than contrasting background levels of economic and social capital. Equality of condition can be seen to be significantly more ambitious regarding the attainment of equality than the principle enunciated in the White Paper. The attainment of this is a worthy mission for adult education. Were the field informed by equality of condition it would combine personal development with a social justice vision, a much more complex undertaking and not without challenges to everyone involved. However, equality of condition and, increasingly, even the lesser categories of equality, are countered by the widespread adoption of an opposing force - human capital - which gains its momentum from the sway of neo-liberalism.

An exercise in colonisation: Human capital and lifelong learning

The concept human capital made its inaugural appearance in Europe, – stealthily and unobtrusively - in 1995 with the publication of the White Paper: *Teaching and Learning: Towards the Learning Society* (European Commission, 1995). It originated elsewhere. Among those who first promoted human capital prior to this was Theodore Schultz, an economist at Chicago University School of Economics. In December 1961, Schultz opened his Presidential address[3] to the annual meeting of the American Economic Association (AEA) as follows:

> Although it is obvious that people acquire useful skills and knowledge, it is not obvious that these skills and knowledge are a form of capital, that this capital is in substantial part a product of deliberate investment, that it has grown in Western societies at a much faster rate than conventional (non-human) capital, and that its growth may well be the most distinctive feature of the economic system. Investment in human capital is probably the major explanation for this difference. (Schultz, 1961, p.1)

The concept was subsequently inserted into the mainstream of economics by Gary Becker[4], a colleague of Schultz's at the Economics Department, University of Chicago. Since then, economists and management gurus have fastened onto human capital as a convenient, semantic category to cover all the dynamics affecting the capacity of a workforce and it has largely attained uncritical currency. As an inevitable corollary, the idea has been extended

---

[3] This was six years before the OECD study Investment in Education; it took some 40 years before adult education became thoroughly colonised by the concept.

[4] Human Capital: A Theoretical and Empirical Analysis, with Special Reference to Education.

pervasively into the unwitting consciousness of the individual who is persuaded to assume greater responsibility for her/his so-called human capital.

Unsurprisingly, the Organisation for Economic Cooperation and Development (OECD) has long embraced and promoted human capital which it defines as follows:

Text Box 4.4: Human capital defined

Human capital is broadly defined as a combination of individuals' own innate talents and abilities and the skills and learning they acquire through education and training. The business world, which has eagerly embraced the concept of human capital, tends to define it more narrowly as workforce skills and talents directly relevant to the success of a company or specific industry.(OECD, 2007. p. 2)

The caveat inserted by the OECD concerning the business world's appropriation of the concept clearly indicates that, within the economic system, ownership of the 'capital' in question is deemed to reside in the organization. To postulate this is to reduce the members of the workforce to the status of expendable foot-soldiers in a battleground dominated by the rallies and retreats of market forces. This is a reality that has been repeatedly visible in contemporary Ireland whereby some multi-national companies have been quick to abandon their operations here when cheaper 'human capital' presents as satisfying their requirements elsewhere. Human capital, reposing in the ownership of business, can be seen to objectify the human by introducing this complex notion of value as determined by future income-earning potential.[5]

Definitions of human capital, including – especially – Schultz's, reveal its core premise. As with the Irish government some half-century later (discussed below), Schultz located it exclusively within 'the economic system', noting its growth and its contribution to the 'national output' as well as identifying it as a decisive 'factor of production'. Indeed, in the competitive environment being negotiated by nation states – and confederations of same, such

---

[5] It is not too fanciful to suggest that definitions such as those of Schultz and the OECD are evocative of one of Freire's pronouncements: 'The oppressor consciousness tends to transform everything surrounding it into an object of its domination. The earth, property, production, the creations of people, people themselves, time - everything is reduced to the status of objects at its disposal.' (Freire, 1970, p. 40)

as the EU – enhancement of knowledge and skill sets[6] is the overriding motif within the notion of human capital. The market-driven need for such enhancement inevitably gives rise to human capital development. Enhancement can only be obtained by exposure to learning, be that informal and incidental or formal, invariably entailing third-party facilitation. However, the learning entailed in human capital development is very circumscribed, being focused on the needs of production or administration in the workplace or market, with specific objectives, accordingly. These are overwhelmingly concerned with applied knowledge, skills, capacities and talents. Within such parameters, human activity is reduced to commodification. It becomes open to quantification and measurement through changes registered in output. This has given rise to such mechanistic approaches to learning as can be noted in the emergence of Mager-type behavioural approaches to the formulation of learning objectives[7]. There is invariably no pretence that learning for human capital development relates to any areas of human activity other than those within the economic domain. The knowledge and skills involved are all linked symbiotically with the demands of the marketplace. Accordingly, education is increasingly coerced into being instrumental and policy is forced to adjust accordingly leading to programmes that are increasingly utilitarian in orientation.

O'Sullivan (2005, p. 114), offers an outline of the development of human capital theory and its impact on educational policy to contemporary times which he characterises as part of the shift towards the positivism that now prevails. He collates this in a table (which he adapted from Marginson, 1997, p. 116, Table 4.2). In this a series of 'waves' is delineated. The following table is an extrapolation.

---

[6] The neologism 'upskilling' being the most commonly encountered indicator.

[7] A behavioural objective should have three components: (i) Behaviour – the behaviour should be specific and measurable (ii) Condition – the conditions under which the behaviour is to be completed should be stated, including what tools or assistance is to be provided and (iii) Standard – the level of performance that is desirable should be stated, including an acceptable range of answers that are allowable as correct. Mager, R. F. (1961). *Preparing Objectives for Programmed Instruction*. California: Fearon Publishers.

Table 4.3: Human Capital Theory and the Policy Process

Theory	Main Theoretical Assumptions	Government Practices
First Wave Human Capital Theory (the 1960s, as indicated above).	Education leads to productivity and investment in education leads to economic growth	Expansion of education provision, supported by funding; equal opportunity to maximise human capital
Screening theory (1970s – 1980s)	Education credentials are a surrogate for individual productivity; education is a screening device that distributes jobs	Cessation of increases in expenditure; programmes linking education to work; standardisation of qualifications
Second Wave Human Capital Theory (1990s)	Education augments the capacity to handle new technologies and other innovations	Selective investment in education in high technology and management areas
Market Liberal Human Capital Theory (personalised and episodic)	Individuals invest in education until costs exceed the expected benefits, mostly, future earnings	Programmes and policies to secure self-managing individual development: the selective use of student assistance, 'talking up' participation, income contingent fees and loans schemes etc.

O'Sullivan/ Margison (2005) offer a revealing indication of the extent to which human capital has colonized education and, as a corollary, impacted on its ethos during the period in which lifelong learning also evolved as a notional holism. The most recent stage in its evolution reveals a development whereby much of the responsibility for accumulating human capital is transferred onto the individual.

The imposition of the idea of human capital on the consciousness of the workforce has long since reduced much of adult education to a market commodity. Combined with the growth of individualism, this has given rise to alienation from education for social purpose thus serving to reinforce rather than undo the stratification of society. Side by side with the emergence of human capital, neo-liberalism has also grown apace, much of it also the product of the Chicago School of Economics so that they have become inseparable bedfellows colonising education in the interest of market forces.

Apart from adult-cum-further education, human capital theory has informed much of what has passed for general education policy in recent times. As the field of education is one in which power has always been at play, an issue then is to try and establish how the concept of lifelong learning facilitated this and how this plays out particularly in state-funded adult education.

As the title of the Kenny Report indicated, the notion of lifelong learning had some currency in Ireland in the early 1980s. However, it came to maturity elsewhere.

Lifelong learning as a concept had been promoted by UNESCO (education permanente, 1972) and the OECD (recurrent education, 1973). However, these promptings largely went unheeded until the European Union began to take an interest. Eventually, its revival was clearly signalled in 1993 with the publication by the EU of its White Paper *Growth, Competitiveness, Employment: The Challenges and Ways Forward into the 21st Century*. As a harbinger of what was to come, Chapter 7 was titled *Adaptation of Education and Vocational Training Systems*. In the course of this it was proposed to overhaul these systems and re-direct them towards a more utilitarian function. The thrust of the paper is best illustrated in the first of its general objectives for the 'reform of education and vocational training systems' (European Commission, 1993, p. 119) which states 'the main principle of the various types of measures to be taken should be to develop human resources throughout people's working lives, starting with basic education and working through initial training to continuing training.' Adult education which depended on EU funding was clearly going to be in the firing line.

Lifelong learning attained vogue status in 1995 with the publication of the White Paper *Teaching and Learning: Towards the Learning Society* by the European Commission. As already noted, this paper included references to human capital. This marked a most significant development as far as adult learning in the member states is concerned. The European Union is precluded from direct engagement in the education systems of member states but Articles 126 and 127 of the Maastricht Treaty (1992) had facilitated a role of advocacy and mentoring and this was to be exercised systematically from this juncture on.

The reincarnation of the idea of 'lifelong learning' at first gave rise to fresh hope for adult education in the expectation it would feature as a constituent part. However, its authors, the

EU Commission, only accorded the field the most cursory attention. Following its publication, the European Parliament and Council declared the following year - 1996 - the *Year of Lifelong Learning*, confirming the centrality of the concept in the Union's strategy for growth. This centrality was soon applied to the so-called Lisbon Agenda agreed by the European Council early in the year 2000, months ahead of the publication of Ireland's *Learning for Life*. The Council had been convened 'to agree a new strategic goal for the Union in order to strengthen employment, economic reform and social cohesion as part of a knowledge-based economy' (European Council, 2000, p. 1). The document heralding the strategy was strongly pragmatic. Predicated on the thesis that the lifeworld experienced by humanity had been transformed by the development of a digitised learning society, the Council ordained that it was incumbent on everyone to recognise this and to deploy digitisation whether for production or consumption.

Among the many measures deemed necessary for the achievement of this vision, education and training loomed large. The member states were all urged 'to take the necessary steps' to attain targets specified as follows:

> ...a European framework should define the new basic skills to be provided through lifelong learning: IT skills, foreign languages, technological culture, entrepreneurship and social skills; a European diploma for basic IT skills, with decentralised certification procedures, should be established in order to promote digital literacy throughout the Union. (European Council, 2000, pp. 8-9)

Lifelong learning was therefore to be at the centre of the strategy but clearly a version to be dominated by human capital development. This was rooted in the unexamined notion that acquisition of the express skills (IT, linguistic, entrepreneurial and social) - combined with accreditation - empowers participants thereby countering social exclusion. The Lisbon strategy did indeed concern itself with the need to promote social inclusion but its standpoint on this is neatly summed up in its own aphorism 'the best safeguard against social exclusion is a job' (European Council, 2000, p. 11).

Ever since, the EU has relentlessly urged its view of lifelong learning on the member states. Although it is precluded - under the founding Treaty of Rome - from directly intervening in the education system of member countries a process known as the Open Method of

Coordination (OMC)[8] was instituted with the adoption of the Lisbon Agenda, in 2000. This allows the EU to make recommendations, a measure which could be viewed as a further softening of the original embargo following that under the Maastricht Treaty. EU Commission staff quickly responded with a *Memorandum on Lifelong Learning*. This was expressly concerned with six 'key messages': New basic skills for all; More investment in human resources; Innovation in teaching and learning; Valuing learning; Rethinking guidance and counselling; Bringing learning closer to home (European Commission, 2000, p. 20)

One notes that there is no reference to either social inclusion or exclusion in this set of priorities but, instead, that the rank order indicates an orientation towards the embrace of human capital theory with its emphasis on skills and human resources. Indeed, the memorandum merely makes one modest gesture towards equality in a passing reference to gender equality and the needs of 'Third Age' citizenry. Notwithstanding this, extensive reference is made throughout the memorandum on social issues and the need for social cohesion. However, the strategy for achieving this reveals a particular mindset, being summarised as follows: 'Education and training have become more important than ever before in influencing people's chances of "getting in, getting on and getting up in life"' (European Commission, 2000, p. 9), in other words gaining a foothold in the existing order.

Over the decade 2000 to 2010 a flood of missives promoting lifelong learning was pressed on the member states by the EU. The Commission followed its earlier memorandum with a further communication in 2001: *Making a European Area of Lifelong Learning a Reality*.

Here it opts for a definition:

Text Box 4.5: Lifelong Learning *a la* the European Commission

> ...all learning activity undertaken throughout life, with the aim of improving knowledge, skills and competences within a personal, civic, social and/or employment-related perspective. (European Commission, 2001, p. 9)

---

[8] OMC is an implementation of a 'participative management by objectives' approach on the European level. ... the OMC basically is a process whereby the European Commission develops certain objectives and a corresponding timeframe in a specific area of (social) policy, which then become the basis for contracts with the member states. (Tuschling, & Engemann, 2006, p. 453).

This document cites valuing of learning as a prime objective within the new 'reality' with, as corollary, 'Valuing formal diplomas and certificates' (European Commission, 2001, p. 16). While some of the other statements had emancipatory potential, notably the valuing of non-formal and informal learning, the emphasis on accreditation tended to foreclose such possibility.

In 2003 the OECD lent its weight to developments with the document *Beyond Rhetoric: Adult Learning Policies and Practices*. Unsurprisingly, the organisation that laid the foundations - in 1966 - for the ultimate colonisation of education in Ireland by human capital theory now explicitly advocated its deployment: 'Enhancing the financial incentives to invest in the human capital of adults, at the individual and enterprise levels, can stimulate adults to participate in learning' (OECD, 2003, p. 9).Equally unsurprisingly, at this juncture also, the World Bank went as far as valorizing human capital as a panacea for the plight of the developing world: 'Investment in human capital is critical for economic growth' (World Bank, 2003, p. 4).

In February 2005, dissatisfied with the rate of progress on attaining the levels of adult learning proposed in the Lisbon agenda of 2000, the President and Vice-President of the European Commission made a lengthy submission to the spring meeting of the European Council. In the course of this they advocated 'Investing more in human capital through better education and skills', (European Commission, 2005a, p. 26). In keeping with this standpoint and also in tandem with the now ubiquitously invoked concept of 'innovation', human capital was invoked throughout, with a stab at quantification:

> Investment in human capital is also necessary because highly skilled people are the ones who are best equipped to work with the most productive capital and to implement organisational changes appropriate for the new technologies. An increase by one year in the average education level of the labour force might add as much as 0.3 to 0.5 percentage points to the annual EU GDP growth rate. (Commission of the European Communities, 2005a, p. 28)

As can be seen, European bureaucracy tended to objectify the people of Europe as repositories of human capital to be cultivated accordingly for the purpose of achieving economic goals, the all-embracing goal. The influence of the EU on member countries is also manifest in the demand made in this document: 'Member States must fulfil their commitment to put in place Lifelong Learning Strategies by 2006' (European Commission, 2005a, p. 27).

Indeed, 2005 was a busy year for the EU's Commission in regard to its lifelong learning mission. On the heels of the document presented earlier to the Council, the Commission staff issued a working paper on education and training in March, 2005. In this, the benchmarks set in 2001 were reviewed. This is a very comprehensive document that reveals a noteworthy concern with social objectives. However, the paper reveals a narrower focus towards the end in the declaration that people and their skills are a form of human capital and an asset so that 'all spending on education and training, from public or private sources, is thus considered investment in human capital' (European Commission, 2005b, p. 60), once again showing a tendency to reify people.

Towards the end of 2005, the Commission submitted a document to the European Parliament and to the Council recommending the adoption of a set of key competences as central to the lifelong learning project. This marked the elevation of human capital theory to a position of primacy within education and theory. The intent is clear in the title of this document[9] – while jobs were to be the solution to all issues as had been trumpeted in the original Lisbon strategy and competences were to be central to lifelong learning. The Council broadly accepted the proposal to develop the key competencies in question and, in the process, agreed to consolidate their role in education and learning 'the development of skills and competences is a key element of lifelong learning strategies' (European Council, 2005, p. 21).

Ultimately these competences – compiled by 'experts' from 31 countries and European level stakeholders – comprised eight in all:

1. communication in the mother tongue;
2. communication in foreign languages;
3. competences in maths, science and technology;
4. digital competence;
5. learning to learn;
6. interpersonal, intercultural and social competences, and civic competence;
7. sense of initiative and entrepreneurship;
8. cultural expression.

(European Commission, 2007, pp. 1-12)

---

[9]Recommendation of the European Parliament and of the Council on key competences for lifelong learning.

Of the eight competences, only one can be deemed to be concerned with social issues and that only in part. Consequently, this prioritising of competences, when contrasted with the absence of a tradition of critical pedagogy in all sectors of education, inevitably works to ensure that social justice issues are fated to occupy the margins. Human capital theory was firmly in the ascendant, the rationale clearly being one of fixing the prevailing system rather than reforming or re-directing it.

The policy position of the EU is largely unchanged since this period of consolidation with human capital theory retaining its unassailable position of centrality.

Following Suit: Ireland

In 2002 the *Report of the Taskforce on Lifelong Learning* was launched by its sponsoring Department: Enterprise, Trade and Employment an event which generated no queries about where the responsibility for learning lay. Everything about the report reflects the impact of human capital theory. While it adopted a vision of lifelong learning that was inclusive, an early assertion in the report that: 'Lifelong Learning forms a major plank of the EU employment strategy and associated Employment Guidelines' (Department of Enterprise, Trade and Employment (DETE), 2002, p. 5) illustrates both the standpoint of the taskforce and its deference to what had become normalised within the EU. The pragmatism at its centre is best revealed in its summary contents: Statistical Overview; The National Framework of Qualifications; Basic Skills; Information and Guidance; Delivery, Access and Funding and; The Workplace.

Human capital theory could now be seen to inform the government-sponsored view of lifelong learning exclusively and, as far as its implementation was concerned, the lifeworld was indeed to be colonised by the system-world (state and business)[10] – both prominent in the membership of the Taskforce on Lifelong Learning. Indeed, one of the more progressive outcomes of the White Paper of 2000 – the establishment of the National Adult Learning Council on an ad hoc basis in 2002 – was terminated two short years later so that there was no longer even a modest shred of pretence at democratic engagement in the shaping of lifelong

---

[10] Both State and Business were strongly represented in the Taskforce which was hosted by the Department of Enterprise. Of the 20 members, eight represented different Government Departments and four different business interests. Three members represented higher education interests, two represented trade union interests and one represented FÁS. The Community and Voluntary Pillar had two representatives.

learning as applied to the adult sector. With that, the potential for an emancipatory narrative within adult education was marginalized.

All relevant national documents that emerged in the interval have relentlessly promoted this new symbiosis between lifelong learning and human capital development. *The Human Capital Investment Operational Programme* (2007-2013) exemplifies this. Adult education is invoked once: 'Adult literacy is the Government's top priority in adult education' (DETE, 2007, p. 54). On the other hand, the government's policy on lifelong learning is unmistakably shot through with human capital theory indicating the form adult education was to take:

> Government is committed to the implementation of a Lifelong Learning policy and to the modernisation of the workplace. Under Towards 2016, it was agreed that one of the high level objectives to be reached is to drive the lifelong learning agenda by enhancing access to training, the development of new skills, the acquisition of recognised qualifications and progression to higher level qualifications. (DETE, 2007, p. 58)

Lifelong learning is therefore clearly seen as designed to support the economy. What then about the twin objective of social inclusion? The short section dealing with this notes that the focus was to be on two specific areas: 'Upskilling the Workforce and the Activation of Groups Outside the Workforce ... delivered to groups such as older people, migrants and ethnic minorities, women, young people and people with a disability' (DETE, 2007, p. 62). Clearly, human capital is perceived as offering the panacea by which social exclusion will become history and social inclusion an all-pervasive condition.

Perhaps it is reasonable to suggest that the coup de grâce to anything approximating to emancipatory education was administered with the publication in 2008 of *Building Ireland's Smart Economy: A Framework for Sustainable Economic Renewal* (Department of An Taoiseach, 2008). With its assertion (p. 74) that 'a particular focus needs to be on efforts to increase participation in lifelong learning by promoting opportunities for education and training, in order to facilitate required upskilling and reskilling', the so-called Smart Economy was billed as the route to lead Ireland out of the socio-economic and fiscal abyss into which it had been plunged.

Finally, the triumph of human capital theory in colonising state-supported adult education is clearly illustrated in the Guidelines for the *Back to Education Initiative (BTEI) Operational*

Guidelines[11] circulated in 2012 by the Department of Education and Skills. Of four aims, the final one (DES, 2012c, p. 3) declaims:

> In the current context, the BTEI enables providers to address the skills needs of unemployed people, in particular the priority groups identified in the Government's activation agenda, and to develop part-time education and training opportunities for low-skilled people in employment to gain qualifications.

This is subsequently seen to translate into a brief outline of approved content within which balance would seem to be struck between lifeworld needs and those indicated by the market while, on the other hand, the priority afforded human capital development surfaces in the accreditation dimensions:

Course content should be relevant to learners' personal, social and cultural needs, prior learning and to labour market needs, underpinned by the National Skills Strategy. Provision should offer access to minor awards related to the key competences of Communications, Mathematics, Information and Communications Technology (DES, 2012c, p. 7)

A pragmatic view would concur with the aims and objectives of the BTEI guidelines but that would be to acquiesce in a dispensation in which the role of state-supported adult education can be seen to be largely unconcerned with issues of social purpose. Instead of being imbued with such a vision, the arrangements are clearly designed to perpetuate the status quo and facilitate, at best, inclusion within the same.

Voices from the field

The most instructive part of a PhD I completed in 2012 arose from consultations I had with twenty-two learners and seventeen educators in the course of fieldwork. These were engaged with the following programmes: Back to Education Initiative (BTEI); Vocational Training Opportunities Scheme (VTOS); Literacy Education; Senior Travellers Training; and

---

[11] BTEI is co-funded by the Irish Government and the European Union under the European Social Fund.

Community Education. Appended are extracts from the Information sheets for both learners and educators to indicate what I hoped to explore in the course of semi-structured interviews.

The adult learners who participated were, for the most part, residents of the North Inner part of Dublin city; a minority resided in an area outside of this in which the local schools are designated disadvantaged. Both areas have traditionally experienced low levels of transfer to higher education. Among the findings that resulted from interviews with the learners were:

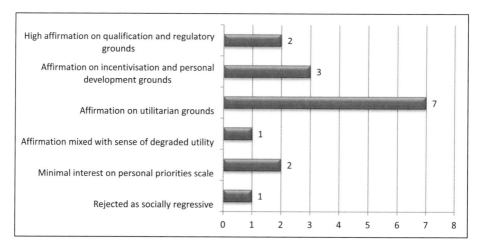

Figure 4.1: Attitudes to accreditation

Of those who commented, the majority (4:1) were in favour of accredited learning on different grounds but within this group, with the exception of three, motivation resulted from factors external to their personal needs such as the expectations of employers and the ever-warming qualifications climate. It is possible to speculate therefore that the widespread neo-liberal narrative, such as that contained in the welfare-to-work mantra constitutes an impetus for engaging in adult education even if the accreditation on offer suggests pathways to work that is short of appeal and reward or inaccessible.

92

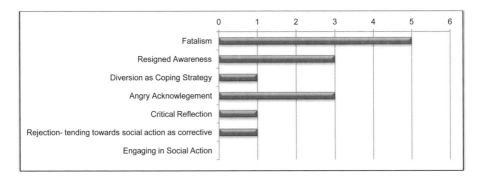

Figure 4.2: Attitudes evinced towards inequality in Irish society

The attitudes towards inequality ranged from feeling disempowered in the majority of cases to more hopeful signs of resistance and outright rejection. Condemnation prevailed particularly among those engaged in VTOS, BTEI and Community Education learning. These last indicated that those deemed to be disadvantaged by virtue of qualifying for state-supported learning are open to acquiring a more enriching skill, that of informed critique, which is ultimately unaccepting of society's prevailing inequality. In particular, the learners in VTOS demonstrated how participative exposure to Sociology was revealing of the inequities that characterised much of their personal experiences and the lifeworlds of their communities.

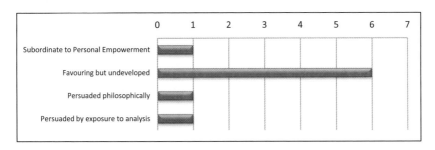

Figure 4.3: Disposition towards criticality as part of Adult Education

Of those who commented on this, the majority clearly showed a disposition to engage in critique. Indeed, it emerged that where educators facilitated this it was both welcomed and enjoyed, although, as indicated in the foregoing figure none had yet reached the stage of engaging in social action as an outcome

The following is a set of comments by an interviewee who showed exceptional capacity for critique throughout our encounter and attributed this to being exposed to the writings of such as Illich, Freire and Fanon by a tutor at an early stage of re-entry to education. It amounts to a thorough repudiation of the neoliberal thrust at the heart of state-funded adult education:

> *...it's one of the things that holds back the inner-cities, and maybe even people in the country, that everything around education is geared towards getting you back into the workforce ... I could never understand that they wouldn't allow the individuals to grow within that education. It's very narrow ... we have computer courses run in order to fit people in with jobs, say for Microsoft and places like that, which further down the road might not necessarily be available in the country no more to employ people ... Which to me is fairly narrow. Instead of giving someone an education programme that opens them up to understanding that there's many different choices in life. Like I always wondered about the programme of Adult Education ... where they train people through a narrow programme for jobs and not train them to understand the world. And what I mean by that is, these people go on and can educate other people in the area, you know? Make that area strong. And then you actually have what is real transformative education.*

It is instructive to juxtapose these comments with what is set out as one of the four objectives of BTEI in the operational guidelines of 2012 and which closely approximates to what Freire designated as banking education:

> In the current context, the BTEI enables providers to address the skills needs of unemployed people, in particular the priority groups identified in the Government's activation agenda, and to develop part-time education and training opportunities for low skilled people in employment to gain qualifications. (DES, 2012c, p. 3)

The educators whom I consulted (tutors in the main plus three administrators) were able to range widely, for the most part, as a result of considerable experience and engagement with adult education.

When asked what they understood by inequality in society there was a surprising range of responses. One tutor confessed:

> *I probably never thought about...an equal society...do you not think there's always going to be the underdog and that...you can never bring everybody up?*

A reflective administrator observed:

...it's the lack of voice really I think is one of the big things...they know they're being done out of something. They may not know what, but people know. From the grassroots.

An enquiry about adult education's potential as a strand in the promotion of equality yielded the following relative unanimity:

I think it can - if it's properly resourced and people are given the space to do it and it's not based specifically around labour market needs.

...if we're looking for equality of condition it's much, much broader than adult education and I think that, given the resources that adult education has in Ireland, we're a long, long way off equality of condition.

Well, I don't think adult education on its own can bring about change. I think it's one strand of work. I believe, anyway, that community development more broadly [pause] campaigning, groups, justice groups, political action, I think all of that's required...

However, the conditions and circumstances constraining state-funded adult education militated strongly against emancipatory education as several asserted:

It's probably not happening in any significant way - no it's not...The kind of adult education we're talking about...[adult education] is still very unequal in itself compared to the rest of the sectors. So if it's unequal within the overall scheme of things - how does it then help to make other things equal...it's already a victim itself.

...we're restricted in a lot of ways because I think education...as it's funded, very often is about moving individuals up the ladder but in a still quite unjust society...it's not about changing society itself...it's really more about fitting in!

Paid tutors certainly wouldn't [foster transitive consciousness] because they wouldn't be allowed to go out and influence change in that particular way, to campaign or to be radical in your community...

That an adult education tutor conceded she had never 'thought about an equal society', while very revealing, is unsurprising given its omission from the narrative and methodological implications as described by others, in two cases colourfully:

Now, when have you gone to a meeting on Adult Education in the VEC when someone has mentioned social justice? They'd turn around and think you were on something...

Never heard anyone mention it - I think they'd fall off the chair if I was at a meeting and raised it - they'd think I was watching too much Oprah or wanted to give them a hug!

...any kind of training is difficult to do because you are working with part-time teachers, who, if you were to put on a training course on a particular day, a lot of them would be working somewhere else that day. So, do they give up the money they would have earned for that day? Do they let those groups down? You can't pay tutors for going to training...to do the kind of in-service you might like to do - it's very hard!...you can't get the people for it - and you can't blame them.

These remarks seem to reveal a combination of practical and ideo-political barriers to the development of emancipatory approaches within adult education. While my fieldwork was concerned with the specific area of state-supported adult education within a very limited spatial area, a more insidious finding was contained in a national report:

> VECs were less likely to use process focused criteria such as participation methodologies, a focus on social/community action or those pertaining to critical analysis, to make decisions about what groups to fund. Yet, these aspects of methodology are, according to the White Paper, what makes community education unique. (Bailey, Breen &Ward, 2011, p. 102)

Many other enlightening findings emerged from the collaborative fieldwork in which I was privileged to engage. Among the great ironies uncovered was the readiness of learners, unsupported and on their own initiative, to engage in social action. This was vividly described by one learner who characterised herself as an unlikely activist when outlining the spontaneous, independent response of her fellow learners to the threatened discontinuation of a valued facility in their community:

> *...the ladies that I was in the group [pause] they were very strong. They'd get together if they needed anything [pause] like the swimming pool down the road there that was being closed by the city council. And the ladies [pause] in the knitting group [pause] and I suppose some of the ladies in the other courses as well, all got together...They all marched down there to the local swimming pool and assembled there with their banners. The whole lot of them...If it's anything to do with the community they'll get up with their banners and they'll be out there....In the rain and snow...[and] they'll go down to the clinic, down there...And ring them up [elected representatives]*

That this action was spontaneous, unsupported and independent suggests that the tutors tend to operate under constraints of the kind identified by one administrator and also highlighted by Bailey (op cit). This was confirmed by another learner within the same programme. When asked if he felt it is possible to introduce social issues into adult education, he replied:

Well they [the learners] do anyway...They're always talking about different things...all the students they discuss everything...Oh, yeah - because they're all adults. And they see what is happening all around them. And they're disgusted.

To the question as to whether those kinds of issues were discussed in the course of the class, he responded:

Oh, yes!

When asked if these were raised by the tutors or the students, his response was:

Oh, no, no - the tutor wouldn't. But they might speak to us after about it - off the record!

One can readily imagine the impact there would be on society were the state and its subordinate bodies mature enough to accommodate the development of critical forms of pedagogy. Ireland might then be likened to progressive Sweden, the one-time Prime Minister of which, Olaf Palme, was recorded as saying 'Sweden is, to a great extent, a Study Circle democracy'.

Conclusion

Current developments in the sphere of further/adult education leave little scope for optimism that meaningful equality will feature within emerging strategy. *An tSeirbhís Oideachais Leanúnaigh agus Scileanna* (SOLAS) now occupies the foremost position in this. That it assumes responsibility for much of the work previously undertaken by the defunct National Training Authority (FÁS) is a clear indication of its likely thrust. Indeed, the explanatory memorandum for the Bill to establish this authority confirms its predominant orientation. Prominent among the functions set out for SOLAS are:

1. To consult the Department of Social Protection and employers to determine the types of education and training programmes...;
2. To advance funding to training bodies and other bodies for the provision of further education and training...;
3. To provide, or arrange for, the provision of training for employment. (Further Education and Training Bill, 2013: Explanatory Memorandum, p. 2)

Human capital rather than a concern with social justice is well placed to maintain its dominance in all state-funded further/adult education so that it continues being deployed to underpin the neo-liberal agenda. If so, as is the case in the following chapters, this is likely to be paralleled by persistent questioning of this blatant colonisation of the lifeworld by the system world.

Of many that can be invoked from other sources, the following seems very fit for present purpose:

> Does the idea of lifelong learning ... present more fundamental challenges to the way that we do things? Are we witnessing the logical extension of well-defined trends in education and training, or does lifelong learning mark a decisive turning point in the way that people and organisations define and manage their learning? And if the changes are important ones...are they entirely positive or, on the contrary, do they pose new and alarming threats? (Field & Leicester, 2000, p. xviii)

Later, Field himself adjudged Western social policy as supportive of the existing social order which inevitably had clear implications for the thrust of policy on state-supported adult learning:

> At its simplest, the changing language reflected a move away from any concern with social change, and an acceptance that capitalism is the only game in town. Rather than struggling against the structural causes of inequality, the new language of exclusion implies that government's task is to promote 'inclusion' into the existing social order. (Field, 2006, p. 21)

One of the more salient recent comments is made by Gilead (2009, p. 555)

> ...under existing conditions there is a deep theoretical incompatibility between the philosophical foundations of human capital theory and the ways in which education seeks to promote social cooperation.

This comment might suffice as the last word except that it prompts questioning apropos state-funded adult education in Ireland. The existing social order being highly unequal how should adult education respond to the challenge set by equality of condition in the theorization of equality that has emerged since the appearance of the White Paper in 2000? In particular, how should state-funded adult education be reformed in relation to the benchmark set by Baker et al. (2009, p. 47) whereby equality 'should be the defining concept in our thinking about social institutions and how they should be changed'? The challenge is clear. If left to the learners

98

and tutors there is some evidence it would stand a good chance of being realized. To use Habermas's model, that then leaves the system world – the political establishment and the agents of the economy – as the targets for change. A daunting task. But even the most enduring hegemony and most utilitarian guidelines are not immune to challenges mounted by emancipatory approaches to learning. In Chile, where Freire formulated much of Pedagogy of the Oppressed, even Pinochet had to give way, eventually.

Extracts from information sheets

In keeping with the requirements of the university's (UCD) protocol for the approval of fieldwork, outlines of the interviews (structured or unstructured) to be pursued had to be submitted. The following are extracts from those which were used to guide the interviews with Learners and Educators (tutors and administrators). These were issued to the respective respondents in advance of each interview and discussed as necessary.

Learners

What is the research about?

Adult education is supposed to help to bring about equality in society. A White Paper in 2000 said it should work most of all with those who had to leave school early. It should help them go back to education and make use of new chances.

In this research I want to ask if adult education can do more than that. I want to find out if adult education helps learners to discuss and think about this unequal world. I also want to find out if it can help people take action to make our society more equal.

What kind of information will I be looking for?

I will be asking you questions like these:

- Does your learning help you feel more confident? How?
- What do you think about getting qualifications, such as FETAC Levels ?
- Does your tutor bring up social issues, such as housing or employment?
- Do you think that kind of discussion should be part of what you do as a learner in adult education?

Educators (Tutors and Administrators)

What is the research about?

Essentially, it's an exploration of the role of adult education in achieving equality. In the White Paper on Adult Education, 2000, equality is set out as one of its three core principles. The Paper recognises various barriers to the emergence of 'a fully inclusive and cohesive society'. It points out that these arise from differences of socio-economic status, ethnicity, disability and gender. Inequalities in education result from these. The Paper's response is that the role of adult education is to target resources on those most in need as a result of 'early school participation and achievement' and so encourage them to return to education and avail of fresh learning opportunities.

Accepting that these measures are very important, this research seeks to explore the extent to which adult education needs to go beyond the provision of such learning opportunities and to support learners - by using critical approaches:

- in making meaning of their world, in recognising the structures that make society unequal

- in coming to an awareness of action that can be undertaken to help bring about 'a fully inclusive and coherent society', beginning with change in the immediate community. Such action could entail more active, participatory democracy or the development of movements in keeping with constitutional rights.

CHAPTER FIVE

WHAT'S IN A NAME? TERMINOLOGY, POWER AND CONTESTATION

Michael Murray

Introduction

The emergence of Further Education and Training (FET) in recent years signifies a decidedly different policy approach towards adult and community education. Many commentators would argue that this is evident in the way further education and training is promoted by policymakers and how it compares - and in many ways, contrasts to – philosophies that guide adult and community education. Central to this are differing and clashing understandings of key terms used in policy, theory and practice.

Defining and framing terms is crucially important. The EU, along with the European Association for the Education of Adults (EAEA), the Adult Learning Working Group (ALWG), as well as the Organisation for Economic Cooperation and Development (OECD), have all called for commonality of the usage of terms in order to facilitate greater understanding of adult learning and further education in order to compare, monitor and efficiently benchmark this area of education. Others, however, view an attempt to impose universal definitions upon adult and further education as an attempt to constrain, control and dominate both formal and non-formal learning.

Put simply, defining terms is an expression of power. One way of conceptualising how power is exercised through terminology is through the use of 'discourses'. Discourses go beyond the notion of texts or instances of speech. They are also what Michel Foucault referred to as 'discursive practices'. He states –

> ...in a society such as ours, but basically in any society, there are manifold relations of power which permeate, characterise and constitute the social body, and these relations of power cannot themselves be established, consolidated nor implemented without the production, accumulation, circulation and functioning of a discourse. (1980, p. 93)

Crucially, as Hunt and Wickham state, 'discourses have real effects'. They inform thoughts, words and actions and indeed, define what thoughts, words and deeds are marginalised - 'They structure the possibility of what gets included and excluded and of what gets done or remains undone...' (1994, p. 8-9). Therefore, in the context of terminology that frames the policy, theory and practice of adult and further education, their specific usage is not arbitrary – they represent attempts at legitimising a particular approach or philosophical position in relation to learning and professional practice, which in turn, produces claims to knowledge to the extent that '...there is no power relation without the correlative constitution of a field of knowledge, nor any knowledge that does not presuppose and constitute at the same time power relations' (Foucault, 1975, p. 27).

While, at any one time, it might appear that one discourse is entirely pervasive – for instance with respect to the view that all education and training should directly benefit the economy – all discourses are constantly challenged – they essentially compete with one another. This is apparent in the context of adult and further education, where there exists much disagreement over what terms mean and at a more basic level, what the purpose of such educational activity should be. This chapter looks at the usage of terminology in order to highlight the competitive terrain in which adult and further education operates. It suggests that this terrain comprises of contesting philosophies, which makes any attempt to universally impose definitions incredibly challenging. There are a number of key factors contributing to this. Firstly, adult and further education, is, by its nature, diverse and fragmented even within individual nation states and different localities. Therefore, the meaning of terms can be very much rooted in a local context. Secondly, there does not simply seem to be enough research on adult and further education currently that could inform any systemic approach to universal definitions. Lastly, and possibly most importantly, the terrain is characterised by very different philosophical or ideological approaches to education and the use of certain terms indicates a continuing struggle for control over the course or direction of this field of education. Therefore, different approaches to adult and further education exist, particularly with respect to discourses emanating from policymakers and local contexts, along with those that are promoted by activists. In order to illustrate the different discursive approaches, four key terms are analysed – the term 'further education' itself, 'learnercentredness', the role of the 'teacher/ educator' and finally the concept of 'critical reflection'. The key argument offered here is that practitioners must be aware that any definition offered by either policymakers or theorists is a product of power and interest and therefore, should never be construed as self evident or even the "truth".

Defining contested terms

The previous chapter has shown that, in recent times, there has been an identifiable drive towards the development of agreed definitions of terms in relation to Life Long Learning, adult learning and Further Education by policymakers. The EU has been at the forefront of this action. The rationale offered here is that an agreed 'European Glossary' of terms would facilitate the development of 'core data for monitoring the adult learning sector...' (NRDC, 2010, pp. 2-3). It would be seen as improving the quality of adult learning provision, increasing transparency and also enabling the transference of skills and qualifications. In addition, the EAEA argues that the development of minimum standards would facilitate '...the movement of personnel and exchange of experience, so that practices can be compared, better local judgements and choices can be made, and innovations can be tried out elsewhere if they promise to tackle real needs better than what is currently doing done' (2006, p. 5) Moreover, The European Commission asserts that 'a common 'language' bridging the worlds of education/ training and work needs to be developed to make it easier for citizens and employers to see how key competencies and learning outcomes are relevant to tasks and occupations' (2009, p. 10).

However, attempts by the EU to come up with working definitions for the purposes of enhancing quality and monitoring have been largely unsuccessful. A key barrier to devising definitions goes to the core of deeply held views on what the field should be about or if it should be treated as a distinct educational "sector" at all. This endeavour is made all the more arduous given that adult learning throughout Europe incorporates a multiplicity of terms, understandings and definitions. This salient point is made by the EU's own 'Adult Learning Working Group' (ALWG) in a study of 31 European countries. Here, the point is made that -

> Compared with other sectors of education and training, adult learning in the 31 countries is more heterogeneous across all its dimensions. It takes place in the context of a great diversity of overarching politics, legislative frameworks, structures, governance arrangements and funding mechanisms. There is a wide range of priorities, aims, learning contexts, organisational forms, learning content and learning outcomes. (2010, p. 8)

The EAEA specifically identify this richness and diversity as a core strength where 'good successful adult education practice is deeply rooted in local conditions and arrangements' (2006, p. 4). The EAEA also point to the potential danger of imposing standardisation – 'Removing the diversity would weaken the capacity of national provision to meet needs where this diversity reflects historical, cultural and political as well as economic differences' (2006, p. 5). Finally, the EAEA warn that –

> It is not sensible or likely to succeed to try to impose, even hostile to introduce, common terms for similar phenomena that may differ in important detail in terms of what they mean and how they work in different national contexts. (2006, p. 7)

A second challenge to developing accepted definitions is more practical – there is simply a lack of research in relation to adult and further education for many European countries. For instance, the European Commission-sponsored report on the development of a common language for adult learning concluded that there currently exists a deficit of both qualitative and quantitative data that could contribute to policymaking. In fact, the authors state that their study relies upon data from the UK and Norway (NRDC, 2010, p. 9). As a consequence of this, the report concludes that 'In a number of fields in adult learning, sufficient baseline data have not yet been gathered and in these fields the lack of clarity in definitions and terminology is particularly apparent' (NRDC, 2010, p.10). This has impacted on attempts to offer working benchmarks in order to monitor adult learning (NRDC, 2010, pp. 13-14). In turn, the ALWG also acknowledge that '...the contribution and benefits of the adult learning sector are not well researched, debated or published' (2010, p. 9).

In the Irish context, FETAC itself has asserted that 'There is a lack of clarity on what comprises the Further Education and Training field...' (2005), and in addition, policymakers rely heavily upon international research. The danger here is one of "creeping standardisation", where, due to a lack of research in individual countries, international standards and definitions become imposed as a consequence. The richness and value of local approaches and knowledge - as well as the specifics of economic and political contexts – are overlooked in this process. Moreover, Connolly makes the argument that the limited amount of existing research that does exist seeks to examine '...what works, rather than any critique or questionings of assumptions or approaches...' (2007, p. 119). In other words, funded research activity is geared towards establishing and maintaining the status quo almost as a self-evident reality, rather than challenging this dominant discourse.

Lastly, there are deeper, more ideological issues at work in terms of attempting to define the activities of adult, community and further education. In one sense, the argument can be made that attempting to define the features of this field of education and learning is also an attempt to control and dominate the discipline. Such attempts at "colonisation" have been met with suspicion and resistance from practitioners. This is a key point echoed in the previous chapter and relates to a central tension within adult and further education between discourses that seek to promote education in broadly economic terms, and other discourses that view adult and further education as a cornerstone of a more just and equal society. This conflict confirms the politicised and contested nature of adult learning where 'Deep philosophical differences about values and priorities reflect in the use and connotation of different terms...' (EAEA, 2006, p. 1).

Adult and further education – A new policy discourse?

The central importance of the EU and OECD in defining policy in the Irish context has been explored in considerable detail in previous chapters. This influence is hardly unusual: in general terms, national policy in a multitude of areas is shaped by transnational political institutions. It is most evident in the Irish context with the imposition of a structural adjustment programme on economic policy as direct consequence of the so-called "bail-out" by the "Troika" (EU, ECB, IMF) from 2008 onwards. While the transnational influence on adult and further educational policy may be less overt, it is nevertheless significant in shaping what could be described as an emerging, dominant discourse which drives national and local policy. Here the EU and the OECD has an '...agenda setting impact' which offers '...crucial reference points and yardsticks for the formation of policy and practice at national level' (Biesta, 2006, p. 170).

In Chapter Four of this book, Hurley alludes to the tension between a human capital discourse and equality in EU policymaking, particularly in relation to Lifelong learning. This tension is also evident in the notion of the 'European Social Model' (ESM). The ESM seeks to promote – '...values that include democracy and individual rights, free collective bargaining, the market economy, equal opportunities for all, and social protection and solidarity. The model is based on the conviction that economic progress and social progress are inseparable: 'Competitiveness and solidarity have both been taken into account in building a successful Europe for the future.'[1]

The importance of the "social" within the ESM is notable and is reflected in much of the EU's adult and further education policy pronouncements. For instance, The EU 'Action Plan on Adult Learning :Achievements and results 2008-2010' points out that -

> While literacy and numeracy provide a foundation for new skills for jobs, developing new skills needed by adults in modern society; digital skills, economic and financial literacy, civic, cultural and environmental awareness, healthy living, etc. also merit significant attention. (2010, p. 3)

Elsewhere, the OECD would appear to echo much of the EU's ethos on adult and further education. For instance, its 2006 publication *'Promoting Adult Learning'* acknowledges that adult learning is, by its nature diverse across different countries, that more needs to be done by way of having skills recognised through certification systems that have credibility with employers (OECD, 2006).

Yet despite the importance of the social dimension to the ESM, many authors have argued that the real driving force or ethos promoted by the EU in relation to adult and further education is the economic imperative (Biesta, 2006), where '...the mentioning of the other functions of Life Long Learning seems to be hardly more than lip-service...' (Biesta, 2006, p. 174). Most pointedly, the ALWG report states that

> ...all evidence points to the need for a highly qualified labour force to achieve the EU's goal of becoming a dynamic and competitive knowledge-based economy. In addition, in the current economic climate, the skills of Europe's workforce are crucial to economic recovery and will be vital in responding to whatever new economic structures emerge post downturn. (2010, p. 7)

Crucially, Biesta argues that Life Long Learning '...seems to have shifted from 'learning to be' 'to learning to be productive and employable' (2006, p. 172). Elsewhere, The EAEA state that the concept of life long learning itself has gradually moved from its 'humanistic' roots

---

[1] http://www.eurofound.europa.eu/areas/industrialrelations/dictionary/definitions/EUROPEANSOCIALMODEL.htm, accessed, 12th May, 2013

towards an ethos which focused on '...the needs of the economy for skilled labour with the necessary competence' (2006, p. 8).

The consequence of this approach is not merely the pursuit of a different philosophical position. Instead, critics argue that it has the potential to seriously impact on quality of life and equality (see Chapter 4 for more detail on this), thereby increasing marginalisation in society. For example, this new ethos or discourse influences what is learned and crucially, what is not in relation to adult and further education. According to Biesta,

> This transformation is not only visible at the level of policy; it also has had a strong impact on the learning opportunities made available to adults, partly through a redefinition of what counts as legitimate or 'useful' learning and partly as a result of the reduction of funding for those forms of learning that are considered not to be of any economic value. (Biesta, 2006, p.169)

Additionally, Brine (2006) points out that this approach to adult and further education exacerbates inequalities through the production of what can only be described as a two-tier system of education. Taking the view that current policy on lifelong learning is geared towards economic rather than social benefits, Brine goes further to argue that EU policy initiatives effectively create a tier of 'High knowledge-skilled' learners (associated with higher education and the 'knowledge economy') and 'Low knowledge-skilled' learners (associated with adult and further education and the 'knowledge society'). The low knowledge skilled workers are viewed as problematic for the EU - they are invariably the most marginalised within society and include the unemployed, disabled, those from ethnic minorities, early school leavers, lone parents, ex-offenders and senior citizens (Brine, 2006, p. 656). This is evident in the EU's assertion that the 'Action Plan on Adult Learning is geared towards '...those who are disadvantaged because of their low literacy levels, inadequate work skills and/or skills for successful integration into society' (2007, p. 3). It is through such policies that these groups are effectively 'classed, gendered and raced' (Brine, 2006, p. 656). They are groups that are problematised because a failure to integrate into society places them 'at risk' and crucially, frames them as 'the risk' to overall political, economic and social stability (Brine, 2006). In other words, these marginalised and disempowered sections of society must be controlled. While the higher knowledge skill learners are viewed as the future in terms of offering an educated workforce that will drive the European economy, the contrast with low knowledge skill learners could not be greater –

The mirror image of the knowledge economy discourse of hope and promise is one of exclusion, risk and fear. Those most at risk from the new (knowledge) economy are themselves constructed as the threat. (Brine, 2006, p 657)

Lastly, Brine argues that this two-tier system ensures that wider societal inequality is set to continue. She points out that the low knowledge skilled learners will continue to work within 'classed and gendered low-skilled' jobs, effectively servicing the needs of the knowledge economy. This is a 'surplus population' who 'move in and out of insecure or temporary employment' (2006, p. 661).

In the Irish context, these important policy perspectives are very much evident and this point has been explored in detail in previous chapters. Given the financial dire straits that the country has recently found itself in, it is understandable that the economic discourse in relation to adult and further education should be so dominant within policy processes and this is evident in the recent Department of Education and Skills statement (alluded to in previous chapters) that 'adult education and training' should be aimed at 'upskilling and reskilling people who are unemployed, where 'Providing skills for work is a priority.'[2]. Elsewhere, it is notable that the successor to FÁS, the national body responsible for skills and training, 'SOLAS', will have 'overall strategic responsibility' for further education in the country, where again, the focus is on economic benefits (DES, 2012d, p. 3).

While the implementation body for adult and further education, the Irish Vocational Education Association (IVEA) – renamed as the Education and Training Boards Ireland – does differentiate between Further Education and Adult and Community Education, the latter provision does reflect the general EU policy discourse of educational provision for disadvantaged groups and communities, where '...,community and voluntary groups deliver a range of educational activities for disadvantaged adults within their community.'[3]

---

[2] www.education.ie, accessed 9th May, 2013
[3] http://www.ivea.ie/services/community_ed/community_ed.shtml, accessed, 22nd May, 2013

Challenging the policy discourse – the adult and community education approach

The EAEA, in its report on trends and issues, makes the following point in relation to how Lifelong Learning is currently being conceptualised –

> What is controversial and philosophically objectionable, even repugnant, to many steeped in the values and tradition of European adult education, is the tendency for lifelong learning, as they see it, to be co-opted to serve liberal economics and a global free trade market.' (EAEA, 2006, p. 6)

This brief statement clearly outlines that terms such as 'lifelong learning' are not accepted as universal concepts, instead they indicate conflicting understandings and ideologies. The historical development of an emancipatory adult and community ethos in Ireland is explored in detail in Chapter Three. However, it is worth pointing out that it is an area of education and learning that encompasses a number of differing philosophical perspectives, which importantly, challenges the growing policy ethos outlined in the previous section. A key moment according to McDonnell is the establishment of the VECs in the 1930s, where the aim was to provide 'continuation education' as 'supplement' to schools in the form of 'practical training for employment in trades, manufacturing, commerce and industrial pursuits' (McDonnell, 2003, p. 48). Yet, this economistic approach to adult education, closely associated with the formal sector, was challenged by the emerging community education ethos in the 1980s. As Connolly discusses in Chapter Three, Women's and Community Education, emerged as a '...response to local learner needs...' and particular barriers for women – 'These barriers included the inflexibility of timetabling, the lack of childcare facilities and the invisibility of women who could not register unemployed as they worked in the home' (McDonnell, 2003, p. 48).

One of the more enduring aspects to this development is the emergence of a "movement" rather than the creation of yet another educational "sector". In this context, adult and community education is viewed '...in its commitment to educationally and socially marginalised groups' (Connolly, 2007, p. 119). Additionally, the questioning and challenging of the social and economic order is viewed as a perquisite to critical and responsible political citizenship. Keogh associates this discourse with a 'radical adult education' position that 'seeks to equip adult learners to challenge and change what are considered essentially unjust structures' (2003, p. 14). Unsurprisingly, Keogh observes that this approach, '...does not always find favour with the state or the economy' (2003, p. 14). Likewise, adherents to the radical position would view current EU and Irish Government policy as driven almost wholly by economic imperatives that have been created by the interests of the market and societal elites. Further, they would suggest that Further Education represents an attempt to regulate and control both tutors and learners through a philosophy that shares many core characteristics with Neoliberalism and Managerialism (Managerialism is explored in detail in the next chapter). Critics assert that it is a philosophy that has an immensely detrimental impact on adult and community education (Finnegan, 2008). As a consequence, the more overtly political aspects of adult and community education, for example the raising of issues of systemic inequalities and injustices in society, are increasingly viewed as merely recreational education and an unnecessary diversion from the pursuit of economic progress.

It is important to acknowledge that while the radical discourse outlined above does enjoy popularity amongst key organisations and agents, it is not the only discourse or ethos that exists within adult and community education. For instance, while AONTAS acknowledges the importance of this ethos within community education, the organisation is also clear that many who avail of adult education are doing so for economic rather than / social/ political reasons.

> Over the past two and a half years, employment in the construction, manufacturing and retail sector has declined dramatically. With little immediate prospects for employment, many of those employed in these sectors have no other option other than to upskill or retrain. Also an increasing number of highly skilled adults have also found themselves unemployed and adult education is providing a gateway for them to change career. This has led to a dramatic increase in the numbers of adults requesting further education and training making the sector one of the largest growth areas of the whole education system.[4]

Additionally, the argument can be made that the radical approach to adult education crosses the line between offering a critical analysis of power relationships to promoting a particular political viewpoint, which in turn, limits the learning experience. As Keogh observes - '...It

---

[4] http://www.aontas.com/information/howtogetinvolved.html, accessed 12th May, 2013.

also stands accused of being at risk of ultimately operating to indoctrinate learners into social action, thereby denying them their independence and self-agency...' (Keogh, 2003, p. 14).

Clashing views – Defining "Further Education"

It will be recalled from earlier that FETAC itself has expressed concern that the concept of 'Further Education' remains somewhat poorly defined (Grummell and Murray, forthcoming). This view is understandable, given that FE is invariably defined in the *negative* – in what it is not – in policy terms. For example, the Qualifications (Education & Training) Act (1999), defines further education and training broadly as 'education and training other than primary or postprimary education or higher education and training'. Likewise, the Teaching Council's own definition also encompasses this negative aspect- '...education and training which usually occurs outside of post-primary schooling but which is not part of the third-level system' (2011, p. 3). This places further education in a vacuum-like position; defined by its absence and lack of being and is also evident in the Department of Education and Skills (DES) definition of further education as embracing 'education and training which occurs after second-level schooling but which is not part of the third level system'. This is similar to UK where further education

> ...is not like higher education (feet on the ground, working with difficult learners, proper 'on the job' teacher training, serving the local community, misunderstood). It is not like schools (adults, part-time students, rescuing school failures, diverse academic-vocational programmes, strong industry-business links). It provides work-based training but is not like private training organisations. (Gleeson, Davies & Wheeler, 2005, p. 447)

One of the key reasons for FE being defined in such terms is that understanding of what is contained within FE, or just as importantly, what aspect of education should FE itself be *contained within*, has shifted much in recent years. This again reflects contested philosophical positions in relation to FE and adult and community education. Historically in countries such as France and the UK, FE has been associated with technical colleges and vocational-based training (Freynet, 1999; Hayes, Marshall & Turner, 2008). However, in recent times, FE has been a term that is utilised in a rather broader context. In the UK since 1992, FE was designated to include 'more clearly defined vocational and qualification courses, access to higher education courses, adult basic education and skills acquisition for those with learning difficulties' (Fieldhouse, 1999, p. 53). Fieldhouse further comments that 'areas of adult

112

education considered most suitable for public funding by the government' are now included within the FE remit, while 'less valued, recreational, social and leisure provision' is defined as adult education (1999, p. 53).

In one sense, the Irish situation mirrors this development. *The White Paper on Adult Education – 'Learning for Life'* (2000) refers to further education *within* the context of Adult and Community education and was an integral part of a "lifewide' commitment in the development of an Adult Education system.' (Chapter Four) More recent treatments of Further Education – and its relationship to adult education – demonstrates a significant shift in ethos however. Here, the perceived purpose of FE would appear to have somewhat narrowed into a training/ reskilling paradigm. For instance, Enterprise Ireland emphasises the centrality of Post Leaving Certificate courses (PLCs). PLC courses '...adopt an integrated approach, focusing on technical knowledge, core skills and work experience. They are designed as a step towards skilled employment and, as such, are closely linked to industry and its needs.'[5] Most significant is that the Department of Education now views adult education and training within the general framing of Further Education and training.[6] The emphasis here overall is on 'providing skills for work', with no mention of the importance of issues outlined in the White Paper such as consciousness raising, cultural development and community building. This, it can certainly be argued, demonstrates an attempt to define not just further education, but also adult and community education within a new managerial paradigm (see Chapter Six for more on this).

Ultimately, it can be argued that the term 'further education' is simply problematic. Kingston (2008) offers the view that 'further' implies 'continuation', but for many adults who have had to endure a sometimes horrendous first experience of education, 'continuation' would be the last thing that they would want. Instead, Kingston argues that adults 'need a title that reeks of a different approach', and while there might not be a single title that might be sufficient, the term 'adult education might go a long way' (Kingston, 2008).

---

[5] www.enterpriseireland.ie – Accessed 26th May, 2013.
[6] http://www.education.ie/en/The-Education-System/Further-Education-Training/ - accessed 26th May, 2013.

Learner-centeredness

One of the key features of adult learning that seeks to differentiate itself from, for instance, second-level education, is that the former is driven by a learner-centred approach to learning. It is an approach that informs the philosophical underpinnings of adult and community education and constitutes a critique what is termed the 'banking system' of education (see Chapter Three for more discussion on this). Here, the content of the learning, is, by definition, conceived and imposed by the educator or educational institution and is characterised by learning strategies of memorising and reproducing "legitimated" knowledge, rather than encouraging the development of creative, critical thinking.

Malcolm Knowles, in his seminal writings on andragogy (as opposed to pedagogy), characterises this approach through different stages in the learning process. For instance, he suggests that students should be actively involved in the planning of their own learning, with the teacher '...serving as procedural guide and content resource' (1988, p. 48). and in the 'mutual evaluation' of learning with the teacher (1988, p.49). In the context of FET, Knowles would certainly argue that an andragogical approach would also be appropriate for youth education – 'what is required, if youth education is to produce adults who are capable of engaging in a lifelong process of continuing self-development, is a whole new set of assumptions about the purpose of youth education...'(1988, p. 58). Additionally, adult education theorists such as Jack Mezirow would argue that a dialogical and deliberative relationship between educator and students in the classroom or learning space is integrally involved in developing the skills and capacities necessary for democratic citizenship. (Mezirow, 2003, p. 62). In other words, learner-centredness is not merely a learning tool, it is an exercise in democracy and equality, which ultimately benefits society by encouraging active, and most importantly, critical citizenship.

The learner-centred approach is also reflected in a number of key policy documents, not least in the Bologna Process –

> We reassert the importance of the teaching mission of higher education institutions and the necessity for ongoing curricular reform geared toward the development of learning outcomes. Student-centred learning requires empowering individual learners,

new approaches to teaching and learning, effective support and guidance structures and a curriculum focused more clearly on the learner...[7]

Elsewhere, the EU's Communication on competencies states that 'education and training systems must... become much more open and relevant to the needs of citizens...' (2009, p. 2), while the European Commission's 'Action Plan on Adult learning' specifically identifies a focus on the adult learner as a key characteristic of good governance in adult learning (2007, p. 5). In the Irish context, the IVEA has asserted that 'Lifelong learning focuses on people learning, rather than merely being recipients of education'[8] Moreover, FETAC itself states clearly that 'establishing and maintaining the centrality of the learner is now recognised as critical...' (FETAC, 2005, p. 4).

However, in practice, this translates into a discernibly narrowed understanding of learner-centeredness in comparison to the adult education discourses outlined above. Here, learner orientation seems to be focused on a consultative rather than participatory approach to student involvement in their own learning. For instance, the FETAC 'Learners charter' mentions consulting with learners on '...the development and review of policies, awards and our service' (FETAC, 2009, p. 6). Elsewhere, and quite strikingly, one FE college equates 'learner-centredness' with 'independent learning', which effectively means that students should have access to certain resources such as computers and the internet, in order to be able participate on certain courses[9]. Overall, it can be argued that the mere imposition of a FETAC-styled assessment/ awards process negates any meaningful consideration of learner-centredness. Biesta points to a fundamental contradiction in this respect – '...while individuals are being made responsible for their own lifelong learning, the 'agenda' for their learning is mainly set by others' (2006, p. 176).

The role of the teacher/ educator

The other side of the learning relationship of course involves the educator or teacher. The terms 'teacher' and 'adult educator' are important in themselves, but are by no means interchangeable. They can equate to very different learning environments, philosophies and

---

[7] http://www.ehea.info/article-details.aspx?ArticleId=147, accessed 29th May, 2013
[8] http://www.ivea.ie/services/further_ed/further_ed.shtml, accessed 22nd, May, 2013
[9] Limerick College of FE, http://www.lcfe.ie/About-Us/General-Information.aspx, accessed, 26th May, 2013

outcomes. A key differentiating factor between adult education and, for instance, second level education is focused on the power dynamics of this relationship. In contrast to the learner-centred approach discussed above, the more traditional pedagogical perspective is geared towards '...the transmittal of knowledge and skills that had stood the test of time' (Knowles, 1988, p. 40). Again, it is notion of legitimated knowledge that is effectively closed from scrutiny or criticism that forms the learning curriculum. Within the "teacher" paradigm, Knowles asserts that the learner is conceptualised as dependent upon the teacher, the learner's own life experience is minimised in terms of relevance and learning occurs from a standardised, subject centred curriculum (1988, pp. 43-4). At a more fundamental level, teacher/ learner power relationship is characterised by the teacher doing the talking and the student listening, students working in isolation and it is the teacher solely who will evaluate the learning.[10] In contrast, an adult learning approach lends itself to self-directed learning where the teacher's role is '...redefined as that of a procedural technician, resource person and co-inquirer; more a catalyst than an instructor, more a guide that a wizard' (Knowles, 1988, p 48). Knowledge is challenged and critiqued and not merely accepted and reproduced which has far reaching implications for the notion of working from a standardised curriculum. Group work is critically important here too, where learners act a support and resource for each other, communicating without teacher monitoring and co-evaluating learning along with the adult educator.[11]

The dynamic of the educator/teacher interacting with the learner in the context of further education is recognised by the Teaching Council, who state that

> Teaching in further education is characterised by learner-teacher relationships based on mutual respect and equality. There is recognition of the professional role of the teacher in responding directly to the individual and collective needs of the learners. (Teaching Council, 2011, p. 9)

While this statement would appear to favour a teaching/ learning approach that differs from the more hierarchical approach outlined above, meaningful deviation from this paradigm can,

---

[10] http://www.nclrc.org/essentials/goalsmethods/learncentpop.html, accessed, 8th April, 2013

[11] http://www.nclrc.org/essentials/goalsmethods/learncentpop.html, accessed, 8th April, 2013

in practice, prove rather problematic given the context in which FE currently operates. At a fundamental level, much of the educator's approach to working within the FE environment is pre-defined by external structures that seem to favour teaching to fixed, measurable outcomes over facilitation and dialogical learning. For instance, County Kildare VEC, in its handbook for tutors, clearly outlines the parameters (as defined by QQI) in which a teacher must develop a 'scheme of work'. These include referring to a generic programme descriptor that defines the duration of a module, the objectives of a module and the learning outcomes (Kildare VEC, 2013, p. 18). Working within a rigid system of learning which emphasises performativity rather than critical thinking is obviously going to impact on how much teachers can "facilitate" rather than "teach". This in turn impacts on the learning environment, as well as the educator's relationship with the learner. Drawing on the UKs experience, Hayes et al. make the following observation on how the need to meet predetermined learning outcomes impacts on teaching and learning –

> This means lessons cannot be left to develop in an open-ended manner as a result of issues emerging but need to be predetermined to avoid digressions. Likewise, learning outcomes cannot be concerned with understanding as this is too ambiguous to be demonstrated at the close of the lesson. Instead outcomes need to be framed in such a way as to enable students to prove a competency gained during the course of the teaching period: naming, listing, reciting, giving an example or showing. The emphasis upon predetermining the course of the lesson goes against the principles of andragogy... (2008, p. 40)

Critical reflection

Critical reflection is a fundamental concept in adult learning and is viewed by theorists and policymakers alike as a cornerstone of the Further Education learning experience. However, as with other concepts and terms explored in this chapter, it is a term that lacks any universally agreed understanding and at the same time underlines very different philosophical approaches to adult learning and FE. As Smith, E. observes – '...it is fair to see that the purposes of critical reflection are diverse and potentially opposing' (2011, p. 214). However, it is worth reiterating once again that the differing discourse of concepts such as critical reflection are indicative of conflicting philosophies and power relationships – they represent very different interpretations of what adult and FE *should* be about.

At one level, it can be argued that critical reflection is concerned with '...learning to reason and reflect about life and the society and culture that we live in' (Connolly, 1996, p. 36). However, the term itself encompasses both variety and commonality within differing educational contexts. For instance in the second level context, McGrath and Coles (2011) emphasise the important of critical reflection in professional teacher practice. According to Ghaye, this should include an examination of personal and professional values –

> The art of teaching is one that needs constant renewal and reworking, in order that it does not disintegrate, it is imperative that this process coheres around a set of educational values that can be justified by being held under constant review....A teacher's values should be derived from the nature of what constitutes effective and ethical practice.' (2011, p. 92)

For its part, a report commissioned by the Teaching Council identifies critical reflection as a principle that underlines 'quality teacher education' (Conway, Murphy, Rath & Hall, 2009, p. xviii). Additionally, the Teaching Council states, in its guidelines for teacher education programmes that teachers should have the competency to 'describe and critically reflect on the particular features of teaching and learning in the further education sector', as well as be able to 'reflect critically on their own teaching skills' (Teaching Council, 2011, p. 12). The importance of this concept is also reflected in individual learning centres around Ireland, where for instance, one centre states that it is '...dedicated to facilitating learning, personal growth and critical reflection.'[12] Elsewhere, County Kildare VEC assert that –

> The reflective process involves thinking and analysing actions with the aim of improving practice. This requires consideration of what has been done, the process and the outcome...A tutor should promote the idea of the reflective process with learners. By doing this, they will begin to recognise what has and has not worked for them and then apply it to other tasks. (2013, p. 22)

What is common here is critical reflection is geared towards good professional practice on the one hand, and as a learning skill on the other. "Critical reflection" has become part of the assessment criteria for many FETAC courses. For instance, on the 'Working with groups' module descriptor, there is an assessment of 'critical reflection, analysis and evaluation of

---

[12] http://portarlingtonaec.ie/about/, accessed April 10th 2013

own participation and experiences'[13]; for 'Intercultural studies', students are required to engage in 'critical reflection, insight and evaluation of learning process'[14]; likewise on the 'Career planning' module, students are required to include critical reflection as part of their learning journal[15].

Within the discipline of adult and community education, critical reflection encompasses various discourses. For instance, one such discourse views critical reflection as very much an individual endeavour and concentrates upon a psycho-therapeutic perspective, which focuses on '...the identification and reappraisal of inhibitions acquired in childhood as a result of various traumas' (Van Woerkom, 2010, p. 342). The more radical discourse of adult and community education perceives critical reflection in political terms where the emphasis is on '...issues of citizenship and democracy and it could be styled "adult education for change"...' (Keogh, 2003, p. 14). The "critical" aspect asks for consideration of the broader power relationships and structures that contribute to how we construct our worlds, but also and more pointedly, it seeks to transform influences or 'hegemonic assumptions' (Fook, 2006, p. 3) which are conceptualised as inequalitarian, unjust and discriminatory. In this context, critical reflection is associated with 'emanicpatory learning', it is a core component in raising critical awareness of oppressions (Connolly, 1996, pp. 37-8) and constitutes

> ...the ability to understand the social dimensions and political functions of experience and meaning making, and the ability to apply this understanding in working in social contexts. (Fook, 2006, p. 10)

Critical reflection, therefore, represents yet another area of contestation between differing perspectives. While there is something of a consensus between different philosophical positions that critical reflection is an integral part of the educating/ learning process, "context" is again, everything here. Developing the capacity to critically evaluate ideas or one's own practice is obviously important. However, critics of the Teaching Council discourse will argue that the discourse on critical reflection that is being adopted for FE removes any serious consideration of linking education to creating the conditions for a more

---

[13] http://public.fetac.ie/AwardsLibraryPdf/E20143_AwardSpecifications_English.pdf, accessed 10th April, 2013

[14] http://public.fetac.ie/AwardsLibraryPdf/E20169_AwardSpecifications_English.pdf, accessed 10th April, 2013

[15] http://public.fetac.ie/AwardsLibraryPdf/L12570_AwardSpecifications_English.pdf, accessed 10th April. 2013

just and equal society. As a result, critical reflection and learning within FE is essentially about developing study skills, "good practice" and, crucially, adhering to existing economic and societal power relationships rather than challenging them.

Conclusion

It will be recalled from earlier that Michael Foucault conceptualised discourses as largely the product of power which signified attempts at control or domination. An examination of the contested nature of terminology in adult and further education would suggest that attempts at domination have largely failed in this often misunderstood area of education and learning. Instead, it can be argued that conflicting arguments, ideas and philosophies are the order of the day. The nature of this clash of positions is most apparent in the emergence of a managerial/ policymaking discourse which seeks to portray adult and further education strictly in terms of what would be beneficial to economic activity (including flexibility and mobility of workers), which is contrasted with the adult education discourse that seeks to link education to wider issues of power inequalities in society. The development of the policymaking perspective is evident in how adult education is currently positioned as an appendage to further education – this amounts to an astonishing reversal of policy from the government's White Paper in 2000.

This very obvious contestation of philosophies is evident in the examination of terminology offered here. It will be recalled that further education is invariably defined in the negative and is increasingly associated with training and reskilling. This is in contrast to the adult and community education approach which places great importance on development of critical thinking and the central importance that education plays in addressing systems of injustice, marginalisation as well as democratic citizenship. Following on from this, while there is much talk of the centrality of learner-centredness within further education, the very imposition of the FETAC system negates any meaningful learner participation. Likewise, the role of the educator/ teacher is narrowly defined within the FETAC system and bears more than a passing resemblance to a traditional, second level teaching model (hierarchical, the teacher as the custodian of knowledge), particularly given the constraints that educators find themselves working under in the accreditation system. In contrast, the adult and community education approach emphasises the active participation by learners (with educators) in the creation and legitimising of knowledge. This importance of what constitutes useful or relevant knowledge is also evident in the concept of critical reflection, which has a long tradition within adult education and signifies the questioning and challenging of systems of inequality. It can certainly be argued that the current further education discourse on critical reflection has reduced the concept to mere teaching practice or as a study skill.

It is clear, therefore, that some common threads have emerged in this examination of the use of terminology. One view of further education is that its primary purpose is to address the needs of the market. Moreover, this discourse seeks to portray Adult, Community and indeed Further Education as neutral, benign and apolitical. Others would argue the opposite – that education is never neutral, that it is always political and that it actively promotes the interests of certain groups in society – economic elites, marginalised groups or otherwise. Neither perspective constitutes a "correct" or "true" version of what Adult and Further Education is or what it signifies. Instead, these different discourses represent exercises in power and offer very different visions of the kind of society we wish to live in.

CHAPTER SIX

FET: RESPONDING TO COMMUNITY NEEDS OR SHAPING COMMUNITIES TO SUIT A GLOBAL MARKETPLACE IN CRISIS?

Bernie Grummell

Introduction

This chapter explores the implications of recent policy changes for further education in Ireland. Increasingly, neoliberal discourses are driving a performance-based and employment-orientated vision of education. Employability is promoted as the principal objective of sectors such as further education, with success measured by the achievement of awards and progression to employment or higher education. This is driven by a highly disrespectful discourse of NEET (Not in Employment, Education or Training) which removes the learner and learning from education. Further education represents the vocational, technical and practice-based forms of education in Ireland as elsewhere, but this is now being repositioned in a neoliberal era through the auspices of employability, professionalization and performativity. This chapter explores the implications in terms of how further education is conceptualised in the Irish context and in a global neo-liberal reform agenda. Discursive practices of negative comparative definition or an outputs orientation raises interesting questions about the positioning and knowledge claims of further education. As a sector, it is continually defined by *what it is not* (see chapter Five), and hence always reliant and reactive to these other sectors of education, or it is trapped within the constraints of its outputs rather than concentrating on what further education is; its actual knowledge claims, learning processes and distinctive characteristics, to which we now turn. This reflects the contested knowledge and political position of further and adult education. I examine the role of professionalism and performativity in the governance and organizational structure of further education. Changes in these areas have profound impacts on the learning and knowledge base of further education, constraining its social justice and transformative capacity for the learners at the heart of further education.

This chapter reviews the policy development of further education in Ireland and the historical sweep of its development, in light of its current position in the neo-liberal heartland of an austerity-driven political landscape. The implacable drive of neoliberal economics in everyday practice is evident in the current economic and training discourses of further education, which aims to upgrade the employability of low skilled and marginalized sectors of the population. It explores the social justice and equity implications of this seemingly inescapable drive to 'further education', critically examining the consequences for learners, knowledge and knowing.

The evolution of further education in Ireland

As documented in the opening section of this book, further education has emerged historically from the specific context and local logics of its development in Ireland. While its diverse origins are evident, particularly noteworthy are the impact of centralised control structures, including the Catholic Church's ownership of the primary and secondary schools, with the state dominating educational resources (buildings, infrastructures, salaries, curriculum) and institutional structures, especially through the VEC structures.

Socio-economic divisions emerging within are also significant, with the vocational ethos of further education in Ireland, as elsewhere, focusing on the training of the working classes in particular (Anderson, Brown & Rushbrook, 2004), while second level and higher education concentrated on general education and the academic education of the professions. It will be recalled from the previous chapter that Brine (2006) notes a continuance of this stratification in recent decades as key differences emerge between the so-called 'low skilled knowledge' and 'high knowledge skilled' workers. Further education works primarily with those positioned within the so-called 'low skilled knowledge' categories and higher education with the 'high skilled knowledge' workers. The different positions, careers and even the terminology of low-and high skilled knowledge workers raises key questions about the social and class reproduction of further and higher education (Apple, 2004; Baker et al.; 2009; Bourdieu & Passeron, 1990; Bourdieu, 1998). The historic correlation of further education with the working classes and marginalized groups, and the lower level of status and recognition of further education relative to other education sectors has profound social justice consequences. This correlation has been exacerbated by the performativity and professionalism drive which has restricted the scope of further education to the so-called 'low skilled knowledge' work and hence its workers to the lower scales of the knowledge economy (Brine, 2006).

Clear gendered patterns are also evident in further education as the apprenticeship programmes (such as construction or carpentry) train a predominantly male student body. In the wake of the global economic crisis and collapse of the Irish construction industry in 2008, these male-dominated apprenticeship training programmes have been decimated, with a huge concern about the further education and employment challenges for these workers (OECD, 2010, p. 8). The Post-Leaving Certificate sector caters for a largely female student body in the 'feminised' occupations such as hairdressing, beauty and child care (Watson, McCoy & Gorby, 2006, p. 8).

The current organisation of further education in Ireland

In line with the ambiguity arising from definitions of further education, confusion also exists in the organizational structures of further education. As Conroy and O'Leary describe a 'perplexing myriad of funders are engaged with further, adult and community education' (2007, p. 13). This stands in sharp contrast to the systematic and substantial structural funding of school and higher education sectors by the Department of Education and Skills and Higher Education Authority respectively. This complexity is reflected in its organisational structure where two distinct government departments – and logics – operate; the Department of Education and Skills (DES)[1] and the Department of Enterprise, Trade and Employment (DETE)[2]. It is mirrored in the tensions between an education (learning) agenda and employment (training) agenda of these state departments. The education agenda of further education focuses on encouraging access and progression through the education system. Similar to the UK, the employment agenda in Irish further education focused initially

---

[1] As outlined in earlier chapters, the Department of Education and Skills is responsible for the Education Training Boards (formerly VEC) which provide further education. The Department's own nomenclature reflects its own discourses with education, changing over 15 years from the Department of Education to a Department of Education and Science and now a Department of Education and Skills (Lynch, Grummell & Devine, 2012, p. 10)

[2] DETE delivered FE provision mainly through Foras Áiseanna Saothar (FÁS), the National Employment and Training authority established in 1967 as ANCO to provide vocational training for employment mainly through apprenticeships (now SOLAS operating under DES), with all of these organisations undergoing changes of nomenclature in that time to reflect their changing ideology.

on vocational education and more recently on building employability for a knowledge economy (Gleeson et al., 2005; Hardiman, 2012).

Structural confusion and overlaps between these government departments have resulted in a complex organizational structure. Further education operates in the second level education system, through Education Training Boards (formerly the Vocational Education Committee structures). As outlined earlier, the VEC and newer ETB structures are centralized and hierarchical in nature, following a linear line of command towards the CEO of local ETBs. Given this centrifugal bureaucratic structure and hierarchy, further education has often been dependent on 'commitment on the part of a particular CEO, VEC committee member, school principal or individual member of a school's staff' (O'Sullivan, 2005, p. 518). Further education often occurs within the broader structures, premises and culture of a second level VEC school, drawing on a differing set of educational logic and system. In other cases, further education is provided in the context of commercial providers and governed by commercial logic. Smaller numbers again are organized under community structures and a community education ethos. Consequently, further education has been heavily reliant on specific local logics of the school, community or industry sector, whilst also centrifugally influenced by state discourses and structures.

Further education's philosophy and pedagogy

The tensions between the different foundations of further education are also evident in its philosophy, pedagogy and students. Further education students differ from second and higher level students as they are typically non-traditional[3], interested in vocational and experiential education and accessing education in alternative ways and for different reasons. Consequently, their education requires a philosophical and pedagogical approach that is rooted in the participative and learner-centered ethos of adult and community education. The linear rigidity of progression within the formal education sector from primary, second towards higher education level does not match these students' need for flexibility, alternative

---

[3] The European Lifelong Learning Project Report (2009) 'Access and Retention: the experience of non-traditional learners in Higher Education' 2008-2010 (RANLHE) defines 'non-traditional' as students who are under-represented in higher education and whose participation is constrained by structural factors: including students from low income families, first generation entrants, students from (particular) minority ethnic groups, students with disabilities and mature students. (http://www.dsw.edu.pl/fileadmin/www-ranlhe/files/MerrillGonzalezMonteagudo_ICERI2010_finalpaper.pdf; accessed 28 June 2013)

progression routes and learner-centred approaches. As noted earlier, further education is positioned at the latter stages of second level and the initial stages of higher education, offering alternatives to the hierarchy of the formal education track. This highlights the philosophical rationale for its unique position and complex organisational structure in Irish education. Adult education and further education cater for a diverse and often marginalised group of learners from a social justice perspective. Hence it needs to maintain flexibility and responsiveness, creating alternatives to the hierarchical pathway of educational progression. However, a structural tension inherent in this remains unresolved as further education 'offer[s] a non-traditional pathway to a traditional provision; and a student-centered preparation for a subject-centered enterprise' (Metcalf 1993, pp. 10-11 as quoted in Coffield & Vignoles, 1997, section 5.5).

The tensions between second level and adult education logics are also evident in the pedagogy of further education. The sector is staffed by educators valued for their experiential knowledge as practitioners, rather than formal teaching or other academic qualifications. The practitioner emphasis is typical of adult and community education rather than the formal schooling or higher education sectors where professional qualifications are valued. Staff in further education tend to come through two distinct tracks – the initial teacher education route where they trained as teachers in the second level system or an employment track where they worked in industry before moving into further education (Hardiman, 2012). These dual pathways into the profession create tensions as the 'unique biographies, broken careers, deflections and diversions (of many further educators) are all passed over in favour of the singular and progressive sense of a cognitively conceived vertical and linear-based career progression' (Gleeson & Knights, 2006, p. 282). Staff recruited directly from industry or community who have practical experience of a vocational area are often valued by the institution and students. This is similar to the first wave of professionalism in the UK where Gleeson and Mardle (1980) describe the significance of the former trade and occupational identities of further education practitioners. This employer focus is also evident in employer representation on further education colleges' boards of management. However this is increasingly undermined by the professionalism demands discussed later.

This privileging of the employment agenda has important implications for pedagogy and knowledge base of further education which still tends to favour a vocational and practice-based orientation. While many of these staff have now undertaken additional education training, most do not have specific training in the pedagogy of adults. Structurally, the lack of formal recognition for experiential and practice-based knowledge results in less secure working conditions and status for those working in the sector. Further education staff are often employed on casual and temporary contracts with poor entitlements, which contributes to the low status and insecurity of the sector (Jeffers, 2012). As Gleeson et al. (2005, p. 450) point out, while

> part-time and contractual work offers a flexible response to market fluctuations it also increases distinctions between core and periphery practitioners with knock-on effects in terms of pay, pension and conditions of service. Part-time and contractual work offers a flexible response to market fluctuations it also increases distinctions between core and periphery practitioners with knock-on effects in terms of pay, pension and conditions of service.

This stands in comparison to primary, second level or higher education; all of which have a clear professional structure, working conditions and pay scales, secure funding and governance structure, centralized curriculum and accreditation systems, strong representative bodies and a clear process for public recognition of their staff as teaching professionals.

How further education performs? The demands of a global neo-liberal reform agenda

Given this insecurity and confusion, a key question in education policy and governance has been how to capture the performance of further education? What learning occurs for individual learners and for society? In the Irish context, this has been filtered through an employment discourse of the government as further education is asked to contribute to the employability of the labour force. This is set within the wider demands of performativity and global neo-liberalism (Apple, 2004; Lynch et al., 2012; Power, O'Flynn, Courtois, & Kennedy, 2013). Further education is asked to contribute to the National Skills Strategy's targets for the labour market by 2020 where:

- 48 percent of the labour force should have qualifications at NFQ Levels 6 to 10;
- 45 percent should have qualifications at NFQ levels 4 and 5; and

- The remaining 7 percent will have qualifications at NFQ levels 1 to 3 but should aspire to achieve skills at higher levels. (AONTAS, 2011:4-5)[4]

Such market-orientated discourses and employment targets have refined the further education agenda from a broad vocational ethos to a targeted training for employability. This shapes the community to respond to the needs of global politics and a marketplace in crisis, rather than responding to learner or community needs. The language of performativity is significant in further education, with emphasis placed on readiness to work rather than actually becoming employed. Performativity, in this sense, is 'a technology, a culture and a mode of regulation that employs judgments, comparisons and displays as a means of incentive, control, attrition and change – based on rewards and sanctions (both material and symbolic). The performances (of individual subjects or organisations) serve as a measure of productivity or output or displays of 'quality'' (Ball, 2006, p. 144). This distilling of learning into measureable outputs or displays of quality disguises the question of why and who is making these judgments about what learning is measured and how its quality is defined. Many researchers and students argue that the structures and governance of education are being re-shaped under the auspices of performativity requirements of statutory agencies and commercial forces rather than the actual needs of learners (Ball, 2006; Hardiman, 2012; Lynch et al., 2012).

Education has become orientated towards the market and in many cases driven by commercial forces (Lynch et al., 2012; Lynch & Moran, 2006). For example, in the further education sector, many private providers operate including the EDEXCEL awarding body, an awarding body for NQAI certified qualifications (NFQ Levels 1-9) which is owned by Pearson PLC, the international media and education company)[5]. The expansion of a commercial orientation in education has been widely critiqued for its narrow emphasis on profitability and the economic value of people as workers and consumers rather than a holistic developmental focus on people learning in social context (Apple, 2004; Giroux, 2006). The employability discourse holds enormous potency through the austerity discourse

---

[4] AONTAS 2011 Submission about Contribution of Further Education Sector, accessed July 2013 http://www.aontas.com/download/pdf/aontas_submission_to_des_feb_11.pdf

[5] http://www.edexcel.com/international/europe/Pages/ireland.aspx

that currently guides government policy and public belief, particularly resonant in a time of uncertainty, risk and recession (Lynch et al., 2012; Power et al., 2013).

Many public educational agencies including ETBs now tender to provide educational services to employers and in many ways have adopted the ethos and priorities of their commercial competitors. This has implications for the kind of education provided in further education. Burke (2007, p. 3) contends that this has led to an 'almost unstoppable trend towards thinking largely in quantitative terms about teaching/learning...and the utilization of business language and concepts in education debates and policy documents'. This is evident in the language of outcomes and performativity that now permeates all sectors of education. For instance, The Department of Education and Skills adopts a defining strategy of an output orientation that lists different types of programmes and providers such as Post Leaving Certificate (PLC) Courses, Vocational Training Opportunities Scheme (VTOS), Youthreach programme for early school leavers, Back To Education Initiative (BTEI), adult literacy and community education.[6] Similarly the Further Education and Training Bill defines further education firstly in terms of its outcome of qualification level: "education provided for the purpose of obtaining an award within the meaning of the Qualifications and Quality Assurance (Education and Training) Act 2012 at a level that is not higher than level 6 specified in the National Framework of Qualifications" and secondly in terms of what it is not – in this case also excluding education provided by other professional bodies ..."does not include (a) higher education within the meaning of the Higher Education Authority Act 1971, or (b) further education within the meaning of the Solicitors (Amendment) Act 1994, the Veterinary Practice Act 2005, the Medical Practitioners Act 2007 or the Nurses 5 and Midwives Act 2011" (Oireachtas Bill, 2013 pp. 5-6).[7] This is a further negation where education by professional bodies is also delineated from further education; raising questions about the limits to the professionalism being envisaged for the further education sector.

Outcomes-based systems were first introduced to increase employability based on standards that could be validated with transparent procedures to ensure quality at national and international level. While transparency and quality were welcomed criteria, what remained

---

[6] http://www.education.ie/en/The-Education-System/Further-Education-Training/; accessed 31 May 2013

[7] http://www.oireachtas.ie/documents/bills28/bills/2013/513/b513d.pdf; ; accessed 25 June 2013

unquestioned were the perspectives and elements of education that were being measured and valued – and equally what was rendered invisible and not valued? The focus on operational definitions in Irish public policy directs attention towards educational outcomes rather than processes; training rather than learning, and clients rather than learners. This is similar to what has occurred in the UK with the introduction of the 'national learning and skills strategy, reinforced by audit and inspection regimes, through which standards of FE provision are promoted, judged and assessed' (Gleeson et al., 2005, p. 447). Outcomes-based systems tend to privilege employer perspectives and as such acts as a mechanism for social power (Wheelahan, 2009, p. 203). Learning outcomes are often separated from the processes of learning. The focus is on outcomes that the learner can produce rather than on the learning process or how this learning applies to life. This has significant implications for the kind of teaching and learning that occurs as it emphasises individual achievement, products and performance rather the communal or participative aspects of learning processes. The focus is on the performance and outcomes of education rather than the learner or learning.

This performance measurement focus is evident in the ongoing debate over recognition of awards. Certification in further education was offered by National Council for Vocational Awards (NCVA) established in 1991. This did not fulfil the diversity of provision in the further education field, so many providers offered certification from UK and other bodies (such as EDEXCEL's BTEA awards mentioned earlier). The National Framework Qualifications (NFQ) simplified this process by introducing 'a single, nationally and internationally accepted entity through which all learning achievements may be measured and related to each other in a coherent way and which defines the relationship between all education and training awards' (NQAI in Tierney & Clarke, 2007, p. 132). FETAC (the Further Education and Training Awards Council) had responsibility for awards from levels 1 to 6 on the NFQ, while HETAC was responsible for awards at higher education level. In 2012 Quality and Qualifications Ireland (QQI) was established as the single awarding national agency monitoring standards and quality of teaching programmes. This formalizing of educational outcomes into these qualifications structures has placed enormous pressures on further education students and staff who struggle to capture the complexity of learning into the measurable performance categories of FETAC. There is an inherent structural tension as non-traditional experiential knowledge has to be slotted into a traditional structure of recognition; and student-centered learning experiences are set within a performativity subject-centered approach. The onus on accessing and matching personal learning to the system requirements is left to the individual student or educator to achieve, rather than the system matching learner needs. This shift to performativity is further consolidated by the State's adoption of standards of professionalism for the further education teaching staff to which we now turn.

The formative influence of professionalism in further education

The State plays a key role in re-constituting the professional status of further education through educational legislation and policies. In recent years, some level of professionalism has been welcomed within the field of further education, given the impact of casualisation, low status, pay and conditions of further education staff (Jeffers, 2012). However, the specific type of professionalism being encouraged has important consequences for learning, knowledge and working conditions of further education. As Ball, Maguire and Braun (2012, p. 3) remind us, 'Policies rarely tell you exactly what to do, they rarely dictate or determine practice, but some more than others narrow the range of creative responses.' This narrowing of the range of creative responses in the translation from policy to action is crucial for further education. How performativity and professionalism are translated into practice are elements of the policy relationship that are often subjective and opaque.

As with other sectors of education, professionalism is often associated with 'technical expertise' rather than any other forms of knowledge (Schön, 1996, p 29). The designated holders of instrumental and technical expertise (particular outcomes) in a given profession are awarded a status in society which reflects the dominant ideological interests of society (Collins, 1996; Gramsci, 1971) in an 'alliance between the state, professions and capital' (Hughes & Tight, 1995, p. 297). Gleeson and Knights (2006) and Avis (2003) describe how public professionals increasingly are governed by licensed autonomy and positioned as 'trusted public servants than empowered individuals' (Avis 2003, p. 329).

This is evident in the Teaching Council's accreditation process for the Postgraduate Higher Diploma in Further Education and the professional registration for further education teachers in 2013. The Teaching Council requirements focus on 'professional practice' and particular types of knowledge. The knowledge base being constituted for further education professionals is largely defined according to existing professional standards and processes for second level teaching qualifications. Adult and further education colleges submitting programmes for Teaching Council recognition have had to legitimate their content and pedagogy in light of these considerations. Providers had to defend the relevance of an adult and further education pedagogy that emphasizes the participatory learning and critical thinking methods that address the inequalities which constitute the lived realities for many of our learners. However, teacher professionalism seems to be about measurable teacher-outcomes and a second level initial teacher education (ITE) orientation, where participatory learning, equality issues and critical thinking are rendered invisible.

For example the Teaching Council's requirements for teaching, learning and assessment outcomes focus on a decontextualised notion of pedagogy and learning. The learner remains invisible, apparent only in the encouragement to apply teachers 'knowledge of learners' backgrounds, identities, experiences and learning modes to his/her teaching, insofar as he/she is aware of these' (Teaching Council 2011, p. 14). This assumes an unproblematic application of pedagogy to learners' reality, which ignores the classed and gendered context of many further education students. The restructuring of further education professionalism along similar lines to second level ITE raises other issues, with particular types of educational knowledge being privileged at second level such as an expert teacher rather than the participative learner-orientated approach of adult education. The inclusion of particular content in the curriculum also had to be defended, including the inclusion of a module on gender studies by Maynooth University. Given the earlier discussion of the gendered nature of participation in further education by students and staff, this is obviously still a pertinent social justice issue for further education to consider. The invisibility of gender equality issues in second level ITE provision reflects the normative acceptance of gender inequality in the highly feminized profession of teaching and hegemonic masculinity of senior management in the formal education sectors (Drudy, 2008; Lynch et al., 2012; Smith, J., 2011).

Performativity has further divided the formal and informal processes of learning, with the formal learning processes being recognised and accredited, while informal learning that is at the heart of further education is more difficult to fit within the performativity radar of learning outcomes. A low status and recognition is given to experiential knowledge that is at the heart of much of adult and further education – what Schön (1996) calls the 'tacit' or 'implicit' knowledge of everyday life. The learner-orientation that is promoted focused on consultation rather than learner participation and control over their own curriculum and learning processes. Tacit, experiential and affective knowledge that is associated with the private sphere is disregarded in favour of the political, economic and technical knowledge that dominate public spheres (Grummell, 2007; Lynch, 2010).

Accrediting knowledge in further education

What is recognized as legitimate knowledge and who are the accredited 'knowers' in Irish further education is currently being renegotiated and formalized through the performativity and accreditation process of statutory agencies such as QQI and the Teaching Council. As Ball points out 'The issue of who controls the field of judgment is crucial. One key issue of the current educational reform movement may be seen as struggles over the control of the field of judgment and its values' (Ball, 2006, p. 144). The governance structure and policy base of further education is being re-structured through the new statutory agencies of ETBs, Solas and the web of interagency responsibilities with Intreo and other groups as outlined in earlier chapters. This latter shift occurred in response to accountability demands in the wake of public controversy over excessive public spending surrounding the previous statutory body FÁS. The nature and extent of these shifts is not being examined. What knowledge is being promoted and what has been negated in these reforms is not being explored. While reform was needed, the incremental creep of a market based system for the 'knowledge economy' has created another unquestioned reality of further education as the provider of training for jobs in this new economic landscape. The neo-liberal shift to a global transient marketplace remains largely unquestioned in this transformation.

This is set within the context of consensual politics and social partnership agreements between the main groups in Irish society which co-opted business, statutory and community groups into the processes of governance, through professionalisation, negotiation and accountability (Coate & Mac Labhrainn, 2008; Somers & Bradford, 2006). This raises challenges for community groups, including adult and further education, to 'maintain trusting and participative relations with their local communities and to retain their social justice and advocacy objectives' (Grummell, 2007, p. 9). The consequences for learners are profound, particularly the focus on individual responsibility for their own learning and capacity-building in a market economy. It 'leads to an over-reliance on the individual rather than

133

social movements as the agency of social change, and consequently, to an inadequate and false sense of emancipation' (Inglis, 1997, pp. 6–7). It is allied with a streamed approach of encouraging access for marginalized or 'risk' groups to certain routes and types of education (including further education) which discourage the sense of collective responsibility, trust and action necessary for civil society.

This shift is not completely unquestioned, as many within the further education sector and wider society question these changes as we see in the final section. Lynch et al., (2012) outline critiques emerging from existing actors such as trade unions and education bodies. A strong line of protest has also emerged from tutors and learners within the adult education and community development sectors[8]. In other cases, it has emerged from representative bodies in the area, especially from AONTAS (Irish National Adult Learning Organisation) and NALA (National Adult Literacy Agency) who have held a learner-centred ethos and a focus on the experiential knowledge of tutors at the heart of their lobbying for the further education sector. As Shamir (2008, p. 3) notes it is 'a complex, often incoherent, unstable and even contradictory set of practices'.

It highlights the need for a situated view of professional knowledge that is located in the micropolitics and culture of the workplace, reflecting a 'recurrent set of unstable conditions, in a variety of localized circumstances' (Gleeson & Knights, 2006, p. 283). Further education in the Irish context is not only stretched across different education sectors in terms of the historical evolution of the field, acting in the sectors of second level, post-compulsory and higher education, but is now stretched in terms of these demands of accountability, performativity and professionalism that do not easily fit with the learning culture, knowledge base, pedagogy and structures of further education. They are also constrained by the discourses and definitions of further education outlined earlier that limit its learning potential, status and transformative capacities. As Deakin-Crick and Joldersma (2007, p. 83) point out the 'accountability move has profoundly reshaped the curriculum, the character of teaching

---

[8] Protests against government cuts in community development sectors include the Communities Against Cuts campaign (http://www.cwc.ie/2012/11/communities-against-cuts-pre-budget-protest/; accessed 24th October 2013), as well as a host of protests against cutbacks in the mental health, special needs, disability, family support and other social inclusion and equality groups since 2008.

and the nature of learning by markedly narrowing what constitutes knowledge, teaching and learning.'

Lynch et al. (2012, pp. 14, 22) highlights the devastating consequences for education

> In a market-led system, the student is defined as an economic maximiser, governed by self-interest. There is a glorification of the 'consumer citizen' construed as willing, resourced and capable of making market-led choices. Education becomes just another consumption good (not a human right) paralleling other goods and the individual is held responsible for her or his own 'choices' within it. The State's role is one of facilitator and enabler of the consumer and market-led citizen (Rutherford, 2005). Neo-liberalism embeds not only a unique concept of the learner in education, it also maps on a new set of goals to education… The focus is the product not the person, both in terms of what is attained and what is counted and countable. A culture of carelessness is created [in education].

A commercial and economic drift towards employability is combined with the performativity, accreditation and professionalism processes to narrow the scope of knowledge and learning in further education. This filtering effect endangers the social justice, caring and transformative possibilities of further education which are core to its ethos as explored in the final section of this book in terms of further education practice.

SECTION THREE: PRACTICE

CHAPTER SEVEN

PHILOSOPHICAL IMPERATIVES WITHIN FURTHER EDUCATION AND TRAINING

Anne Ryan

As Further Education and Training (FET) takes its first steps into the world of professionalization this chapter critiques the importance of retaining a key characteristic that has shaped FET and the wider adult education sector; that is the tradition of radically interrogating 'schools and other pedagogic sites' (Apple, 2011, p. 36) to determine who benefits and who does not benefit from how they currently operate, and to explore how to better serve the educational needs of those who do not benefit.

This chapter considers the significance of education in terms of the social and economic benefits that accrue to those who do well in the formal system. Taking into account the system's on-going poor track record in promoting equality and addressing disadvantage, despite concerted efforts to do so, the chapter highlights the importance for FET of creating positive learning opportunities that actively seek to benefit all learners. The chapter argues that to do so FET needs to maintain the kind of radical interrogatory stance that has characterised adult education theory and practice. This stance will ensure that FET will continue to explore ways to promote inclusiveness while at the same time withstanding the growing impetus towards a neoliberal perspective on education where the needs of the economy override those of society. This chapter outlines the importance of creating learning systems that acknowledge, value and consciously seek to reaffirm the identity, lived experiences and ways of knowing of all involved; it reviews the powerful role of the teacher/ educator as an agent of change; and calls for pedagogical expertise on the part of the educator that transcends that of the mainstream classroom teacher.

The benefits and beneficiaries of education

In considering how FET might position itself within the wider education provision it is necessary to consider the capacity of the current provision, especially formal education, to meet the needs of learners. There is no doubt that employment prospects and general quality of life are greatly improved for those who complete formal education and especially for those who proceed to higher education. Even if graduates find it difficult to find work in their chosen field, they continue to fare better than those with lesser academic qualifications (Ryan, 2011). It is widely accepted that those who do not complete second level school are most likely to face the risk of poverty and social exclusion (European Commission 2011). They have a higher risk of experiencing a range of disadvantages including being unemployed or in precarious employment, earning least, being dependent on social welfare throughout their lives, having literacy difficulties and spending time in prison (Youth Forum Jeunesse, 2008, p. 11).

It is also widely recognised that educational achievement is closely linked to socio-economic status. Therefore those students least likely to complete second level and proceed to third level and least likely to perform well are those who come from the most disadvantaged backgrounds. Gilbert (2011, p. 188) noted that within the context of the OECD's PISA programme (the Programme for International School Assessment) the background of students is a key factor that determines performance, with schools that serve those from higher socio-economic groups doing best. He also notes (Gilbert, 2011) that conventional approaches to improving performance in schools such as increases in funding and reduction in class size do not result in diminishing the impact of socioeconomic inequalities. The persistence of these inequalities was evident in study in Scotland where Furlong and Cartmel (2005) found that social background among graduates with the same results was a key factor in determining how well they fared in the realm of employment. Those from the most disadvantaged backgrounds were most likely to be unemployed and if employed, were most likely to earn less than their counterparts from better off backgrounds.

Education and inequality

Numerous studies have noted the persistence of inequalities across the formal education sector (AHEAD, 2005; Battell, 2004; Corradi, Evans & Valk, 2006; HEA, 2008; Lynch, 1999; and O'Connell, Clancy, & McCoy, 2006). The potential for mainstream education to address socioeconomic disadvantage has been disputed by many commentators with some arguing that mainstream education in fact further entrenches disadvantage. Furlong and Cartmel (2006, p. 15) went so far as to claim that:

…most industrialized nations organize educational provision in ways that lead to a virtual social apartheid. In the post war period all developed countries have made attempts to break down these social barriers, yet in some cases efforts have been somewhat superficial and in most cases ineffective.

The ineffectiveness of these efforts to address disadvantage are starkly demonstrated by statistics relating to access to university in Britain were '…around 33 per cent of 18-year-olds, for example, go to university, but this percentage is in the 80s for higher social class groups and is less than five for children who have ever been in care' (Wilson, 2010, p. 77). Freire, whose great strength as an educational theorist was the insight he gave into the often occluded impacts of everyday practices within schooling, claimed that what is required to address persistent inequality is a critique of educational discourses and practices that maintain and sustain the current system. He also claimed that interventions to address inequalities which do not lead to dismantling exclusionary practices are not benign but in effect serve to further bolster and sustain existing marginality (see Chapter 3). Such interventions tend to focus on the disadvantaged individual and provide supports so that he or she can participate but do little to address the deficiencies in the system that excluded them in the first place. In the main these efforts make provision to include and support these 'outsiders' to 'fit' the system while the system itself remains stable (Crowther, Galloway & Martin, 2000; Tett, 2006).

Freire's emphasis on interrogating systems called for a capacity on the part of learners and educators to engage in analysis that aims to reveal the discourses and values that determine the politics of education. He contrasted this with what he termed 'educational pragmatism' – a technical approach to learning that is primarily concerned with the acquisition of skills, already known facts and information and that shies away from systemic questions:

> The new educational pragmatism embraces a technical training without political analysis, because such analyses upset the smoothness of educational technicism. … To the educational pragmatist, other social and critical preoccupations represent not just a waste of time but a real obstacle in their process of skills[1] banking. (Freire, 1994: xii).

---

[1] The on-going emphasis on skills is particularly evident in the government departments which have included the word in their title – Department of Education and Skills (currently used in Ireland and Wales and formerly used in the UK from 2001 to 2007).

Freire also pointed to the eminently predicable propensity for this type of education to serve some sectors of the population well and others badly. Educators, especially those working with students who have had negative educational experiences in the past, know that replicating approaches that emphasise skills banking is unlikely to result in significantly different outcomes for these students.

> 'Unless critical education is premised on equality, in the sense of accepting that everyone counts and everyone thinks, it will result in an unintended exercise of domestication'. (Hall et al., 2012: xi)

Freire used the term 'domestication' to describe pedagogical practices that leave learners passively unquestioning and enthralled to a system that failed them.

Wilson (2010, p. 117) elaborated on the detrimental impacts of such a 'technical' approach within the British education system. He noted that the strictly guarded tight boundaries that demarcate disciplines and the competition between schools engendered by publishing league tables of performance have combined to promote a situation where: 'teachers 'teach to the test' and the wider benefits of education – indeed it can even be argued that the fundamentals of learning for students – are lost'. In a similar vein Davies (2007, p. 1) described education as hidebound by 'tightly focused curriculum frameworks and testing regimes' that deflect attention from bigger questions to do with their relevance and the challenge of promoting educational success for all students. In both cases these writers are bemoaning the lack of emphasis on students learning in favour of adherence to procedures that standardise the system. Educators in FET regularly comment on the frustration they feel with the culture of standardised tangible outcomes that they must achieve. Within this culture the success of a programme is measured in terms that are often at odds with the educational needs of the learners with whom they are working and in the main the reporting framework allows no space to record and therefore afford value to the real and important learning that they know has taken place.

The limitations caused by structures and procedures were also commented in the Irish context with regard to the sectoral delineation of education into formal, non-formal, primary, secondary, higher, adult, community and now further education. The *White Paper on Adult Education* (2000, p. 69) described:

...the hermetic nature of the different educational sectors / levels in Ireland, [as] giving rise to little inter-sectoral learning in areas such as methodologies and a continuous tendency in the early school years to seek in-school solutions to what may be out-of-school problems. (Department of Education and Science, 2000, p. 69)

It was proposed in the White Paper to overcome these divisions by using the concept 'lifelong learning' to provide a conceptual framework for all educational provision (see Chapter 4). This did not happen and the fragmentation continues with particular and detrimental consequences for the most disadvantaged students and for those who seek to progress through system in unconventional ways.

The replication of mainstream education globally makes it all the more difficult to challenge dominant discourses and practices.

Across the globe, schools and mass education at the beginning of the twenty-first century are part and parcel of the same 'common sense' logic that created them, a logic grounded in a passion for rationality that has seduced the imagination of Northern Europe and its extended cultural spheres for more than two centuries. (Dressman, 2008, p. 13)

While Dressman, like Freire, highlighted the need to critique common sense logic in order to see through it and to interrupt it, critiquing a system that enjoys general acceptance is not easy. The lure of 'common sense' logic is such that a particular way of seeing reality is accepted as a 'truth', a part of the natural order, the accepted rules of the game, and is unquestioned even by those it does not serve well (Borg & Mayo in Steinklammer, 2012) There is therefore widespread acceptance of the system's preferences for competition and individualism, linear progression of same age cohorts within levels and between levels, a 'one-size-fits-all' approach to curriculum and academic acumen over all other forms of intelligences. Within this system there is little room for collaborative group endeavours, for leaving and later resuming education, for anything other than a cursory nod to learner-centred approaches and for learners whose talents are outside the academic arena.

Glimmers of hope

The heretofore hegemonic positioning of mainstream schooling within the broader educational provision, along with similar positioning of other mainstream systems, can no longer be assured unquestioning status. The uncertainties and doubts unleashed by the economic crisis of the late 2000s generated questions to do with the exercise of power, privilege and responsibility. As the crisis deepened there was widespread agreement that what we were witnessing was a 'big system failure', a failure of critical faculty, a failure of leadership and poor governance. There is also a growing awareness that what is needed to ensure good governance is an engaged and informed citizenry and a scepticism with regard to what appears to be unassailable 'common sense' truths. Perhaps now more than ever in the past, there is a very real opportunity to evaluate dominant discourses including those that currently shape education. However, as Duke (2009, p. 172) points out:

> ...*business as usual* is very hard to dislodge. It calls for a society-wide cultural transformation in values as well economic assumptions. Perhaps adult education has something to say, and to do, here. Perhaps, indeed, it should be its central task and duty.

While the time may be ripe for change, change is not guaranteed. Mayo (2012, p. vii-viii) noted that:

> ...neo-liberal perspectives have come to wield increasing influence over the structures of learning and education. Processes of marketisation have been infiltrating the very institutions, including schools and universities that should have been concerned with preserving the space for the production of critical thinking and challenging debates.

In Ireland the influence of the EU has made a major contribution to this process by tying 'the purposes of education so closely with that of the economy' (Lynch, Grummell and Devine, 2012, p. 10). According to Olssen (2008) education within a neoliberal perspective is valued primarily for its capacity to prepare individuals to participate in a versatile workforce characterised by job mobility, technical know-how and adaptability (see Chapter 6). The influence of neoliberalism means that economic considerations are likely to dominate to the detriment of other concerns such as social justice. While access to employment and livelihood is a very important aim of the social justice agenda the problem lies in the priority afforded the needs of the economy over those of the learners especially those who are disadvantaged and the dominance of economic concerns to the exclusion of other concerns. In a time when there is widespread societal concern to enhance employment opportunities it is particularly difficult to assail the apparent 'common sense' truth that positions education as an arm of the economy. Nevertheless at a time when the dysfunctionality of the dominant economic model is receiving attention there is more potential to do so than was the case prior to the current crisis. It is into this turbulent arena, redolent with challenges and possibilities, that Further Education is making its professional debut.

Implementing a pro-equality agenda for Further Education

As outlined in earlier chapters of this book, Further Education has not been ascribed a specific role in overall educational provision. Within the context of mainstream provision FET is largely defined in terms of what it is not – not second level and not higher education. While FET is closer to the mainstream than other aspects of adult education it is not integral to that provision. It could be argued that the vagueness and residual mature of the definition leaves FET in a marginal or peripheral position. It could further be argued that this position reflects the experience of many FET students.

According to the DES website FET students are spread over 1,200 centres offering FET courses and in over 200 FET Colleges. They bring with them a range of life and educational experiences. The reasons students take FET courses are equally varied but anecdotal evidence from students and educators[2] suggests that these reasons fall into one of the following five categories;

(i)   those who want to take specialist courses that can only be undertaken within the FET sector;

(ii)   those who want a qualification which will enable them to access employment on successful completion of their studies;

(iii)   those who completed second level and intend to continue to third level education but who do not have the points needed to proceed directly to it;

(iv)   those who left second level education before completing it;

(v)   those who have been out of the formal education system for some time and who wish to return.

The students who fall into category (i) are a minority within the overall FET provision and are generally, although not exclusively, involved in courses that relate to the arts and other creative endeavours. The FET sector has been particularly adept at providing learning opportunities in these areas. The students who fall into categories (ii) (iii) (iv) and many in

---

[2] This evidence is based on numerous conversations, student research and in class discussion over the 40 years since the Department of Adult and Community Education began working with educators in this sector and delivering off-campus under graduate programmes in a range of subject areas including Return to Learning initiatives.

category (v) tend to be students who were not well served by the formal education system and consequently either left school early or completed second level but did not perform well. They constitute the students for whom the mainstream's emphasis on competition, individualism, linear progression, a one-size-fits-all approach to curriculum and an almost exclusive valuing of academic intelligence over other forms of intelligence, is not an easy fit. Therefore serving the needs of these students calls for approaches to all aspects of provision that are radically different to those in the second level sector.

Putting the students centre-stage

Education that seeks to provide a positive learning experience for all students including those who were poorly served by formal schooling, calls for educators who have not only subject expertise but who also have pedagogical expertise. Crowther et al. (2005, p. 6) described the expertise needed as one based on 'principle and purpose rather than mere technique'. The principle is based on a belief that education is a right for all rather than a privilege to be afforded to some and the purpose of education is to enable learning. It is a pedagogy that respects and is relevant to the contexts of the students' lives; it starts with the students' lived experiences and aims to develop their capacity to actively engage in learning in order to shape the world in which they live. It essentially involves three discrete steps to create learning opportunities that enable students: (i) to 'discover' their experiences; (ii) to 'rediscover' their experiences within a broader social context; and (iii) to apply these discoveries within their lives. Although this process is discussed below in terms of sequential steps it is a cyclical rather than a linear course of action.

Enabling students to 'discover' their experiences

The purpose of creating learning opportunities whereby students can 'discover' their experiences is to enable them to make meaning of their lives. The word 'discover' is used to capture the sense that this is part of a process rather than a mere narration of events and it is an on-going process rather than a terminal event. It begins with individuals telling their personal story and listening to the stories of others. While each individual's story is unique, hearing the stories of others provides opportunities for students to begin to see commonalities and patterns that raise the possibility that these experiences are not chance or haphazard occurrences. These discoveries are especially important for those who may have experienced educational disadvantage and may have assumed that they were at fault or were the unfortunate victim of a particular set of circumstances.

Enabling this kind of learning can pose challenges for the educator not least of which can be managing emotional responses from students whose experiences were particularly difficult. A great deal has been spoken and written by students outlining the widespread and devastating impacts of negative educational experiences on their self esteem and their belief in their capacity to learn. Responding to the needs of students who have had such an experience calls for skill in enabling them to avoid becoming entrenched in a sense of helplessness, hopelessness or debilitating cynicism all of which can inhibit their capacity to critique their experiences.

Enabling students to rediscover their experiences within the broader social context

The purpose of creating learning opportunities whereby students can 'rediscover' their experiences within a broader social context is to enable them to move from personal knowledge to social knowledge, developing along the way a critical sensitivity to their own assumptions about how the world works. In doing so students acquire social literacy in that they deal with the values, beliefs and assumptions that underpin the 'common sense logic' that sustains particular perspectives on how the world works and that eschews other possible perspectives. Creating a learning environment where students can 'rediscover' their experiences by critiquing them in a broader social context is particularly important. The 'rediscovery' step enables students to come to understand how their experiences were coloured by factors such as their socio-economic backgrounds, learning styles, aptitudes or talents, gender, age, ethnicity, religion etc.

If students do not move beyond a personal narrative they are in danger of viewing themselves in terms of 'deficiencies' that need to be overcome. The preference in mainstream education for 'fitting' students into the system tends to favour such a response. Within mainstream education at second and third levels much attention has to date been given to questions such as how to motivate learners to participate, how to integrate literacy skills into other topics, how to build confidence in students who think they are not academically able. These kinds of questions locate the problem firmly within the student. They favour technical responses that assist the student to fit the system. In so doing they endorse the 'common sense logic' of the system and do little to enable students to understand how the world works and how it is revealed through their individual personal experience.

Enabling students to apply their discoveries within their lives

The purpose of creating learning opportunities that enable students to apply what they have learned within their lives is to create active learners who (i) can locate themselves within systems – including the education system, and (ii) can determine how best to manage their future including their educational future. At this stage students need to recognise the cyclical nature of the process – naming their individual experience, critiquing their experience, taking action. Combining knowledge and action which is known as 'praxis' was described by Crowther et al. (2005, p. 7) as: '…learning in order to act but also learning from action…' This kind of approach depicts learning as a dynamic on-going process rather than a finite act. In Freire's words '…the permanence of education lies in the constant character of the search' (1998, p. 93). It is important for students not only to participate in the process but also to consciously experience the learning as it unfolds so that they can continue to engage in the 'search'.

This kind of learning prepares students to participate in all aspects of society including accessing employment. The difference between it and the neoliberal or skill banking approaches is that by not positioning students as passive consumers of knowledge they will not be docile in their experience of systems and they develop the skills that enable them to be reflective and active and therefore better placed to promote the democratisation of society.

Knowledge and the role of the teacher / educator

Enabling the kind of learning described above calls for a radical shift in the traditional roles of the educator and the student. There is an inherent recognition that students know their world; the educator is not merely required to transmit knowledge but rather to create learning opportunities that enable students to recognise what they know and to guide them through the learning process. It further requires educators to undertake a similar process with regard to themselves so that they too come to know the impact of dominant discourses on their beliefs and on the system in which they operate. Without doing so educators are in danger of losing sight of the big picture and the big questions and becoming enthralled within the 'common sense logic' of the dominant forms of curricula, teaching, evaluation and policy.

CHAPTER EIGHT

PRACTITIONER REFLECTIONS ON FET

Jerry O'Neill, Camilla Fitzsimons and Niamh O'Reilly

Introduction

Jerry O'Neill

In this chapter we consider the adult education landscape from our perspective as three practitioners working in its midst. Our three different accounts merely hint at the diversity of adult educator activity and identities within the field. Camilla Fitzsimons works in various adult education contexts but writes here about her work within, and passion and concerns for, radical community education. Niamh O'Reilly, an adult education advocate working for AONTAS, reflects on the various challenges of trying to affect change within the boundaries of a flawed and inequitable neoliberal education system. I worked for several years in Further Education Colleges in Scotland and now, as a tutor working in the adult education services of an ETB, I pause to consider the significance of educator narratives in tutor development.

Each of us has a different story to tell: I endeavour to engage with the plot of my own occupational narrative as an adult educator and wonder if such narrative reflections can contribute to the development of adult educator knowledge, theory and status. Camilla's narrative cautions us against de-politicised and economy-focused approaches to adult education. Such ideas, she feels, can disable critical conversations about the broader function and possibilities of more radical, social-change modes of adult and community education. Niamh's account of her work as an advocate within an adult education NGO reveals how she must constantly perform a delicate balancing act between pragmatism and her principles. Yet, her reflective account of that dilemma represents a way of resolving such paradigmatic conflicts for us all. Acts of critical reflection like this reinforce her principles and provide an explicit ethical and theoretical foundation which allows her to construct the pragmatic possibilities of adult education in addressing social inequities.

The differences between our accounts are possibly less than what a cursory reading of them might suggest. None of us talked to each other about what we would write beforehand. Yet what is clear is that each of us is passionate about the transformative capacity of adult education. We write, along with that passion, with a strong sense of the moral, affective and social capacities and priorities of adult education. We also share a concern about the extent to which the dominance of neo-liberal and economic discourses, policy and structures distort the broader, social and emotional possibilities of adult education. What's more, we suggest I hope, what is different about adult education: a difference which we celebrate in our discussions of the collaborative, dialogic and democratic ways of knowing and learning to be found and nurtured in adult education contexts.

A fundamental point that each of us touches upon, in one way or another, is the importance of creating spaces for adult educators to critically engage and reflect on their work within this wonderfully heterogeneous field. Safe spaces for genuinely critical, and sometimes difficult, conversations about practice and principles are crucial to maintaining the integrity and development of an equitable, democratic and effective adult education. The pages that follow provide one such space to start a conversation.

In search of a clearing: The potential of narrative spaces for adult educator growth

Jerry O'Neill.

So there I was, standing alone amongst the fruit and vegetables in Lidl pondering on the depth of our family's immediate need for an avocado. It wasn't on the list, but I was nearly sure my wife shouted out 'avocado' as I left the house. Or was it 'aubergine'? Struggling with the profound banality of this domestic dilemma, I began to notice a middle-aged man staring at me quizzically. Catching him watching me, he approached with slight embarrassment and ventured,

"Jerry?"

"Em ... yes ..."

It took a moment to draw myself from avocados (or possibly aubergines) and focus on this greying, confused man.

"It's Mark."

Mark. An old friend from school. Although we were close, or so it once seemed, we hadn't seen each other since we walked, or possibly ran, out of the suddenly-impotent school gates of our suburban secondary school in the summer of 1988.

And now, it seemed, poor Mark was middle-aged and shopping for cheap veg in Lidl.

Within the rhythm of the ensuing, slightly awkward, conversation where we vacillated between the familiar and the strange, Mark soon asked, almost inevitably,

"So what are you up to these days? Are you still involved in music?"

Having conversations with people from our past can be odd as their invocations of our former selves defamiliarise our present. I smirked, as I recalled with a certain fondness that former me, and replied,

"No, no. ... I'm a ... I work in ... I'm involved in adult education."

"Really! Wow. That is a surprise. Like teaching and ... stuff ... you were the last person that I'd imagine as a teacher. How did that happen?"

There is so much in this short exchange that touches on many of the occupational nuances, complexities and contradictions of being "involved in adult education": my faltering response and futile millisecond search for an appropriate occupational noun may have something to say about the sometimes precarious identity, and not unrelated economic status, of adult educators; my qualification of the verb 'work' to 'involved' reveals something more than mere paid employment – maybe a hint of an ideological commitment to what I do. Mark's surprise and momentary, unsuccessful struggle to name adult education and his own, misconceived, image of me as a teacher, on the other hand, reveals a wider discursive discomfort and incoherence with adult education that can only be resolved by positioning it, as Mark does here, as a hard-to-signify Other ("and ...stuff") to more traditional forms of education ("teaching").

But, how, as Mark asked, did that happen?

Yes, it is true that, at secondary school, the possibility of a future occupational life in education was something I would have laughed at myself. I was, as they say, able enough at school but by the time I reached Leaving Cert, was jaded with the hysterical priority put on these set of final exams. My interests then, as my old friend quite rightly remembered, lay with music.

Drifting slightly in that summer of 1988 and beginning to feel a thread of anxiety over the possibility of an occupational and educational vacuum within the context of the contracted horizons of a national recession, I was delighted and, it must be said, somewhat relieved, to be offered a place on a Sound Engineering Course in Ballyfermot Senior College. Within a couple of weeks of commencing the course, I was unrecognisable from the apathetic school student from the previous year, as I wholeheartedly immersed myself in the challenges and opportunities presented by a very different type of learning.

So commenced a passionate relationship with adult education, which has endured, in various forms, for 25 years.

In those 25 years I have lived, worked and learned in England, America, Northern Ireland, Scotland and, now, again, Ireland. My career in music didn't quite hit the stellar heights that I imagined as a teenager but I am slowly coming to terms with that now – time is, indeed, the great healer. Instead, a strong, if rather unfocused epistemological impulse, drew me into Higher Education as a mature student in my mid-twenties. Driven by a newly-discovered passion for education and its life-altering possibilities, I embarked on a couple of degrees and a post-graduate qualification in teaching before occupational aspirations and familial circumstances led me to work as a lecturer in the Further Education sector in Scotland.

The several years I taught and learned in colleges in Scotland were rich in terms of my own development as an educator. The college sector was a discursively complex place: at one level they were run, and conceived, as business enterprises which operated, if not for profit, for financial growth. Much of the language, culture and practice of business, as has been pointed out elsewhere, permeated the FE sector there (Coffield, 2009; James & Biesta, 2007; Jephcote, Salisbury & Rees, 2008).

I am reluctant to portray what could be seen as a reductionist dualism between neoliberal managers and emancipatory educators: the reality was more a complex ideological spectrum. I knew many socially-minded education managers and many market-advocating educators. The wide range of vocational and academic subject areas helped to nurture, largely unarticulated, but an equally wide variety of assumptions about the core purposes of further education. And yet despite what practitioners and managers felt or believed, the funding mechanisms and governance structures ensured that colleges were managed with practices and discourses associated with the commercial business world: learning was deconstructed into a complex system of measureable units (i.e. recruitment rates; retention rates at various points; completion rates etc.) which influenced funding streams for colleges and academic and vocational areas within colleges.

Yet, competing against this dominant managerialist discourse, were critical and dissenting, if often heterogeneous and marginal, educational voices embodied in many passionate and committed educators across the sector. Clashes between these discourses, not infrequently, left a trail of occupational victims. But the interesting things that happened in the development of my own knowledge and practice were often found within spaces where I could engage with these clashes. Sensing the worth of such encounters, but also taking heart from scholarly voices such as Penlington (2008) who stressed the importance of institutions embracing dissonance in educator development, some of us endeavoured to create spaces for genuine critical dialogue which, to put it one way, asked questions about the business of further education.

After several years in Scotland, and carrying these questions with me, I returned to Ireland. I still work in adult education (as I name it now) but, as my faltering reply to Mark reveals, my occupational identity and status is less stable these days. Partly by choice, but more by way of lack of opportunity, I do bits and pieces: I do a bit of work as a tutor within the Adult Education services of an ETB; I do some research within the Adult Education field; and I am involved in some Adult Education programmes within the Higher Education sector. Yet, and I nearly neglected to mention this here myself, all of this comes secondary to my primary occupational role in the home: my wife works full-time and I try to juggle my work in adult education around the work involved in the care of our primary school-attending children. This balancing of various lives is, as far as I have seen, commonplace for many adult educators. We slip in and out of different occupational roles and identities numerous times each day.

So, I have, in Ireland, a more fractured sense of occupational coherence and, indeed, as a relatively marginal practitioner in a marginal educational sector, I am unsure about what kind of occupational future in adult education, if any, lies ahead for me. But what sustains me, so far, is the deep belief, nurtured since my days in Ballyfermot, about the social and emotional worth of adult education and its capacity to transform lives and, possibly more pragmatically, that opportunities can come when we attend to our own learning, our own development.

Interesting, maybe. But, to put it bluntly, so what? What's the point of this condensed narrative of one occupational life?

Well, maybe there is no point, but let me explore the possibility of there being, at least, one. For a start, this chance meeting with Mark, his questions which made me step back and consider the narrative of my occupational arc, made my own life feel less familiar. Making strange the familiar, as Wright Mills argued half a century ago, is the central task of a systematic study of society and its constituents, including in this case, adult education (1959). My meeting with Mark allowed me to stand outside the relentless linearity of my lived narrative and look, more critically, at its development. Such reflective and reflexive moments allow us to generalise within our experience and is a concept and practice, as adult educators, we are not unfamiliar with (Brookfield, 2005; Dewey, 1997; Kolb, 1984; Freire, 1996a; Moon, 1999; Schön, 2003). If we acknowledge Eagleton's notion that theory is 'the moment when a practice begins to curve back on itself, so as to scrutinize its own conditions of possibility' (1996, p. 190), then, we might argue that this narrative reflexivity, this curving back, is the starting point for us in creating a theory of our occupational lives as adult educators. Furthermore, rather than seeing theory as dislocated and irrelevant, we start to see it as an activity in critical self-reflection which is, in Eagleton's allure of possibilities, not self-absorbed but rather developmental in its purpose. What we might begin to imagine, then, in acts of narrative reflexivity, to borrow heavily from Thomson (2007) and Connolly and Hussey (2013), is the possibility of a really useful theory for our own practice and development as adult educators.

But it is not enough to start and end with our own narratives as the source of our useful theory. We must also develop this within a community of theoretical voices which speak to our story. Adult educators are familiar with marginal and liminal spaces: our practice, our knowledge, our learners and learning spaces often exist in spaces far from the centre of cultural, societal and institutional authority and validation. As such, it is no coincidence that many of us seek alignment with those who develop theories of the marginal. From the aesthetic and critical narratives of literature, feminism, post-colonialism, post-structuralism, and critical education theories we read the dynamic play and pull of language and power in articulations of knowledge and being (Bakhtin, 1988; Bruner, 1991; Cubitt, 1998; Davies & Gannon, 2005; Eagleton, 1996; Foucault, 2002; Freire, 1996b; hooks, 1994; Horton & Freire, 1990; Joyce, 1968; Kabbani, 1988; Kincheloe, 2008; Kristeva, 1986; Moi, 1985; Polkinghorne, 1988; Richardson, 1994; Ryan, 2001; Said, 1995).

And what we read, or should, from the intertextual resonances between theories and our own narratives is, for one, that our knowledge and ways of being as adult educators is proudly liminal. This liminality enables our ways of knowing as educators to be multidimensional: affective, political, dialogic, creative, compassionate, scientific. Our crooked paths into and around the diverse landscape of adult education allows us, or at least has the capacity if we see its worth, to see the connection between things. And maybe that's where our useful knowledge lies: our own rich educational and occupational narratives have equipped us with this vision to see knowledge as connections, relations. Our interest and our knowledge then, like Heaney's, is often found in the space between things (Cole, 2013). But we know enough also, to know that there is so much we don't know. Occupying spaces of epistemological humility allows us, for example, to acknowledge that not-knowing is a powerful place for learning and development to occur (McCormack, 2013). Or that knowledge ebbs and flows between tutor and student in the adult education environment. And that we grow, as educators, when we continue to explore and extend the boundaries of our own knowledge and practice.

But this exploration into useful theories and knowledge can be a lonely task and wrought with doubt if taken alone. It is important yet not enough to have some worthy but absent theorists as companions on our journeys of growth. As educators we sometimes miss the irony that what we advocate for the good of our students' development as learners, we rarely call for in our own development as educators. Most of us would, in one way or another, believe in and practice a form of pedagogy that had a social and dialogic element. In trying to achieve this, we work hard to create appropriate and safe spaces for such learning to occur. But do we fight as hard to create similarly appropriate spaces, temporal and physical, for our own development as educators? Do we need to be told that much has been written about the capacity for authentic, safe and critical peer-based learning groups in the development of educators across sectors (James & Biesta, 2007; Scales et al., 2011; Snow-Gerono, 2005; Vescio, Ross, & Adams, 2008; Wenger, 1998)? Or do I need to reflect that some of the most important moments in my own learning and development as an educator have taken place in formal and informal dialogic encounters with my peers?

Maybe. But, as I have already suggested, I suspect it does not come as a major surprise to any of us as such environments are the very things we endeavour to create for the development of our own learners. There is then, it seems, a certain responsibility on us to create spaces for such encounters in the vital task of our own development – to find clearings within the relentless pace, density and messiness of our occupational lives in which we can pause to name our practice, our knowledge, our useful theories.

It's important to note that the availability of, and access to, such clearings is not just crucial for our own development; safe, but critically robust spaces are also needed to name and sustain adult education itself. Acts of naming are often, possibly always, political acts. As has been discussed elsewhere in this book, the act of naming adult education is not a neutral one – it is merely part of a wider struggle of values, ideas and purpose at play right now within the broad and heterogeneous field of adult education in Ireland. And it is only if we are allowed to catch our breath in occupational clearings can we reflect on the broader, but fundamental, ideological, structural and educational significance revealed by the semantic tensions between terms such as "FET" and "adult education".

Yet identifying the need for such clearings is, of course, an easier task than actually creating them. Institutional marginality and contractual precariousness, coupled with the occupational, sectoral and ideological diversity of adult educators makes it difficult for us to create these spaces alone.

The nurturing of authentic, peer-led development spaces for educators takes a leap of faith for institutional agents within the sector as it means putting a value (and yes, possibly, even money) behind a commitment to creating temporal and physical spaces for adult educator development. But as Coffield (2009), James and Biesta (2007), Scales et al. (2011) and Wenger (1998) have all pointed out, this requires the need for authentic and creative leadership which acknowledges and validates the centrality of the adult educator, and their development, in the evolution of a high quality service. That, though, is another story.

Let's finish by imagining, instead, what might occur in horizontal, safe and dialogic developmental spaces for educators? Well, as Connelly and Clandinin (1995) suggest, a good place to start would be for educators to share their occupational stories. Such narrative collaboration may just, as Craig suggests, create 'knowledge communities [which] recognize and value teachers' personal practical knowledge and connect individuals to the communal ways of knowing' (1995, p.141).

And in narrating our occupational lives, we may, in embracing the intertextuality of our knowledge and practice, invent encounters in Lidl, to make, a more important point about the conditions and possibilities for our own growth as adult educators

Naming It (Leontia Flynn)

Five years out of school and preachy
with booklearning, it is good to be discovered
as a marauding child.
To think the gloomiest most baffled
misadventures might lead so suddenly
to a clearing - as when a friend
taking me to her well-stocked fridge says:
look
this is an avocado and this
is an aubergine.[1]

---

[1] From Naming It' in Leontia Flynn's *These Days* (2004). Copyright 2004 by Jonathan Cape, London. Used with kind permission of the author

155

Worlds apart? The disunity of FET policy directives and community-based education for social change.

Camilla Fitzsimons

My first job as community educator was with a Community Development Project (CDP) in the late 1990s. It operated out of a vacant social housing unit in a high-rise flat complex in North Dublin, an area often categorised as 'disadvantaged'. With others I set up a learning group for women described as having 'a history of problematic drug use'. In reality, these women continually negotiated their relationship with prescribed and non-prescribed substances as they also managed other roles such as parent, sibling, friend and partner. Paired with a local, 'unqualified' community educator we traversed such topics as local history, women's health, politics, social analysis, computer studies and creative writing. My co-facilitator's legitimate connection to the locality compensated for my unfamiliarity with its cultures and experiences as we drank tea, laughed, cried, discussed, debated and, at times, extended our energies towards tangible community outcomes. These included the establishment of a service-users forum, participation in a demonstration against the closure of the local swimming pool, engagement with employers willing to offer work-placements, and forging links with other activist organisations in addressing community needs. Through this endeavour I was first introduced to group-work as a mechanism for community education; a way of working influenced by Paulo Freire and the Training for Transformation (TfT) movement where methodologies were dialogic, problem-posing, experiential, reflective, and appreciative of the values and experiences brought by each person. Its emphasis on praxis (a cyclical process of action and reflection) also ensured critical-capacities were extended beyond class-room walls towards advancing a more equal world.

I have repeated these processes with a range of groups since; within the same CDP, as tutor in a Vocational Education Committee (VEC), as community educator in a large Housing Association, and as an outreach tutor/facilitator with a Department of Adult & Community Education. Philosophically I identify most with radical concepts infused with humanistic (or person-centered) tendencies. I agree with hooks (1994) affirmation of practice-theory connections interpreting my educational approach as a form of resistance as well as one of 'self-recovery', enacted to encourage 'collective liberation' (hooks, 1994, p.59).

Each time, the process begins by creating certain conditions through lengthy introductions, explorations of personal trepidations, and contemplations on group dynamics. Only then are themes introduced through experiential exercises, personal and shared reflections, and such props as poetry and pictures. Theoretical inputs are guided by these preceding elements and leadership skills are honed in a safe, supported environment. By laying bare subjective experiences, my belief is that comparison, validation and appraisal through theory can deepen understanding and encourage a *structural* over *individual* analysis. Working in this way requires continual tailoring of plans as led by emergent themes and for the facilitator; there is a constant relearning of familiar ideas through dialogic inquiry with students (Shor & Freire, 1987, p. 101). Outward emphasis encourages and supports groups to not only theorize their oppression, but to begin to act on it.

Working in this way I have witnessed particular outcomes. I remember one woman revealing a significant shift in self-interpretation; no longer viewing her circumstances as her fault but rather as prejudiced by a class-based society. I have witnessed the establishment of rights-based forums, the initiation of collective complaints over housing conditions, State-citizen dialogue to influence regeneration plans, and the setting up of support services within communities. I have listened to reflections on the role that gender and ethnicity play in influencing life-chances, and experienced a sense that many who pass through such programmes leave with a renewed and more critical engagement with their socio-economic surroundings. On vocationally-driven healthcare programmes, the inclusion of social analysis has encouraged scrutiny of the medical-model, challenges to hierarchical power-relations, and consideration for the social determinants of health. Consistently, I am humbled when participants reveal their analytical and philosophical potential; a personal reminder to hold firm my belief in people's intellectual abilities regardless of levels of formal education. My commitment is also reinforced through the continual unmasking of negative experiences of school and the heavy burden this can leave, both economic and psychological.

Much of my practice has been within the *Community Sector*; a collection of Community organisations and networks, many of which emerged through bottom-up activism in response to needs on the ground. This sector is commonly described as resting on values of equality and social justice, empowerment, participation and collective action implemented to contribute to the creation of a more equal society. Interpreting myself as ally to those more directly affected by structural inequality, I have elsewhere presented an argument that the Community Sector has been depoliticised in three key ways - its contradictory relationships with the State, co-option through partnership and ideological tensions within (Fitzsimons, 2012). However, it would be disingenuous to suggest a once hot-bed of radicalism blunted by these forces. A more accurate interpretation is to accept that radical elements have always been a minority philosophical undertow (Fitzsimons, forthcoming; Powell & Geoghegan, 2004, p. 156). Also more creditable is the way in which much community work, whilst potentially inclusive of actions to promote participatory democracy, is better described as local service delivery. These services (including community education that addresses personal and vocational concerns) are much needed and it is understandable that money made available to previously neglected areas were used to address the failure by successive governments to provide for basic needs. Many workers within these projects share my ontological perspective on inequality, working tirelessly to create opportunities for people to lift themselves from their life circumstances.

Every effort should be made to ensure an inclusive society and equality-of-opportunity is an important human right. However, managing the symptoms of inequality will always be a limiting perspective as it fails to address the root cause. I interpret inequality as systemic and blame our current epoch of neo-liberalism where trickle-down rhetoric conceals trickle-up economics. Obscured by the language of liberty and freedom, this system has facilitated the transfer of wealth from the majority to an elite, simultaneously limiting civil rights (Giroux, 2006; Harvey, 2005; Klein, 2007). Assisting this, there has been a cultural reproduction of neoliberal capitalism through a cacophony of cultural images, through mainstream media discussion, and through much traditional education. I fight against such efforts to collectively sedate and challenge accusations that to do so is in some way unpatriotic and pessimistic.

In the past, my work has co-existed alongside less-politicised interpretations of community education as I (and others) offer a critical voice within the sector. Part of this has always been about encouraging others to move beyond equality-of-opportunity and service-provision recognizing the need to build communities of struggle. However, it is increasingly difficult to create spaces for this work with events both inside and outside the classroom limiting actions.

Outside the classroom there has been an antagonistic realignment of the Community Sector[2], something that has removed power from local management committees, facilitated the transfer of assets to State-managed structures, and forced project closures. There have also been widespread funding cuts disproportionate to other publically funded entities resulting in pay-cuts and job-losses (Harvey, 2012). It is not surprising that these moves leave many reluctant to show their ideological cards as hostile actions are accompanied by saturating overtures that eulogize apolitical concepts of volunteerism and rewrite social policy as a safety net for the financial sector rather than protection for its citizens. Within this, community education has been cast as supply-chain for the Department of Social Protection's welfare-to-work schemes as unemployment is individualized blaming those out of work for their predicament as well as making them responsible for its rectification.

Inside the classroom there has been both a practical and conceptual onslaught of the belief that only accredited learning is of value. Whilst accreditation brings certain advantages explored elsewhere (Fitzsimons & Dorman, 2013), I struggle with the dominance of Further Education (FE) qualifications in their current guise and the way in which the Common Awards System (CAS) (successor to a range of FE accreditors) was introduced. This process disadvantaged many community education providers, not least through the withdrawal of some qualifications without negotiation. This happened to a component award in *Estate Management*, the only housing related module available and one I was delivering as part of work intended to diffuse power held by Housing Authorities on social housing estates. Despite objections, this top-down decision was not reviewed; the response from FETAC being it was no longer considered relevant. The process of migrating awards is also time-consuming, over-burdening the many community sector organisations whose State-granted funding does not stretch beyond tutor payment for contact hours. This brings newfound reliance on Education and Training Boards (ETBs) for community groups unable to continue to provide direct access. This might seem un-problematic on the surface, but is hugely constraining given reports on the ground that some ETBs are interpreting indicative contents

---

[2] There has been a merger of LEADER and Partnership companies (reducing them from 94 to 52) and the integration of the previously independent Community Development Programme within these new Partnership Companies, now collectively called the Local & Community Development Programme. Responsibility for this programme is being welded into local authority structures under the Department of Environment & Local Government. The Family Support Agency has also been re-aligned within the broader Child and Family Agency.

in programme plans as a compulsory check-list for delivery with tutors held to task if they stray from this format. Reliance on ETBs is also enhanced by the introduction of fees for award validation, and the likely future introduction of fees for retention of accreditation capacities (although the AONTAS Community Education Network are campaigning against this). Community organisations were previously exempt facilitating access for those most in need. A fees structure not only precludes many new entrants, it is likely to prevent community deliverers who have adapted to the CAS from retaining control into the future. This point was consistently and repeatedly put to Quality and Qualifications Ireland (QQI) at each stage of consultation processes and it is demoralizing to realize this fell on deaf ears. These barriers are compounded by the implementation of revised policies on the Protection of Enrolled Learners (something Universities, Institutes of Technology and ETBs are exempt from) again limiting independence and reducing local delivery closest to those most affected.

Implementing the CAS involves over-reliance on copious, preset learning outcomes prescribed by faceless practitioners with no relationship with facilitators or their groups. Modules are over-assessed and the administrative burden involved in integrating coursework and summatively assessing each outcome relegates the centralization of emergent generative themes in favour of teaching to assignments. Conceptually, extensive learning outcomes and their imposing assessment structures encourages the standardization of assignments. This suits banking approaches to education, enhances cultural bias, and stifles diversity and innovation increasing the likelihood that the hidden curriculum of traditional schooling continues uninterrupted in FE tertiary settings.

The use of FE awards also relegates community education to the lower rungs of the National Framework of Qualifications (NFQ), a positioning that encourages behaviourist methodologies; a carrot-and-stick approach concerned with the transference of certain unchallenged skills and predetermined knowledge. This contradicts the analytical and critical philosophies carried by Freirean influenced community educators, keeping these the preserve of those attending Higher Education Institutions (HEIs). These institutions are out of reach to many who access community education due to exorbitant fees for part-time study and excessive registration costs for those who find the time for full-time studies amidst the demands of modern life.

Conclusion

In the opening chapter of *Pedagogy of Hope* (1992) Freire encourages us to continually reflect on whether we, as practitioners, are truly listening to participants; assisting them to draw connections between their lived experiences and the broader fabric of society. I strive to do this by setting aside the dominance of bureaucracy and compliance within much community education practice. I lean on such greats as Freire but also Ghandi's oft cited mantra to 'be the change' and I encourage others to do the same. As educators often working with those most affected by social injustice surely we should question practices implemented from above litmus testing these against the needs and rights of communities within which we work? Our responsibility is also one of advocacy; to encourage policy makers to listen to our generative themes, to learn from our expertise and to value the contribution of community education within the wider tapestry of educational provision.

Principles and pragmatism – advocating for adult and community education within a neoliberal policy framework.

Niamh O'Reilly

Introduction

Advocating for adult and community education through lobbying activities which aspire to influence policy and challenge the dominant discourse is fraught with tension. Both at National and European level, adult education policy is firmly set within the neoliberal ideology, which has been discussed in previous chapters. Trying to advocate for adult learning in a broad sense that goes beyond an instrumental view of adult education is challenging on a number of levels. This is evident in terms of advocating for a low status provider of education, particularly community education which has low visibility, and due to its organic development, can be difficult to place, in terms of policy, within the Further Education and Training System. However, in this chapter I will explore what I perceive to be a pressing, but perhaps a less frequently reported, aspect of adult learning advocacy work: the internal dilemma between one's understanding of the role of adult and community education and the reality of influencing policy, thus the relationship between principles and pragmatism.

Idealism and ideology

My first introduction to adult education was by way of a notice in a shop window seeking volunteer literacy tutors. In the five years of volunteering that followed, I learned about the power of adult learning and the need for a truly learner-centred approach, the results of which were profound to the learner, their family and community. Feeling the need to improve my understanding and practice of adult education I undertook a Higher Diploma in Education Studies, with a specific focus on adult education. Adult education philosophies and methodologies were a revelation to me, the potential of an alternative to schooling coupled with a deep commitment to social justice resonated deeply with me. I had found my calling. Witnessing the result of social and educational inequality during my work at a Local Employment Service I decided to trade disillusionment for the potential to improve the adult education system, this came by way of a job in AONTAS. Perhaps a touch idealist, perhaps a little naïve, I began to work as an adult learning advocate with the desire to improve the educational experience of adult learners. However, over the past nine years this work has been fraught with internal struggles between my conception of adult learning which manifests itself in the principles which inform my work and that of the education policy which I endeavour to change.

Over the course of my work in establishing, developing and coordinating the Community Education Network since 2007, I have been afforded a unique lens to understand the impact of policy on practice. Recently, the startling disconnect between the aspirations of community education and new national policies for further education and training has come into focus. However, this phenomenon is not exceptional to Ireland, as a board member of the European Association for the Education of Adults (EAEA) I have discovered a shared experience with fellow advocates of non-formal adult education in Europe. The disconnect between the philosophies that inform adult education, predominantly a social justice agenda, versus national and European adult learning policy which mainly encompasses the intertwined policy drivers of social, but to a greater extent, economic imperatives is a constant source of debate, disagreement and dissent. As an advocate rationalizing the principles of adult and

162

community education within a neo-liberal policy framework, a pragmatic approach is required but it comes at a cost.

The source of discontent

In the instance of community education the aforementioned principles are not merely aspirational but inform practice. In my view, the practice of AONTAS community education member organisations is characterized as having the following features: the learning process must be cognisant of, and shaped around the life experience of the learner (Dewey, 1938; Knowles, 1980; Lindeman, 1926), and through various learning methodologies and supports, the experience can be transformative at an individual (Mezirow, 1997) and community level (Freire, 1970). The purpose of learning provision is viewed as a right, addresses the desire of the learner to become more fully human, to become conscious of the world (consentization), and to address the inequities in the process of action and reflection (praxis). This alternative politicized education process (Illich, 1971; Freire, 1970) has value at personal and collective level in terms of personal discovery and development, confidence, increased agency and capacity to shape one's world and community. The result of such learning can have a systemic effect through how individuals, families and communities view develop and transform themselves. This conception of community education is in keeping with the principles which inform my work. However, this view of education is diametrically opposed to the new world of FET policy, in which it responds to the needs of a changed and changing economy, whereby education is not a right but a tool which harnesses liberal values of independence and autonomy that facilitate a flexible, responsive individual who can adapt to this uncertain and market driven economy. Rather than participating voluntarily at a time and stage which is spurred by one's own life and aspirations, within the new FET process learners are directed to take up the opportunities available to them or risk the loss of unemployment payments.

Chipping away or becoming part of the mould?

From my experience advocating for radical adult and community education, based on a social justice agenda that is contrary to the ideology of the policies which you endeavour to influence, calls for two approaches. Firstly, at a macro-level, by advocating for an alternative discourse to the dominant instrumental view of adult learning; and secondly, at a micro-level, by influencing aspects of national policy that impinge on adult and community education practice.

Chipping away to find the cracks

At macro-level, broad scale attempts to challenge the dominant instrumental view of adult learning involves identifying cracks within what often appears to be an impermeable, common sense, view of adult education being a tool for the economy. As an adult learning advocate it involves such activities as: identifying potential spaces of influence; providing an evidenced position; uniting with allies of a similar agenda; but also continually reflecting on one's practice and advocacy actions. I have found that there is a constant need for reflexivity to ensure that advocacy work stays true to the principles of adult learning in order to continually push through an alternative concept of adult learning. Avenues of influence include general promotional work to the wider public and advocacy work at National, European, and International level. The benefit of a far reaching approach is that you broaden the net of influence to include actors who shape the perception of adult learning, e.g. OECD, and influence national policy. This more broad scale influence can also include challenging the concept of adult learning within the European policy arena as this can act as a future barometer for national policy.

Efforts to influence the prevailing conception of adult learning is challenging as we, including policy makers, are constantly bombarded with the instrumental view of learning from prominent research bodies such as the OECD. It is perhaps unsurprising that a philosophical understanding of adult learning is broadly unknown. Even in my experience of being a student and lecturer in higher education, I am often confronted by other students who study education. However adult education, and in particular community education, remains an unknown territory. Therefore, I believe we cannot be too judgmental regarding policy makers many of whom do not have an adult education background. I believe it is the responsibility of adult learning advocates to share a holistic, radical view of adult learning.

The limitations of this approach are evident, for example there is only a limited reach and influence. Attributing advocacy work to conceptual change is difficult as direct correlation to one activity is rarely possible, however, it may be due in part to a long-term sustained drive for a wider understanding of adult learning. However, as the task is so great, and the alternative voice so weak, there is a need for allies across the adult and community education system to unify in developing the debate, influencing the discourse, and promoting the broader understanding of adult learning. Academics, advocacy NGOs, voluntary community based providers as well as statutory adult education providers can create an alternative collective voice which can chip away at the instrumental view of adult learning.

Being part of the mould?

Engaging in activities which seek to influence national policy could be viewed as merely an attempt to modify the dominant system rather than effecting social change. I often feel such advocacy is merely addressing symptoms of social injustices rather than addressing the cause. Furthermore, lobbying on a specific issue within the further education and training system could be construed as consolidating the existing hegemonic arrangements that perpetuate a neoliberal stance on adult learning rather than challenging it. Therefore, I frequently feel that I am part of the mould.

However, my internal theoretical debate is overcome by the reality of adult learning practitioners and their need for immediate policy change to ensure provision for learners. In my work, this approach involves responding to the reality of AONTAS members; for practitioners regarding how national policy impacts on their education provision; for learners with respect to how their right to quality adult learning can be achieved within the adult and community education system. Such advocacy involves long-term development work with grassroots practitioners and learners in order to offer a depth and breadth of knowledge and understanding that can then afford the advocate, and the associated NGO, a legitimate representative position. Through this long-term work I develop a relationship with the practitioners and learners, their issues become my issues. The impact of certain adult education policies is real; the very existence of an education organization can be at stake. I feel it is not the time for an internal debate on the theoretical understanding of adult learning, but a time for pragmatic lobbying so that the group can be funded and learners can effectively engage in learning. In order to influence policy within this context, a decision has to be made to be at the table to influence, and thus be a part of the system.

By being at the table to lobby involves an engagement with the system and also the dominant language of policy makers. Like the relationships I develop with AONTAS members for representative work, advocacy work also requires the development of relationships with policy makers. I see it as effecting change from inside the system.

In the process of advocacy work policy issues raised by AONTAS members are reconfigured into a language, and an evidenced position, that can influence policy. This leads to the struggle of using the language of the market to influence policy, to relate to policy makers, and to demonstrate the value of adult and community education including how it meets national priorities for FET. I experience this as acting in a pragmatic manner to influence policy that supports radical adult and community education whilst being acutely aware of the paradox.

Challenges for the adult learning advocate - a personal dilemma

On a personal level, successes in chipping away at the cracks or effecting policy can be bitter-sweet. Any gains made feel like an achievement, however with an academic lens, the internal grapple between concepts of co-option, incorporation or hijacking of social justice aspects of adult learning in order to meet economic imperatives are never far from one's mind. It can seem that no reward is fulfilling.

Furthermore, the internal conflict between one's perception of being a 'sell-out' and dedicating your working life to fighting a losing battle can arise. Lobbying, which is essentially about being part of the system, can be construed as being too conformist to both academics and radical adult and community education practitioners as you are perpetuating the unchanged system rather than transforming it. It could be argued that lobbying from within the system is merely compensatory, that ultimately 'second chance' learners exist because of social inequalities which manifest in unequal educational experience and attainment. If I were to take a Freirean approach, I would struggle to address deep rooted structural inequalities through action rather than make amendments to the system which is ineffectual in addressing oppression. On the contrary, I lobby within a neo-liberal policy framework that uses public services e.g. education to address the requirements of the private sphere e.g. the market. This notion of education proposes that courses must be congruent with the market; provision must be monitored for cost effectiveness and achieve the standards of a professional understanding of FET provision. Therefore, it is often challenging to lobby for radical adult education within the constraints of current FET policy.

The message of promoting education as a public good, which is difficult to measure, describe, or relate to within the current policy discourse and therefore a challenge to advocate

166

for can be deemed too radical for policy makers. Furthermore, it is difficult to ascertain how effective advocacy attempts are in chipping away at dominant discourse of a market driven view of adult education. However, by holding on to one's principles, being aware of the dichotomy of advocacy work and maintaining the position of adult learning for social justice, acting in a pragmatic manner can be acceptable in that the means can justify the ends.

Making a difference or maintaining the status quo?

In addition to the internal dilemma of advocacy, comes the challenge of making a difference. The role of adult learning, and currently FET, as a tool for the economy becomes a common sense approach: its purported ability to address mass unemployment, to equip individuals to take ownership of the learning opportunities available and become responsible for their ability to gain employment is difficult to overcome. Furthermore, the unequal power relations of both adult learners and adult and community education providers which have low visibility and status within the broader education system exacerbates the challenge.

There is no easy answer as how to advocate for a low status provider of education and one that seeks to liberate the oppressed in an unequal world in the face of the enormous power of hegemonic capitalism that permeates the media and public policy. Knowles partly attributed the 'survival' of adult education to institutional dimensions (1977, p. 258). In the Irish context, I believe that the survival of adult and community organisations is due to the consistent lobbying work of practitioners and learners, who are not only educators/participants but are advocates themselves. That's what makes this small distinct form of education different, those involved believe deeply in the principles which underpin this kind of holistic, political and powerful education making the challenges of a pragmatic route to advocacy worth navigating.

CHAPTER NINE

CONCLUSION: FURTHER EDUCATION AND TRAINING: THE TROJAN HORSE

Anne Ryan

To conclude, this chapter considers the challenges and opportunities inherent in the repositioning of FET as part of the state's overall educational provision. This positioning provides an unprecedented opportunity for FET to interact with the formal sector on the big issues pertaining to the purpose of education in the twenty-first century. This chapter calls on FET to respond to this opportunity in ways that draw on its long established preference for educational provision that favours dialogue, inclusiveness and collaboration. To date the professionalization of FET in terms of initial educator training and the terminology used in all aspects of this training are drawn directly from the formal education sector. As FET develops within this new context, it is crucially important that educators maintain the kind of radical interrogatory stance that has heretofore characterised such provision (see Chapter Seven). This invariably includes an awareness of power relationships – both within and exterior to the learning environment – as well as an understanding that educators can play a key role in affecting positive change within the FET system.

Introduction

As FET dons the mantle of professionalism, it can be viewed as a fairytale ending for a sector that was once referred to as the 'Cinderella' of education. It could also be a viable opportunity for FET to influence the pedagogical agenda of mainstream education. The title of this chapter 'The Trojan Horse' is an attempt to convey the notion of gaining access to an otherwise somewhat impenetrable citadel. In Virgil's Aeneid, the Greeks built a wooden horse to conceal an invading force and left it at the gates of the city of Troy. The unsuspecting inhabitants of Troy took in what they thought of as a fitting trophy only to find that it would ultimately destroy them. In this analogy and in the context of the developments in FET it is not about destruction but about influence. The proposal is that FET act as a Trojan Horse that carries the radical education agenda to the heart of mainstream education to transform it. In this chapter I propose that FET plays an active role in making this happen.

This idea directly relates to core arguments offered in this book, where the notion of influencing the FET policy discourse from within illustrates the contested nature of education provision in general. It emphasises the view that educational provision is never politically neutral in the sense that differing viewpoints reflect alternative ways of understanding education's relationship with the economy, culture and society. But it also underlines the notion that "contestation" offers up the possibility to actively challenge and change characteristics of education that facilitate systems of inequality, non-critical thinking and an overreliance upon preformativity.

The path to professionalization

The FET path to professionalization was paved with good intentions but not all translated into reality.

What was meant to happen

The decision to professionalise the FET sector was made in the White Paper on Adult Education in 2000. It was made within the context of a lifelong learning framework that included all forms of education, formal, non-formal and informal. This use of 'lifelong learning' was in keeping with how UNESCO employed the term when it was first popularised in the 1960s and 70s (Walters et al, 2004, p. 143). Regarding formal education the White Paper stated (Department of Education and Science (DES), 2000, p. 31): 'A lifelong learning agenda redefines the school as one of many agencies and learning sites involved with the learner in a much more fluid and less time specific way than has been the case traditionally.' An all embracing approach to education was to be characterised by the following features:

- An holistic curriculum, focussed on a broad sphere of learning and on catering for the learner's educational and personal needs in a way which reflects his/her cultural and community context and experience;
- A view of the student as a self-directed, self-motivated learner;
- A recognition of the student as the centre of the learning process, being supported by teachers and other learners rather than as one in pursuit of the learning which others have already acquired – i.e. learning as *construction* rather than *instruction*. Participative models for identifying and adapting provision to learner needs are central to this process;
- A core learning objective of preparing the learner for a life of learning rather than for a terminal, end-of-learning examination;

170

- New models of assessment and greater fluidity between the educational sectors themselves and between these and the other domains particularly of work and home.... (DES, 2000, p.31)

Furthermore formal education providers were called on to 'pay more overt attention to such features'.

What did happen

In the fourteen years that have passed since the White Paper was published the move to professionalise FET is finally underway and the use of the term lifelong learning to encompass all forms of learning is well and truly abandoned. Its meaning is now much reduced and it is used interchangeably with other terms that refer to education outside the formal school and HE systems. This shift was largely driven by the OECD and the EU's use of the term in ways that no longer emphasised creating structures and institutions to meet the needs of the learner – which UNESCO had emphasised – and instead focused on the learner taking courses to acquire skills to fill gaps in the labour market. Walters et al. (2004, p. 144) described this shift as having a 'predominant ingredient, neoliberalism' at its core. The shift in usage in the Irish context was largely uncontested and its 'new' meaning was in widespread use, even within the FET sector, a year or two after the publication of the White Paper in 2000. As the meaning of the term 'lifelong learning' was compressed it left a practical and conceptual vacuum – there is now no way to refer to all forms of education. The term education cannot play this unifying role because it is commonly understood to refer to formal provision. In the university sector it is generally used to refer to second level schooling with other sectors qualifying the term – pre-school education, primary education, third level education, adult education etc. Furthermore no moves have happened that require formal education to 'pay overt attention' to the list of characteristics cited above. The abandonment of the all-embracing approach to education as envisioned in the White Paper has created an utterly altered philosophical and practical environment as the context in which the professionalization of FET is now happening.

The experience of professionalization

The absence of a shared conceptual framework across the educational system has been starkly evident as the professionalization of FET has proceeded. This is particularly so in regard to the following: (i) the nomenclature drawn on is firmly embedded in the organisation of the formal education sector; (ii) the body overseeing the registration of FET professionals is the Teaching Council. The Council's 37 members includes no FET sector representatives and (iii) the Council's guidelines for developing initial teacher training courses in FET closely mirror those for teacher training in the formal sector (see Chapter Five).

While the professionalization process could be seen as affording the formal sector a dominant position within the overall educational system, the challenge for FET is to identify opportunities inherent in this new reality – a reality where it has a closer connection with mainstream education than ever before – and use this new positioning to further its objective of enhancing the educational experiences of all learners across the educational spectrum. This is all the more important in that: (i) the emphasis on preparing students for 'employment' within the FET sector is also featuring in formal education discourses; and (ii) the shift in terminology within the FET sector is concurrent with a decreasing focus on inherent inequalities within mainstream education provision (see Chapter Four).

Engaging with mainstream education

In the past FET has always been aware of the other players involved in educational provision. This awareness is due in some large measure to FET's work with learners who for whatever reason found themselves adrift from mainstream education – needing help to reconnect and often damaged by their earlier experiences. Up to now the focus has tended to be on the differences and in particular the shortcomings of the formal sector. The possibilities of the different sectors working together to create a less fractured and more cohesive learner-centred provision peaked at the time of the government White Paper (outlined above) but has since waned.

In the intervening years and particularly in the past six years, much has happened to raise public awareness of the fallibility of dominant neoliberal discourses in the areas of economics, education and politics. In chapter Seven there was some discussion on the role of FET in working towards the kind of cultural transformation that would build on this awareness. Duke (2009, p. 172) remarked that although there is widespread awareness of the major flaws, transformation will not happen automatically because *'business as usual* is hard to dislodge' and he proposed that enabling change in the values and assumptions that led to the current crisis should be the central task and duty of FET. The challenge for the FET sector is (i) to find ways to re-engage in a system-wide dialogue and (ii) to ensure the dialogue is meaningful. What is called for is an engagement that (i) includes but is not restricted to the exchange of expertise and methodologies and (ii) most importantly seeks to reveal and explore the overarching social, political, economic and cultural purposes of education in local, national and global contexts. Such an engagement is not just about a finite outcome (though being able to shape outcomes is vitally important) but about an on-going process of dialogue. For FET such a process is not without its risks – not least of which is being subsumed into the larger dominant system. However, not engaging in the process also has risks; the main one is being consigned to the margin of educational provision and not having a voice in shaping the future of education in the state. It is important to state too that this does not amount to "engagement at any price". Anyone who is or has been involved in official consultation/ deliberative processes will be keenly aware that engagement requires good will and trust on all sides, otherwise such processes can be easily become "rubberstamping" exercises that merely affirm the predetermined wishes of policymakers. In such circumstances, questions must be asked as to the value of engagement.

The 'rules' of engagement

The above argument notwithstanding, undertaking a process of engagement means that the FET sector needs to draw on a number of key principles that inform its pedagogical stance. FET practitioners from the radical tradition are keenly aware of the role of dominant discourses in shaping and sustaining systems and in influencing the assumptive worlds of those who work within them.

> Those involved in any learning situation whether as educators or as students, come to their tasks enmeshed in the contexts which form part of their wider environment. Hence they are both knowingly and unknowingly influenced by the web of conflicts, dilemmas and power differentials which are part of their system of origin. (Ryan & Walsh, 2004, p.112)

This is an important consideration for all kinds of engagements including those that involve building partnerships between agencies, institutions and organisations. The individuals who represent these bodies and the bodies themselves all operate within assumptive worlds. When it comes to engagements between sectors involved in the provision of education it is likely that consciously or otherwise they may not share a common view on education. There are likely to be differences in the values and beliefs that determine the experience and

173

positioning of each sector with regard to the nature of knowledge and learning, how to structure learning environments, models of assessment, the value that is attributed to different forms of intelligence, how diversity is perceived and responded to and many other features. These differences, unless acknowledged and appreciated, can inhibit engagement or reduce it to adversarial posturing.

Freire (1972, p. 37) used the term 'nostalgia' to capture the desire to avoid having to accommodate different ways of seeing the world and different ways of operating, to keep things as they are – essentially the desire to stay within one's comfort zone. By using the term Freire was acknowledging that it is difficult to sustain the intellectual and emotional dexterity and stamina needed to resist the allure of uncritically accepting the status quo. However, if nostalgia takes hold there is a danger that those who are attempting to engage will retreat into entrenched positions where the 'other' is seen as 'not knowing' and where meaningful dialogue is not possible. In such circumstances the objective of the engagement is likely to become one of domination rather than exchange.

Of equal importance and intrinsically related to the need to appreciate different philosophical positions, is an appreciation of systemic considerations within the different sectors – how they are structured, how power is exercised, how they respond to change, how they respond to perceived threat and the likely 'hot spots' that may trigger a sense of threat. An understanding of the separateness and identity of each sector as defined by the concept of boundary is useful in this regard (Ryan & Walsh, 2004). A healthy system is defined as having a sufficiently loose boundary to enable an exchange of ideas and perspectives with its environment and a sufficiently tight boundary to maintain its coherence and identity. If the boundaries are too tight the system is in danger of becoming cut off from its environment and becoming self-referential. If the boundaries are too loose it is in danger of being subsumed by more powerful systems within its environment. With regard to the different educational sectors, discussions in earlier chapters point to a formal sector that exhibits tight boundaries leaving it slow – or some would claim unable – to respond to the changing needs of twenty-first century society. In the case of the FET sector the danger is for it to be subsumed into the formal system. As there is no longer a conceptual or 'real' overarching educational framework (as lifelong learning was intended to be) to act as a point of reference for each specific sector, there is a danger that one sector will assume that mantle and seek to influence

174

and control other sectors. Based on the professionalization of FET experience, the most likely sector to assume that mantle is the formal sector. FET needs to have an awareness of and a capacity to manage the dissonance and tensions inherent in such a situation if any engagement is to be meaningful and productive.

Promoting transformative engagement between the education sectors

The most likely sector to lead a venture that promotes sectoral engagement is FET. Doing so is in keeping with its preference for dialogue, inclusiveness and collaboration. It is also an undertaking that could further its preference for learner-centred provision that allows for flexibility in progression between sectors and in delivery of courses, linkages between the world of learning, home, community and work and a curriculum that reflects the learners' educational needs while also reflecting their personal lived experience. Bringing the sectors together is crucial if these aims are to be realised.

The over-arching goals of such a venture would be: (i) to promote engagement between the sectors thereby overcoming what the *White Paper on Adult Education* (DES, 2000, p. 69) described as the 'hermetic nature of the different educational sectors' in Ireland and (ii) to transform the nature of the engagement that takes place in order to better disseminate the knowledge, experience and concerns of these sectors and the learners and communities with whom they work. The term 'transformative engagement' is used to highlight the change that will result in how each sector engages with the other and the change that is likely to ensue within each sector as a result of engaging with the others.

The first task for FET is to seek out ways to begin the dialogue. The professionalization of FET has opened a door to further dialogue with the formal sector. Part of this dialogue should be to explore ways to promote engagement. Hwang and Christensen (2007) noted that 'transition can be triggered by a 'disruptive' or 'catalytic' innovation, one that addresses the needs of those not served by the dominant intuitional and organisational systems'. The repositioning of FET could be seen as trigger to 'disrupt' both FET and the formal sector; and there is no doubt that across all the education sectors there are many who are not well served by the fragmentation of the current provision. There is equally no doubt that there are many involved in the provision of education who would support a more cohesive approach to provision.

Those who participate in such an engagement need a range of skills to manage the different philosophical positions of the different sectors and the tendencies of systems to resist change as outlined earlier. These skills would include being able to interpret their own assumptive world and the assumptive worlds of those with whom they engage in order to appreciate and accommodate commonalities and differences in perspectives; they need to be able to identify plausible short-term or mid-term goals so that working together shows tangible results which can inspire further engagement; they need to be able to mobilise support and build links and understanding in order to establish trust and thereby deepen the engagement; finally they need to be able to imagine what does not exist, communicate it to others so that they can 'buy into' it and work towards its emergence.

If FET can lead such a process it may well 'invade' the mainstream in order to engender dialogue that challenges the hegemonic dominance of neoliberal thinking as not only the best way but the only way to provide education.

> There is a sense of urgency about all that needs to be done, but it is impossible to have an overnight revolution and make things instantly different. We have to cope or survive in the present as well as critiquing and resisting what is wrong. And all the time we have to keep an eye to the future and what we could create.... To simultaneously engage in coping, critiquing, resisting and creating may seem impossible, because they involve contradictory actions of involvement and transcendence, continuity and change. (Ryan, 2009, p. 25)

'The multiplicity of tasks described in the quote above, is akin to what is required of the Freire-inspired educator' (Ryan, 2011, p. 98) and therefore is well within the capacity of the FET sector.

176

APPENDIX 1: LIST OF ACRONYMS

ACOT	An Comhairle Oiliúna Talamhaíochta: the farming authority
ACCS	Accumulation of Credits and Certification of Subjects System
ADM	Area Development Management Ltd.
AEO	Adult Education (Organiser) Officer
AEA	American Economic Association
AHEAD	Association for Higher Education Access and Disability
ALO	Adult Literacy Officer
ALWG	Adult Learning Working Group
ANCO	An Comhairle Oiliúna: the predecessor of FÁS
AONTAS	Aos Oideachais Náisiúnta Trí Aontú Saorálach: National Adult Learning Organisation
BIM	Bord Iascaigh Mhara: Fishery Board
BTEC	Business and Technology Education Council
BTEI	Back to Education Initiative
CAN	Community Action Network
CAP	Common Agriculture Policy
CAS	Common Awards System
CDP	Community Development Project
CEDEFOP	European Centre for the Development of Vocational Training
CEF	Community Education Facilitator
CEN	Community Education Network
CEO	Chief Executive Officer
CERT	Council for Education Recruitment and Training for the hospitality sector
CIF	Construction Industry Federation
CPA	Combat Poverty Agency
CPD	Continuous Professional Development
CSO	Central Statistics Office
CSW	Commission on the Status of Women
DATI	Department of Agriculture and Technical Instruction)

DATE	Dundrum Adult Training and Education
DE	Department of Education
DEE	Department of Enterprise and Employment
DETE	Department of Enterprise Trade and Employment
DETI	Department of Enterprise Trade and Innovation
DES	Department of Education and Science or Department of Education and Skills
DSP	Department of Social Protection
EAEA	European Association for the Education of Adults
EC	European Commission
ECB	European Central Bank
EEC	European Economic Community
EGF	European Guidance Fund
EGFSN	Expert Group on Future Skills Needs
EMPLOYMENT	Umbrella title for three EU funded projects NOW, Horizon, Youthstart
ERDF	European Regional Development Fund
ESF	European Social Fund
ESM	European Social Model
ETB	Education and Training Board
EU	European Union
FÁS	An Foras Áiseanna Saothair - National Training Authority
FE	Further Education
FET	Further Education and Training
FETAC	Further Education and Training Awards Council
GAA	Gaelic Athletic Association
HE	Higher Education
HEA	Higher Education Authority
HETAC	Higher Education and Training Awards Council
IALS	International Adult Literacy Survey
IAOS	Irish Agricultural Organisation Society
IBEC	Irish Business and Employers Confederation
ICA	Irish Country Women's Association

ICEA	International Council for Adult Education
ICT	Information Communications Technology
IFA	Irish Farmers' Association
IITD	Irish Institute for Training and Development
IMI	Irish Management Institute
IMF	International Monetary Fund
IOT	Institute of Technology
INTERREG	EU initiatives to promotes cross-border, trans-national and inter-regional co-operation
IPA	Institute of Public Administration
IT	Institute of Technology
ITABE	Intensive Tuition in Adult Basic Education
ITE	Initial Teacher (Tutor) Education
IUQB	Irish Universities Quality Board
IVEA	Irish Vocational Education Association
KLEAR	Kilbarrack Local Education for Adult Renewal
LALB	Local Adult Learning Board
LEADER	Liaisons Entre Actions de Development de l'Economie Rural
LWL	Longford Women's Link
MACE	Maynooth Adult and Community Education
MIC	Mary Immaculate College
NALA	National Adult Literacy Agency
NALC	National Adult Learning Education Council
NCEA	National Council for Education Awards
NCI	National College of Ireland
NCVA	National Council for Vocational Awards
NCWI	National Women's Council of Ireland
NDP	National Development Plan
NEAP	National Employment Action Plan
NEET	Not in Employment, Education or Training
NFQ	National Framework of Qualifications
NOW	New Opportunities for Women

NQAI	National Qualifications Authority of Ireland
NQF	National Qualifications Framework
NRB	National Rehabilitation Board
NRDC	National Research and Development Centre for Adult Literacy and Numeracy
OECD	Organisation for Economic Co-operation and Development
OMC	Open Method of Coordination
PISA	Programme for International School Assessment
PLC	Post Leaving Certificate Programme
QQI	Quality and Qualifications Ireland
RTC	Regional Technical college
RTE	Radio Teilifís Éireann
SILC	Survey on Income and Living Conditions
SOLAS	An tSeirbhís Oideachais Leanúnaigh agus Scileanna: National Further Education and Training Authority
STANCE	Strategies to Advance Networks Collective Empowerment
TIC	Technical Instruction Committee
TfT	Training for Transformation movement
UCC	University College Cork
UCG	University College Galway
UI	United Irishwomen
UK	United Kingdom
UN	United Nations
UNESCO	United Nations Educational, Scientific and Cultural Organization
URBAN	EU initiative to support integrated development in disadvantaged urban areas
VEC	Vocational Education Committee
VTOS	Vocational Training Opportunities Scheme
VPTP	Vocational Preparation and Training Programme
WENDI	Women's Education Networks Development
WIT	Waterford Institute of Technology

APPENDIX 2:GLOSSARY OF KEY PLAYERS IN THE FURTHER EDUCATION AND TRAINING SECTOR

Luke Murtagh

An Ceard Comhairle

An Ceard Comhairle was established in 1960 following the passing of the Apprenticeship Act (1959) to regulate the apprenticeship system in Ireland. It was an executive Agency of the Department of Industry and Commerce and was empowered to designate certain trades where the apprenticeship system would apply. The Ceard Comhairle was abolished in 1967 when ANCO was set up.

ANCO

An Comhairle Oiliúna (ANCO) was established in 1967, following the passing of the Industrial Training Act, as an executive agency of the newly established Department of Labour and as a consequence of Ireland's accession to the EEC. Its remit was much wider than that of an Ceard Comhairle and had responsibility for apprenticeship, training for individuals and also provided a training advisory service.

AONTAS

AONTAS is the national representative body for adult and further education players and those interested in Adult Education. There are 474 members, fifty-four per cent who are FET organisations and forty-six per cent who are individuals. It had a budget of ⌐917,720 in 2012 of which ⌐887,000 is core funding from DES. The affairs of the association are managed by an executive committee supported by a Director and nine other staff members (AONTAS, 2013, p. 11).

AONTAS secured private sector funding in 1974 to appoint a fulltime director. In 1980 it organized the first adult education week. In the same year the organisation published a *National Directory of Adult and Community Education Agencies*. This publication evolved into 'What Next' a comprehensive, interactive, online guide to training and education courses for adults in Ireland.

A feature of AONTAS during its formative years was engagement with international adult education. In 1970 it joined the European Association of Adult Education (EAEA); in 1972 it organized a study visit for members to Denmark and France while in 1979 AONTAS hosted a similar visit for 36 learners from Wisconsin (AONTAS, 2009b). Engagement with international adult education is very evident. According to the website 'AONTAS is an active member of the EAEA,.. is represented on the Board... [and] is active at global level through the ICAE, the International Council for Adult Education'.

During the last 30 years there has been a focus on innovation. The first innovation was in women's education as a result of research in 1976 on the structures and meaning of women's participation in Adult Education (AONTAS, 2009b). Women's education supported by AONTAS evolved over three decades.

The first phase saw the establishment of community-based women's groups during the 1980s. EU funding was secured in 1992 for the New Opportunities for Women (NOW) project. With the completion of the NOW project, further funding led to the WENDI (Women's Education Networks Development) project to provide management training for women's groups and build their capacity. STANCE (Strategies to Advance Networks Collective Empowerment) continued to develop the capacity of the sector and addressed barriers to women's active citizenship. STANCE ran from 2001 to 2003 and was co-funded by DES and the Department of Social, Community and Family Affairs.

To consolidate women's education the Women's Community Education Quality Assurance Framework project, which ran from 2003 to 2005, was established. As a consequence AONTAS published a Women's Education Quality Assurance Framework in 2005 to ensure that women's groups could ensure quality and have a resource which:

- Frames the social analysis and distinctive practice of women's community education
- Builds a shared language for women's community education
- Quality assures the practice of women's community education.

(AONTAS, 2005a)

The organisation developed expertise in community education through its women's education initiative. One of the first indications of a commitment to community education was

182

organising a conference on the topic in 1982 and a second conference in 1985. The most significant contribution was influencing the treatment and status given to community education in both the Green (Department of Education and Science, 1998) and the White Paper (Department of Education and Science, 2000). In recognition AONTAS was commissioned in 2003 to deliver the Training and Support Programme for Community Education Facilitators for the Department.

Support for community education continued and the 'Community Education' Report (AONTAS, 2005b) was published and the Community Education Network was established in 2007. The Network comprises over 130 community education organisations working collectively to gain recognition for community education, raise its profile and lobby to ensure it is adequately resourced. It holds three national meetings per year and is the only national network dedicated to independent voluntary community education groups committed to social change (www.aontas.com).

Finally, in its submissions to SOLAS and in meetings with the SOLAS executive AONTAS drew attention to the fact that community education was largely ignored in the initial SOLAS proposals. Its representations were successful and resulted in an explicit recognition of community education.

In recent years AONTAS has focused on the needs of the learners evident in the *Annual Report and Financial Statements 2012*. A section of the report is dedicated to raising the voice of the learner because

> Learners are central to the work of AONTAS and we are committed to supporting the capacity of learners to influence policy and practice in adult and community education. (AONTAS, 2013, p. 15)

A key strategy is to ensure the learner's voice is heard through establishing an Adult Learners' Forum in 2010 and appointing a Learner Support Officer in 2012. An indication of progress was the holding of a 'Lobby for Learning' day where learners met the Minister for Education and Skills (AONTAS, 2013).

CERT

Cert was established in 1964 as an executive agency of the state to provide training for hotel, catering and the tourism industry. Its courses were certified by the National Tourism Certification Board. It was abolished in 2002 and its functions were taken over by Fáilte Ireland the state tourism body.

College of Industrial Relations

The College of Industrial Relations, which later became the National College of Ireland, was founded in 1951 by Fr Edward Coyne SJ with an enrolment of 103 students. By 1965 that number had increased to 1800 students.

An Cosán

An Cosán is a voluntary community organisation based in West Tallaght with a staff of 130. The founders set out with a vision 'to create, in the face of poverty isolation inequality and disadvantage, a distinctive model of community-based education'.

An Cosán has three separate complimentary services (1) The Shanty Education and Training Centre for adult and community education (2) Rainbow House, the early childhood education and care facility and Fledglings, the Social Enterprise Centre which provides early childhood education. The philosophy of An Cosán is by 'using the power of transformative education through learning, leadership and enterprise to end the injustice of poverty' (www.ancosan.com, 2013).

The annual budget (2012) is ⊏3,012,163. Almost ⊏2 million is provided by the state through Pobal, HSE, Co Dublin VEC, Irish Aid, Co Dublin VEC and the Departments of the Environment, Community and Local Government, Family and Social Affairs and the Department of Children and Youth Affairs. ⊏109, 828 was generated through the operations and the balance came from corporate donations and fundraising.

The model of transformative education seeks to ensure that all individuals who attend reach their full potential and grow their capacity to take responsibility for social change in their communities, contributing to the eradication of poverty and social injustice.

The holistic, learner-centred approach and the range of adult learner supports, facilitate participants to:

- Progress along an individual path of lifelong learning
- Develop personality
- Enhance their skills
- Access progression routes in terms of education and employment
- Become even more informed and active citizens.

In 2012 just over 600 students were placed by An Cosán. Thirty-eight per cent attended non accredited programmes where they were accessed second chance education for the first time. Sixty-eight percent attended accredited programmes, thirty-eight percent per cent attended FET courses, twenty-eight per cent third level courses and 4 per cent courses in IT. The third level programmes on offer reflect the organisation's community based philosophy. The courses were

- BA in Leadership and Community
- BA in Applied Addiction Studies and Community Development
- BA in Early Childhood Education and Care
- Special Award in Child Care and Development (level 7).

A survey of learners starting in 2012 revealed the reasons they had for taking a course were:

- 62% to build self confidence
- 45% to enhance employment prospects
- 42% to gain educational qualifications.

County Committees of Agriculture

County Committees of Agriculture were established under the DATI in 1900. Their role was strengthened in 1931 under the Agriculture Act. They had a role in FET in agriculture. They were replaced by ACOT in 1980.

Department of Agriculture and Technical Instruction (DATI)

The Department of Agriculture and Technical Instruction was established in 1900 following the passing of the Agriculture and Technical Instruction (Ireland) Act in 1899. DATI was abolished with the establishment of the Irish Free State and its responsibilities were transferred to the Department of Agriculture and Education.

Dublin Institute for Adult Education

The Dublin Institute for Adult Education was founded in 1950 by the Catholic Church to provide education for trade unionists on church teaching on matters relating to work and employment.

Education and Training Boards

Sixteen Education and Training Boards (ETBs) were established under the Education and Training Boards Act, 2013. The legislation abolishes 33 Vocational Education Committee (VECs) and transfers their functions to 16 ETBs. It provides for ETBs to deliver FET in their area of operation and the transfer of FÁS training functions to them (DES, undated, An Action Plan for SOLAS).

Farm Apprenticeship Board

The Board was established in 1964 to provide apprenticeship training for young farmers. It was wound up in 2004.

Further Education Section (FE) of DES

The FE section of DES is an important FET player responsible for developing and implementing FET policy. It was not always so. The FE section started as a Unit within another section of DES. The Unit's work consisted mainly of the administration of adult education grants to statutory and voluntary bodies and managing EU funded projects such as Youthreach and VTOS. A significant step in the expansion of the FE Unit's role was the appointment of a Minister of State for Adult Education.

Willie O'Dea adopted a proactive role as that first minister and decided to publish both a Green Paper and a White Paper on Adult Education. Apart from being an important development for adult education, the decision meant that the FE Unit changed its role from an administrative one to a policy role. This policy role, coupled with the growing importance of adult education led to the appointment of the first Principal Officer with sole responsibility for adult education. The FE Unit then became the FE Section of DES. Following the publication of the White Paper on Adult Education (2000) the FE Section was responsible for implementing its recommendations.

As a result of these developments and the implementation of the National Adult Literacy Strategy, the roll out of the Back to Education Initiative, the establishment of a Community Education Service through the appointment of Community Education Facilitators and the growth of PLCs, the FE Section continued to grow in status.

The FÁS scandal, which became public in 2008/9, led to a fundamental reappraisal of training in Ireland. As a result the government decided to dissolve FÁS. Its services for the unemployed were transferred to Intreo, an executive agency of the Department of Social Protection. The FÁS training services were transferred to the DES in 2010 (DES, 2012b) and are now provided by SOLAS, an executive agency of DES.

These decisions were significant for the status of FE in DES. The Labour Market Policy Section, the Employment and Strategy Unit and the responsible Assistant Secretary General in the Department of Enterprise Trade and Innovation (DETI) transferred to DES. This included transferring the direct training functions from DETI, the management and oversight of European Social Fund (ESF) and European Guidance Fund (EGF) as well as reporting on and monitoring educational measures in the National Development Plan (NDP) aided by the EU Structural Funds and the European Regional Development Fund (ERDF).

As a result FET is now managed by the Skills Development division of DES headed by an Assistant Secretary General with the following sections headed by a Principal Officer:

- ESF/EGF Policy and Operations
- Further Education
- NDP/EU Structural Funds, SOLAS Liaison, Training and Education Estimates

Intreo

Intreo is a new service, established in 2012 by the Department of Social Protection as an executive agency. The FÁS employment services were transferred to the new body as part of the process of dissolving FÁS. It is a single point of contact for all employment and income supports and is designed to provide a more streamlined approach to employers, employees and jobseekers. INTREO offers practical, tailored employment services and supports for jobseekers and employers alike.[3]

The services provided to FET are categorized under four main headings, Work Programmes, Internships Education and Training and Self-employment Supports as shown in Text Box Appendix 2.1.

Text Box Appendix 2.1: Intreo FET Linked Programmes 2012

	Million(€)
Work Programmes	
• Community Employment	24,000
• Rural Social Scheme	2,500
• Tus Community Workplace Programme	3,800
• Job Initiative	1,200
• Part-time Job Initiative	200
Internships	
• National Internship Scheme (Job-bridge)	5,000
• Work placement Programme	200
Education and Training	
• Back to Education Allowance	26,000
• Part-time Education Option	N/A
• Education Training and Development	N/A
• Activation Family Support Programme	N/A
• Technical Assistance and Training Scheme	N/A
• Technical Employment Support Grant	N/A
Self- Employment Supports	
• Not directly relevant	
• DSP Core business imperatives: control, income maintenance, activation	
TOTAL COST	**€873.84 Million**

---

[3] http://www.welfare.ie/en/Pages/office/Intreo-Centre-Dun-Laoghaire.aspx

Irish Management Institute

The Irish Management Institute (IMI) was founded 1952 by a group of businessmen with the support of the state. Training for managers is at the core of its existence and as a result IMI established an education and training committee. By 1957 IMI had appointed a full time director. An indication of the scale of the IMI operation is that by 1967 2,600 people were attending IMI courses annually and in 1972 it took over responsibility for supervisory management training in Ireland (Cox, 2002). Today IMI operates from a purpose built campus in Sandyford Dublin.

NALA

The National Adult Literacy Agency (NALA) is a voluntary organisation committed to making sure people with literacy and numeracy difficulties can fully take part in society and have access to learning opportunities that meet their needs. According to the last international survey, one in four - that is, about half a million - Irish adults have problems reading and writing (NALA, 2013). NALA's vision is for Ireland 'to be a place where adult literacy is a valued right and where everyone can develop their literacy and take part more fully in society'.

The membership of NALA is 514 members served by a staff of 34 through a head office in Dublin, a regional office in Cork and its website. The NALA budget is €2,068,133. €1,908,949 of that budget is received from the Government (NALA, 2013).

NALA aims to improve literacy levels, advance literacy policy, remove barriers to learners with literacy problems and provide representation for students by

- Creating awareness of literacy and numeracy as a reality for many Irish people
- Developing teaching materials
- Providing distance education materials
- Influencing policy at local, national and EU levels
- Carrying out research into aspects of literacy and numeracy
- Engaging in campaigns to raise awareness about literacy issues in Ireland
- Providing tutor training.

NALA has made a major contribution to the development of the national adult literacy service through influencing policy. The recommendations on literacy in the White Paper (DES, 2000) were influenced by NALA. DES recognized that reality by making NALA the executive agency to implement the National Adult Literacy Strategy. It has also influenced government policy and the level of funding made available for literacy by:

- Putting adult literacy on the political agenda
- Establishing the first national intensive basic education programme (ITABE)
- Contributing to securing increased funding for the VEC Adult Literacy Service from €1 million in 1997 to €30 million in 2010
- Securing national funding to establish the first national adult literacy fund under Des
- Securing the first dedicated workplace basic education fund to support adults who wanted to improve their basic skills in the workplace.

Another contribution was working with the VECs to increase participation in the literacy services. The numbers benefiting from the service increased from 5,000 learners in 1997, when the International Adult Literacy Survey (IALS) was published to c. 56,800 (NALA, 2013). The increase has also been helped by a distance education option, www.writeon.ie. By the end of 2012

> There were 26,768 learning accounts on the site, an increase of almost 9,000 since 2011. During 2012, 14,183 different people visited the site almost 56,000 times, spending an average of 22 minutes per visit. (NALA, 2013, p. 30)

Participation has increased significantly through the 12 TV adult literacy series, and information and advice given on the Freephone support line.

While increasing awareness, influencing policy and increasing participation are important, the quality of the teaching for students is critical. NALA has worked consistently to support literacy tutors through initial and continuous professional development, providing regular opportunities for students, Adult Literacy Organisers and tutors to meet, developing programmes for specific target groups, providing supports for providers through a quality framework and issuing guidelines for good adult literacy practice.

NALA has recognised that its efforts should extend beyond the education and training systems through the Plain English campaign. 'By using plain English, organisations can reach more people – in particular those with literacy difficulties – and enable them to fulfil their potential, access entitlements and better use services.' The plain English service helped a range of organisations to make their written information easier to understand.

Clients included:

- hospitals and other bodies under the Health Service Executive such as the National Cancer Screening Service;
- public sector bodies such as the Office of the Director of Public Prosecutions, the Equality Authority and the Food Safety Authority of Ireland;
- voluntary organisations such as the Irish Council for Civil Liberties and the Irish Cancer Society; and
- private companies such as MSD, Electric Ireland and Abbott Pharmaceuticals.

(NALA, 2013, p. 45).

Literacy research has been at the heart of NALA's work and it has participated in a wide range of research projects with third level institutions.

A recent development has involved increased co-operation with Aontas. During 2012 NALA and Aontas co-operated in making a submission to SOLAS; organising a joint learner event with the Minister of State for Training and Skills and representatives from DES, FÁS and the VECs as part of the AONTAS Adult Learner's Festival. They also made inputs into learner events in October and November and agreed a memorandum of understanding. During 2013 both organisations agreed to work on the theme of the 'Learner Voice'.

National Rehabilitation Board

The National Rehabilitation Board was set up in 1967 as an executive agency of the Department of Health to co-ordinate training and rehabilitation services for people with disabilities. It was replaced in 2000 by the National Disability Authority following the passing of the National Disability Authority Act 1999.

Quality and Qualifications Ireland (QQI)

QQI was established in 2012 under the Qualifications and Quality Assurance (Education and Training) Act, 2012. The authority is created by the amalgamation of four bodies that had awarding and quality assurance responsibilities: the Further Education and Training Awards Council (FETAC), the Higher Education and Training Awards Council (HETAC), the National Qualifications Authority of Ireland (NQAI) and the Irish Universities Quality Board (IUQB). Crucially, QQI is responsible for

Promoting, maintaining further developing and implementing the National Framework of Qualifications as well as advising the minister of quality assurance in education and training and ensuring providers have effective quality assurance procedures in place. (www.qqi.ie, 2014).

Most qualifications offered by FET providers and funded by the state fall within the qualifications' framework and are from level one to level six inclusive, with the majority of them offered between level three and level six on the framework.

The People's College

The People's College was founded in 1948 by the trade union movement to provide education and training for members. The establishment of the college was inspired by the Workers' Educational Association (Roberts, 1986).

SOLAS

SOLAS was established in 2013 by the Further Education and Training Act 2013 and has three strategic objectives:

- Leading and co-ordinating the change management process of integrating FET institutions and programmes;
- Co-ordinating and managing the funding and performance management of FET programmes;
- Leading the modernisation of FET programmes to ensure that they are focussed on the lifelong needs of learners, especially jobseekers, and are flexible and relevant to the needs of the labour market. (www.solas.ie, 2013)

Sometimes it is difficult for a service user or staff member to unravel the complexity of the broader system within which the service operates. That is particularly true of FET which is undergoing radical reform. The next section attempts to unravel the complexity.

Technical Instruction Committees (TICs)

Technical Instruction Committees were established in 1900 to provide technical education through local technical schools, support technical and scientific education in primary and secondary schools and to provide adult education courses for agriculture and industry. They were funded from the rates and by way of a grant from DATI. There were 72 TICs in Ireland originally. Following the establishment of the Irish Free State there were 48 TICs in the new Irish State. They were abolished in 1930 following the passing of the Vocational Education Act 1930 and replaced by 38 Vocational Education Committees.

Vocational Education Committees

Following a Commission on Technical Education which reported in 1927, the 1930 Vocational Education Act was passed and provided for 38 Vocational Education Committees. These Committees were funded through the rates and a grant from the Department of Education. They ran Continuation and Technical schools as well as providing adult education. The Committees were abolished in 2014 with the establishment of 16 ETBs.

APPENDIX THREE: FURTHER EDUCATION AND TRAINING TIME LINE

Luke Murtagh

YEAR	EVENT
2014	Solas publishes its first Further Education and Training Services Plan
	Educate Together opens its first Post Primary school
2013	Solas formally established as the new Further Education and Training Authority in Ireland. It is responsible for funding, planning and co-ordinating training and further education programmes
	ETBs formally established to provide education and training programmes in their administrative areas.
	Education and Training Boards Bill published which gives 16 Education and Training Boards (ETBs) a remit for FET and training in their administrative area
2012	The passing of the SOLAS legislation, establishes SOLAS as an executive agency of the Department of Education and Skills
	From April 1st all FE teachers paid by the DES, delivering FETAC level 4-6 courses are required to register with the Teaching Council. To register they have to complete a recognised Post Graduate Diploma in Adult and Further Education at level eight of the National Framework of Qualifications
	Report by Expert Group on Teacher Training
	Qualifications and Quality Assurance (Education and Training) Act 2012
	Report on the Forum of Patronage and Pluralism in the Primary Sector published
2011	First Cabinet Minister for Children and Youth Affairs appointed
	National Strategy for Higher Education published
	Decision to establish SOLAS
	Decision to amalgamate VEC's and establish 16 Local Education and Training Boards
	National Strategy to improve Literacy and Numeracy among Children and Young People
2010	EU, ECB and the World Bank (the Troika) provide a financial assistance package for Ireland under certain conditions
	Responsibility for FÁS transferred from the Department of Enterprise and Employment to DES
2009	Emergency Budget introduced by the Government to deal with the financial crisis
2008	Collapse of the Irish banking system
2007	Expert Group on Future Skills recommends a national skills strategy
	Government approves the establishment of Community National Schools under the patronage of the VEC's

PHASE 5: 1993 - 2006 The Era of Reform	
YEAR	**EVENT**
2005	Recommendations for a Traveller Education Strategy published
	Delivery Equality of Opportunities in Schools (DEIS) programme launched
2004	The Education for Persons with Special Needs Act provides for the inclusion of those with special needs in the education system and extends the remit of the National Council for Special Education
	Whole School Evaluation starts in Post-Primary Schools
2003	Mc Iver Report on PLC's published
	National Access to Higher Education Office established
	State Examination Commission appointed
	National Adult Learning Council (NALC) is suspended by DES
	Whole School Evaluation commences in Primary Schools
	Prison education curriculum reviewed
2002	National Education Welfare Board established
	National Council for Special Education established
	Taskforce on Lifelong Learning Reports
	Community Education Facilitators (CEF's) appointed to VECs
	NALC established
	Back to Education Initiative (BTEI) introduced
2001	National Qualifications Authority of Ireland (NQAI) and HETAC and FETAC established
	Vocational Education Amendment Act passed – major changes in the way the VECs operate
2000	White Paper on Adult Education published
	Cromien Report highly critical of the way DES is organised
	Education Welfare Act provides for the establishment of the Education Welfare Board
1999	Skillnets established
	Qualification (Education and Training) Act passed
	White Paper on Early Childhood Education issued
	New Primary School Curriculum published

1998	Good Friday Agreement signed
	A Social Inclusion Unit is established in DES arising out of the First National Anti-Poverty Strategy
	The First Principal Officer for Adult Education is appointed in DES
	Green Paper on Adult Education published
	Education Act passed
1997	National Anti-Poverty Strategy published
	Willie O'Dea is appointed as the first minister for Adult Education
	Green Paper on Voluntary Activity published
	International Adult Literacy Survey Report (IALS) issued
	Supreme Court vindicates the right of a child with severe mental and intellectual disability to have an education provided by the State
	Universities Act passed
	Women's Education Initiative funded by the DES
1996	A Strategy for Equality Report of the Commission on the Status of People with Disabilities published
1995	White Paper on Education - Charting our Education Future published
	Report of the Steering Committee on Higher Education
	Teastas (Qualification Authority) established on an ad hoc basis
1994	Introduction of the Early Start Programme
	First students take the Leaving Certificate Vocational Programme (LCVP)
1993	Industrial Development Act provides for the establishment of the Forbairt, IDA and Forás
	National Education Convention takes place
	Special Education Review Committee Reports

PHASE 4: 1966 – 1992 Increased Role for the State after Investment in Education

YEAR	EVENT
1992	Green Paper on Education published
	Regional Technical Colleges Act passed
	Introduction of Home School Liaison Scheme
1991	National Council for Vocational Awards established
	Twelve Area-based Partnership Companies established
1990	Report of the Industrial Policy Review Group (Culleton Report)

1989	New Opportunities for Women (NOW) Scheme introduced
	First Community Development Programme provided by the Department of Social Welfare
1988	Teagasc established
	New Junior Certificate Programme introduced
	VTOS (Vocational Training and Opportunities Scheme) introduced
	National Disability Authority established
	First Social Partnership Agreement signed
1987	Single European Act passed involving reform of the Structural Funds and Coordination with European Social Fund and Regional Development Fund
	Youth Reach established
	FÁS established
	National Council for Curriculum Development established
1984	Kenny Report on Adult Education issued
	First adult literacy and community budget allocated to VECs
	ACOT established to provide training and services for agriculture
	White Paper on Educational Development published
	Major extension of Vocational Preparation and Training Programme (VPTP) which led to the development of PLC's
1980	NALA established
	White Paper on Educational Development published
1979	First Adult Education Organisers (AEOs) appointed to VECs
1978	Bord Iascaigh Mara (BIM) established with a training remit
	First Educate Together Primary School opened in Dalkey (the Dalkey School Project)
1976	Central Applications Office (CAO) established
1975	National Institute of Higher Education (NIHE) Dublin later DCU established
1974	First Senior Travellers Training Centre opened
1973	Murphy Report on Adult Education
	Ireland joins the EEC
1972	National Council for Education Awards (NCEA) set up to be the awarding body for RTCs
1971	Technical subjects examined for the first time in the Leaving Certificate
	New Curriculum introduced in Primary Schools
1970	Thomond College becomes part of NIHE
	NIHE Limerick established. It later became UL
	Document proposing the establishment of Community Schools by the Department of Education issued

1969	First Regional Technical College opens
	AONTAS, the first dedicated advocacy organisation for adult education, established
1968	Higher Education Authority (HEA) established on an ad hoc basis
	Third Level student grants introduced
	Points system for entry into courses at third level introduced
	Prison Education starts in Shangannagh
1967	ANCO established to be the industrial training authority following the passing of the Industrial Training Act
	Rehabilitation Board established
	Free second level education introduced coupled with a free transport scheme
	Common Basic Salary Scale introduced for all teachers
	Guidance counselling introduced to post primary schools
	Commission on Higher Education Report Published
	Steering Committee on the Establishment of Regional Technical Colleges Reports
1965	Investment in Education published setting the agenda for Irish education until at least the 1990s
1964	Farm Apprenticeship Scheme introduced
	Psychological Service established in the Department of Education

PHASE 3: 1922 – 1965 The Irish State adopts the Westminster model of government; embraces Catholicism and cultural nationalism; stagnates and finally begins to re-emerge from its slumber.

YEAR	EVENT
1963	CERT established to provide training for the hospitality industry
1959	Apprenticeship Act allows for the new National Apprenticeship Board to designate new trades
1958	First Programme for Economic Expansion is published
1954	An Grianan, a residential adult education college, is opened by the ICA
1952	The Irish Management Institute (IMI) is established
1951	The College of Industrial Relations (later NCI) is set up
1950	The Dublin Institute of Adult Education opens its doors
1948	The Peoples College is established
1947	Group Certificate Examination introduced for continuation students in Vocational Schools
1946	UCC introduces its University Extension programmes which serve as a model for other Universities
1936	Department of Education introduces a range of trade examinations
1931	Agricultural Act passed abolishing the Department of Agriculture and Technical Instruction and setting up County Committees of Agriculture
	Apprenticeship Act passed designating certain trades and establishing apprenticeship committees

1930	Vocational Education Act establishes the VEC system which remained in place until 2013 when they were replaced by the ETBs
1926	Report of the Commission on Technical Instruction recommended the establishment of VECs and legislation for apprenticeship
	Report on Primary Education (published following the Second National Programme Conference held during the school year 1925/26) reflects the cultural nationalist ideology of the new state
1924	Ministers and Secretaries Act regulates the operation of government departments in the Free State
	Department of Education established to oversee Primary, Secondary, Technical and Higher Education
	1878 Intermediate Education) (Amendment) Act introduces a revised method of payment of grants to secondary schools Certificate
	Report of the Dáil Commission on Secondary Education paves the way for the introduction of the Intermediate and Leaving Certificate Examinations and reform of secondary School programmes to reflect the cultural nationalism of the new state
1923	Civil war ends
1922	Irish Free State established on the 6th of December 1922

PHASE 2: 1800 – 1922 Laying the Foundations of a denominational Anglophone system

YEAR	EVENT
1919	McPherson Bill, which proposed integrating all aspects of education into a Department of Education and establishing local education authorities, is strongly resisted by the Catholic Church and Sinn Fein. The Bill is defeated
1913	The Department of Agriculture and Technical Instruction devises its own examination system for technical schools
1910	The United Irish Women's Organisation is set up
1908	Universities Act establishes the National University of Ireland and University Colleges in Dublin, Cork and Galway
1900	Department of Agriculture and Technical Instruction established as well as local Technical Instruction and Agriculture Committees
	Revised Programme for Primary Schools introduced
1899	Agriculture and Technical Instruction Act passed
1898	Local Government (Ireland) Act establishes a local government system and provides for local authorities to levy a rate of one penny in the pound for technical instruction
1896	Recess Committee appointed on the initiative of Horace Plunkett
1894	The Irish Agricultural Organisation Society is established
1887	The first technical school in Ireland opens in Kevin Street, Dublin (Cooke, 2009)
1884	GAA founded
	Second Report of The Royal Commission on Technical Education Published recommends raising of school leaving age , technical subjects in Primary Schools and the establishment of municipal and local authority technical schools (Cooke, 2009)

1883	Conradh na Gaelige set up
1881	Royal Commission on Technical Instruction established and publishes its first report
1878	Intermediate Education Act allows the state to fund secondary schools based on their examination results
1875	First Catholic Teacher training college is established in St Patrick's, Drumcondra, Dublin
1872	Payment by results introduced to primary schools
1869	The Irish Church Act disestablishes the Church of Ireland
1850	Queens University with colleges in Cork, Dublin and Belfast established
1838	Teacher Training College established in Marlborough Street, Dublin to train primary teachers
1832	First Primary School Inspectors appointed
1831	The National School system is established
1829	Catholic Emancipation
1811	Kildare Place Society is established to support school provision open to all
1800	Act of Union

PHASE 1: 1591 – 1800 Before the Act of Union	
YEAR	**EVENT**
1795	Maynooth College established
1792	Relief Act removes the need for a licence to run a Catholic school
1700 – 1831	Growth of Hedge schools to circumvent penal laws and educate Catholic children
	Charter School movement establishes a system of voluntary schools under a charter given to the Incorporated Society for the Promotion of English Protestant Schools in Ireland
	A system of voluntary catholic secondary schools was established from 1771 by religious orders and diocesan authorities
1695	Penal Laws enacted which prohibit Catholic education
1591	Trinity College established

REFERENCES

Adult Learning Working Group (ALWG). (2010). *Action plan on adult learning 2007-2010. Final report of the Adult Learning Working Group*. Brussels: GHK.

AHEAD (Association for Higher Education Access and Disability). (2005). *Participation of and services for students with disabilities in Institutes of Technology 2004-2005*. Dublin : AHEAD.

Ahern, N. (2000, February 23). Dail Debates. Retrieved January 15, 2014, from http://oireachtasdebates.oireachtas.ie/debates%20authoring/DebatesWebPack.nsf/take s/dail2000022300028#N82

Alcock, P. (2003). *Social policy in Britain* (2nd ed.). Hampshire: Palgrave Macmillan.

An Cosán. (2014). Retrieved January 15, 2014, from www.ancosan.com

Anderson, D., Brown, M., & Rushbrook, P. (2004). Vocational education and training. In G. Foley (Ed.), *Dimensions of adult learning: Adult education and training in a global era*. Maidenhead: Open University Press.

AONTAS. (2005a). *Women's community education quality assurance framework*. Dublin: AONTAS.

AONTAS. (2005b). *Citizen learner conference report*. Dublin: AONTAS.

AONTAS. (2009a). *Flower power: AONTAS guide to best practice of women's community education*. Dublin: AONTAS.

AONTAS. (2009b). *Many happy returns: AONTAS celebrating 40 years 1969-2009*. Dublin: AONTAS.

AONTAS. (2013). *Annual report and financial statements 2012*. Dublin: AONTAS.

Apple, M. W. (2004). *Ideology and curriculum* (3rd ed.). London: Routledge.

Apple, M. W. (2011). Paulo Freire and the task of the critical educational scholar/activist. In A. O'Shea, & M. O'Brien (Eds.), *Pedagogy, oppression and transformation in a 'post-critical' climate*. London: Continuum.

Avis, J. (2003). Rethinking trust in a performative culture: The case of post compulsory education. *Journal of Education Policy, 18*(3), 315-332.

Bailey, N., Breen, J., & Ward, M. (2011). *Community education: More than just a course: Exploring the outcomes and impact of Department of Education and Skills funded community education*. Dublin: AONTAS.

Baker, J., Lynch, K., Cantillon, S., & Walsh, J. (2009). *Equality: From theory to action* (2nd ed.). Hampshire: Palgrave Macmillan.

Bakhtin, M. (1988). *The dialogic imagination: Four essays*. Austin: University of Texas Press.

Ball, S. J. (2006). *Education policy and social class*. London: Routledge.

Ball, S. J., Maguire, M., & Braun, A. (2012). *How schools do policy enactment in secondary schools*. London: Routledge.

Bamber, J. (2010). *Effective community development programmes: A review of the international evidence base*. Dublin: Centre for Effective Services.

Battell, A. (2004). *(Report Compiler) Pathways effective support for early school leavers*. Dublin: National Youth Federation.

Biesta, G. (2006). What's the point of lifelong learning if lifelong learning has no point? On the democratic deficit of policies for lifelong learning. *European Educational Research Journal, 5*(3 & 4), 169-180.

Bourdieu, P. (1998). *The state nobility: Elite schools in the field of power*. Stanford: Stanford University Press.

Bourdieu, P., & Passeron, J. (1990). *Reproduction in education, society and culture*. London: Sage.

Brine, J. (2006). Lifelong learning and the knowledge economy: Those that know and those that do not - the discourse of the European Union. *British Educational Research Journal, 32*(5), 649-665.

Brookfield, S. (2005). *The power of critical theory for adult learning and teaching*. Maidenhead: Open University PRess.

Bruner, J. (1991). The narrative construction of reality. *Critical Inquiry, 18*(1), 1-21.

Burke, A. (2007). Crosscurrents in the competencies/standards debate in teaching and teacher education. In R. Dolan, & J. Gleeson (Eds.), *The competencies approach to teacher professional development: Current practice and future prospects*. Dublin: Marotone.

Byrne, K. (1999). Laying the Foundations: Voluntary and state provision for technical education 1730-1930. In J. Logan (Ed.), *Teachers Union: The TUI and its forerunners 1899-1994* (pp. 16-36). Dublin: A & A Farmar.

Cannon, C. (2013). Address at VITA conference. Dublin: AONTAS. Retrieved January 15, 2014, from http://www.aontas.com/download/pdf/minister_ciaran_cannon_address_at_vita_confe rence.pdf

Carey, L. (1979). *The history of AONTAS: A review of adult education*. Dublin: AONTAS.

CEDEFOP. (1995). *Teachers and trainers in vocational training, Volume 2: Italy, Ireland and Portugal*. Luxembourg: Office for Official Publications of the European Communities.

Central Statistics Office . (2011). *Survey on income and living conditions (SILC)*. Dublin: Central Statistics Office .

Chang, H. (2010). *23 things they don't tell you about capitalism*. London: Allen Lane.

Coate, K., & Mac Labhrainn, I. (2009). Irish higher education and the knowledge economy. In J. Huisman (Ed.), *International perspectives on the governance of higher education*. London: Routledge.

Coffield, F. (2009). Rolling out 'good', 'best' and 'excellent' practice. What next? Perfect practice? *British Education Research Journal, 35*(3), 371-390.

Coffield, F., & Vignoles, A. (1997). Report 5: Widening participation in higher education by ethnic minorities, women and alternative students. In R. Dearing, *Reports of the National Committee of Inquiry into Higher Education*. Retrieved September 2013, 11, from http://www.leeds.ac.uk/educol/ncihe/

Cole, H. (2013). Seamus Heaney: A poet of in-between. *The New Yorker*. Retrieved December 9, 2013, from http://www.newyorker.com/online/blogs/books/2013/08/seamus-heaney-a-poet-of-in-between.html

Collins, M. (1996). On comtemporary practice and research: Self-directed learning to critical theory. In R. Edwards, A. Hanson, & P. Raggett (Eds.), *Adult learners, education and training 1: Boundaries of adult learning*. London: Routledge/Open University.

Combat Poverty Agency. (2014). *About Us/History*. Retrieved January 15, 2014, from http://www.combatpoverty.ie/aboutus/history.htm

Community Education Network. (2014). *What is community education?* Dublin: AONTAS.

Connolly, B. (1996). Community development and adult education: Prospects for change. In B. Connolly, T. Fleming, D. McCormack, & A. Ryan (Eds.), *Radical learning for liberation*. Maynooth: MACE.

Connolly, B. (1999). Group work and facilitation skills: A feminist evaluation of their role in transformative adult and community education. In B. Connolly, & A. B. Ryan (Eds.), *Women and education in Ireland Vol. 1*. Maynooth: MACE.

Connolly, B. (2007). Beyond the third way: New challenges for critical adult and community education. In B. Connolly, T. Fleming, D. McCormack, & A. Ryan (Eds.), *Radical learning for liberation 2*. Maynooth: MACE.

Connolly, B. (2008). *Adult learning in groups*. Maidenhead: Open University Press.

Connolly, B., & Hussey, P. (2013). The war against people: Adult education and practice for critical democracy. *The Adult Learner*, 75-87.

Connolly, F. M., & Clandinin, D. J. (1995). Personal and professional knowledge landscapes: A matrix of relations. In D. J. Clandinin, & F. M. Connolly (Eds.), *Teachers' professional knowledge landscapes*. New York: Teachers College Press.

Conroy, P., & O'Leary, H. (2007). *Community development and policy learning in further education in Ireland*. Dublin: Combat Poverty Agency.

Conway, P., Murphy, R., Rath, A., & Hall, K. (2009). *Learning to teach and its implications for the continuum of teacher education:A nine-country cross-national study*. Cork: UCC.

Coolahan, J. (1981). *Irish education: History and structure*. Dublin: Institute of Public Administration.

Corish, P. J. (1995). *Maynooth College 1795-1995*. Dublin: Gill and Macmillan.

Corradi, C., Evans, N., & Valk, A. (Eds.). (2006). *Recognising experiential learning: Practices in European universities*. Estonia: Tartu University Press.

County Kildare VEC. (2013). *Guidelines for tutors of programmes leading to QQI (FETAC) awards*. Kildare: Kildare VEC.

Cox, T. (2002). *The making of managers: A history of the Irish Managment Institute*. Dublin: Irish Management Institute.

Craig, C. (1995). Safe places on the professional knowlege landscape: Knowledge communities. In D. J. Clandinin, & F. M. Connolly (Eds.), *Teachers' professional knowledge landscapes*. New York: Teachers College Press.

Crowther, J., Galloway, V., & Martin, I. (2000). *Popular education: Engaging the academy. International perspectives*. Leicester: NIACE.

Cubitt, G. (1988). *Imagining nations*. Manchester: Manchester University Press.

Culliton, J. (1992). *A time for change: Industrial policy for the 1990s*. Report of the Industrial Policy Review Group . Dublin: Stationery Office.

Daly, M. (2002). *The first department: A history of the Department of Agriculture*. Dublin: Institute of Public Administration.

Davies, B. (2007). *Developing sustainable leadership*. London: Chapman.

Davies, B., & Gannon, S. (2005). Feminism/poststructuralism. In B. Somekh, & C. Lewin (Eds.), *Research methods*. London: Sage.

Deakin-Crick, R., & Joldersma, W. (2007). Habermas, lifelong learning and citizenship education. *Studies in Philosophy and Education, 26*(2), 77-95.

Department of Agriculture and Technical Instruction for Ireland. (1908). *Seventh annual general report of the Department*. Dublin: Her Majesty's Stationery Office.

Department of An Taoiseach. (1987). *Programme for national recovery*. Dublin: Stationery Office.

Department of An Taoiseach. (2008). *Building Ireland's smart economy: A framework for sustained economic renewal*. Dublin: Stationery Office.

Department of Education. (1926). *Report of the Department of Education for the school year 1924-25, and the financial and administrative years 1925, 25, 26*. Dublin: Stationery Office.

Department of Education. (1935). *Report of the Department of Education for the school year 1933-4*. Dublin: Stationery Office.

Department of Education. (1938). *Report of the Department of Education for the school year 1936-37*. Dublin: Stationery Office.

Department of Education. (1966). *Investment in Education*. Dublin: Stationery Office.

Department of Education. (1969). *Steering commitee on technical education: Report to the Minister for Education on the establishment of Regional Technical Colleges*. Dublin: Stationery Office.

Department of Education. (1970). *National adult education survey: Interim report*. Dublin: Stationery Office [Interim Murphy Report].

Department of Education. (1973). *Adult Education in Ireland: A report of a committee appointed by the Minister for Education*. Dublin: Stationery Office.

Department of Education. (1983). *Lifelong learning: Report of the Commission on adult education [Kenny Report]*. Dublin: Stationery Office.

Department of Education. (1994). *Report of the National Education Convention*. Dublin: Stationery Office.

Department of Education and Science. (1997). *International adult literacy survey: Results for Ireland*. Dublin: Stationery Office.

Department of Education and Science. (1998). *Adult education in an era of lifelong learning: Green paper on adult education*. Dublin: Stationery Office.

Department of Education and Science. (2000). *Learning for life: White paper on adult education*. Dublin: Stationery Office.

Department of Education and Science. (2001). *Report of the action group on access to third level education*. Dublin: Stationery Office.

Department of Education and Science. (2004). *Interim review of the role and functions of the National Adult Learning Council* . Unpublished: Department of Education and Science.

Department of Education and Science. (2012d). *Explanatory note on the general scheme of the Further Education and Training Authority (SOLAS) Bill 2012*. Dublin: DES.

Department of Education and Skills. (2012a). *Report of the International review panel on the structure of initial teacher training provision in Ireland: Review conduction on behalf of the Department of Education and Skills*. Dublin: Department of Education and Skills.

Department of Education and Skills. (2012b). *An action plan for SOLAS: The new further education and training (FET) authority*. Dublin: Department of Education and Skills.

Department of Education and Skills. (2012c). *Back to education initiative (BTEI): Operational guidelines 2012*. Dublin: Further Education Development Unit.

Department of Enterprise and Employment. (1997). *White Paper: Human resource development*. Dublin: Stationery Office.

Department of Enterprise, Trade and Employment. (2002). *Report of the taskforce of lifelong learning*. Dublin: Stationery Office. Retrieved January 15, 2014, from http://www.djei.ie/publications/labour/2002/lifelonglearning.pdf

Department of Enterprise, Trade and Employment. (2005). *Lisbon Agenda: Integrated guidelines for growth and jobs - National reform programme*. Dublin: Department of Enterprise, Trade and Employment.

Department of Enterprise, Trade and Employment. (2007). *Human capital investment operational programme 2007-2013*. Dublin: Stationery Office.

Department of Equality and Law Reform. (1993). *Report on the Second Commission for the Status of Women*. Dublin: Stationery Office.

Department of Finance. (2006). *National development plan 2007-2013: Transforming Ireland - A better quality of life for all*. Dublin: Stationery Office.

Department of Social Welfare. (1997). *Supporting voluntary activity: A green paper on the community and voluntary sector*. Dublin: Stationery Office.

Department of Social, Community and Family Affairs. (n.d.). *The national community development programme: A handbook*. Dublin: Stationery Office.

Dewey, J. (1938). *Experience and education*. New York: Macmillan.

Dewey, J. (1997). *Experience and education*. New York: Touchstone.

Dressman, M. (2008). *Using social theory in educational research*. New York: Routledge.

Drudy, S. (2008). Gender balance/gender bias: The teaching profession and the impact of feminization. *Gender and Education, 20*(4), 309-323.

Dublin and Dun Laoighaire Education and Training Board. (2014). Retrieved January 15, 2014, from http://www.ddletb.ie/Footer/Education-centres/DATE-Dundrum-Adult-Training-and-Education.aspx

Duke, C. (2009). Please, no more 'Business as Usual': What the harsh new world means for adult and higher education. *Adult Education and Development, 72*, 171-194.

Durcan, T. J. (1972). *History of Irish education from 1800: With special reference to manual instruction*. Bala, North Wales: Dragon Books.

Eagleton, T. (1996). *Literary theory: An introduction* (2nd ed.). Oxford: Blackwell.

European Association for the Education of Adults (EAEA). (2006). *Adult education trends and issues in Europe*. Brussels: EAEA.

European Commission. (1993). *Growth, competitiveness, employment: The challenges and ways forward into the 21st century*. Luxembourg: Office for Official Publications of the European Communities.

European Commission. (1995). *White paper on teaching and learning: Towards the learning society*. Luxembourg: Office for Official Publications of the European Communities.

European Commission. (1997). *Proposals of employment guidelines for Member States' employment policies for 1998*. Luxembourg: Office for Official Publications of the European Communties.

European Commission. (2000). *A memorandum on lifelong learning*. Luxembourg: Office for Official Publications of the European Communities.

European Commission. (2001). *Making a European area of lifelong learning a reality*. Luxembourg: Oiffice for Official Publications of the European Communities.

European Commission. (2005a). *Working together for growth and jobs: A new start for the Lisbon strategy*. Luxembourg: Office for Official Publications of the European Communities.

European Commission. (2005b). *Progress towars the Lisbon objectives in education and training*. Luxembourg: Office for Official Publications of the European Communities.

European Commission. (2007). *Key competancies for lifelong learning*. Luxembourg: Office for Official Publications of the European Communties.

European Commission. (2009). *Key competencies for a changing world*. Brussels: European Commission.

European Commission. (2010). *Action plan on adult learning: Achievements and results 2008-2010*. Brussesl: European Commission.

European Commission. (2011). *Progress towards the common European objectives in education and training: Indicators and benchmarks 2010-2011. Commission staff working document.* Luxembourg: Publications Office of the European Union.

European Council. (1996). *A strategy for lifelong learning.* Brussels: Council of the European Community.

European Council. (2000). *Lisbon European Council 23 and 24 March 2000: Presidency conclusions.* Luxembourg: Office for Official Publications of the European Communities.

European Council. (2005). *Education, youth and culture.* Brussels: Press release 14061/05.

Expert Group on Future Skills Needs. (2007). *Tomorrows skills: Towards a national skills strategy.* Dublin: Stationery Office.

FÁS. (1998). *Annual report and financial statement 1997.* Dublin: FÁS.

Ferriter, D. (2004). *The transformation of Ireland: 1900-2000.* London: Profile Books.

FETAC. (2005). *Further education and training in Ireland: A quantitative analysis of the sector.* Dublin: FETAC.

FETAC. (2009). *Information for learners; Guidelines for providers.* Dublin: FETAC.

Field, J. (2006). *Lifelong learning and the new educational order.* Stoke on Trent: Trentham Books.

Field, J., & Leicester, M. (2000). *Lifelong learning: Education across the lifespan.* London: Routledge Falmer.

Fieldhouse, R. (1999). Futher education. In P. Federighi (Ed.), *Glossary of adult learning in Europe.* Hamburg: EAEA and UNESCO.

Finnegan, F. (2008). Neo-liberalism, Irish society and adult education. *The Adult Learner,* 54-73.

Finnegan, R. B., & Wiles, J. L. (2005). *Women and public policy in Ireland: A documentable history 1922-1997.* Dublin: Irish Academic Press.

Fitzsimons, C. (2012). Social change community education: Where are we now? *The Irish Review of Community Economic Development Law and Policy, 1*(4). Retrieved January 15, 2014, from http://eprints.nuim.ie/4027/1/NCLC-E-Journal-Issue-4-Volume-1.pdf

Fitzsimons, C. (forthcoming). *Community education in Ireland: Views from practitioners.* Maynooth: On going PhD Dissertation.

Fitzsimons, C., & Dorman, P. (2012). 'Swimming in the swamp'- inquiry into accreditation, community development and social change. *The Adult Learner,* 44-58.

Flynn, L. (2004). *These days*. London: Jonathan Cape.

Foley, M. (2011). Leixlip Women's Studies: Were they needed at all? Retrieved January 15, 2014, from http://www.kildare.ie/leixliphistory/archives/2012/03/leixlip_womens_studies_were_t h.html

Fook, J. (2006). Beyond reflective practice: Reworking the 'critical' in critical reflection: Keynote address. *Standing conference on university teaching and research in the education of adults*. University of Leeds. Retrieved June 5, 2013, from http://mcgraw-hill.co.uk/openup/fook&gardner/resources/5.c.pdf

Foucault, M. (1975). *Discipline and punish: The birth of prison*. London : Penguin Books.

Foucault, M. (1980). *Power/knowlege: Selected interviews and other writings*. New York: Pantheon Books.

Foucault, M. (2002). *Archaeology of knowldege*. (A. Sheridan Smith, Trans.) London: Routledge.

Frazer, H. (2007). Promoting social inclusion: The EU dimension. *Administration Journal, 55*(2), 27-60.

Freire, P. (1970). *Pedagogy of the oppressed*. New York: Herder and Herder.

Freire, P. (1972). *Pedagogy of the oppressed*. Hammondsworth: Penguin.

Freire, P. (1994). Foreward. In D. Macedo, *Literacies of power*. Oxford: Westview Press.

Freire, P. (1996a). Paulo Freire - An incredible conversation. International Literacy Institute. Retrieved from http://www.literacy.org/media

Freire, P. (1996b). *Pedagogy of the oppressed*. London: Penguin.

Freire, P. (1997). *Pedagogy of hope*. New York: Continuum.

Freire, P. (1998). *Pedagogy of the heart*. New York: Continuum.

Freynet, P. (1999). Continuing and further education. In P. Federighi (Ed.), *Glossary of adult learning in Europe*. Hamburg: EAEA and UNESCO.

Furlong, A., & Cartmel, F. (2005). *Graduates from disadvantaged families: Early labour market experiences*. Bristol: Joseph Rowntree Foundation/The Policy Press.

Furlong, A., & Cartmel, F. (2006). *Young people and social change*. Buckingham: Open University Press.

Garavan, T., Costine, P., & Heraty, N. (1995). *Training and development in Ireland: Context, policy and practice*. Dublin: Oak Tree Press.

Ghaye, T. (2011). *Teaching and learning through reflective practice* (2nd ed.). Abingdon, Oxon: Routledge.

Gilbert, I. (2011). *Why do I need a teacher when I've got Google.* Abingdon, Oxon: Routledge.

Gilead, T. (2009). Human capital, education and the promotion of social cooperation: A philosophical critique. *Studies in Philosophy and Education, 28,* 555-567.

Giroux, H. (2006). *America on the edge: Henry Giroux on politics, culture, and education.* VA, USA: Palgrave Macmillan.

Gleeson, D., & Knights, D. (2006). Challenging dualism: Public professionalism in 'troubled' times. *Sociology, 40*(2), 277-295.

Gleeson, D., Davies, J., & Wheeler, E. (2005). On the making and taking of professionalism in the further education workplace. *British Journal of Sociology of Education, 26*(4), 445-460.

Gleeson, D., Mardle, G., & McCourt, J. (1980). *Further education or training? A case study in the theory and practice of day-release education.* London: Routledge and Kegan Paul.

Government of Ireland. (1997). *Sharing in Progress: National Anti-Poverty Strategy.* Dublin: Stationery Office.

Gramsci, A. (1971). *Selections form prison notebooks.* London: Lawrence and Wishart.

Grummell, B. (2007). The 'second chance' myth: Equality of opportunity in Irish adult education politicies. *British Journal of Educational Studies, 55*(2), 182-201.

Grummell, B., & Murray, M. (forthcoming). A contested profession: Performativity and professionalism in Irish further education. *Journal of Educational Administration and History.*

Gunnigle, P., Heraty, N., & Morley, N. J. (2006). *Human resource managment in Ireland.* Dublin: Gill and Macmillan.

Hall, B., Clover, D. E., Crowther, J., & Scandrett, E. (Eds.). (2012). *Learning and education for a better world: The role of social movements.* Rotterdam: Sense Publishers.

Hantrais, L. (2000). *Social policy in the European Union.* Houndmills: Macmillan Press.

Hardiman, F. (2012). *Finding a voice: The experience of mature students in a college of further education.* Maynooth: Unpublished Ed.D Dissertation. Retrieved July 1, 2013, from http://eprints.nuim.ie/3908/1/F._Hardiman_Thesis.pdf

Harvey, B. (2012). *Downsizing the community sector: Changes in employment and services in the voluntary and community sector in Ireland.* Dublin: Irish Congress of Trade Unions.

210

Harvey, D. (2005). *A Brief History of Neoliberalism*. Oxford, New York: Oxford University Press.

Hayes, D., Marshall, T., & Turner, A. (Eds.). (2008). *A lecturer's guide to further education*. Buckingham: Open University Press.

Heverin, A. (2000). *The Irish Countrywomen's Association: A history 1910-2000*. Dublin: Wolfhound Press.

Higher Education Authority (HEA). (2008). *National plan for equity of access to Higher Education 2008-2013*. Dublin: National Office of Equity of Access to Higher Education. HEA.

Higher Education Authority. (2012). *Part-time and flexible Higher Education in Ireland: Policy, practice and recommendations for the future* . Dublin: HEA.

hooks, b. (1994). *Teaching to transgress: Education as the practice of freedom*. New York: Routledge.

Horton, M., & Freire, P. (1990). *We make the road by walking: Conversations on education and social change*. (B. Bell, J. Gaventa, & J. Peters, Eds.) Philadelphia: Temple University Press.

Hughes, C., & Tight, M. (1995). The myth of the learning society. *British Journal of Educational Studies, 43*(3), 290-304.

Hunt, A., & Wickham, G. (1994). *Foucault and law*. London: Pluto Press.

Hurley, K. (1998). Towards an inclusive, effective model. *The Adult Learner*.

Hwang, J., & Christensen, C. M. (1992). *Irish Educational Documents Volume 2*. Dublin: Church of Ireland College of Education.

Hyland, A., & Milne, K. (1987). *Irish educational documents* (Vol. 1). Dublin: Church of Ireland College of Education.

Hyland, A., & Milne, K. (1992). *Irish educational documents* (Vol. 2). Dublin: Church of Ireland College of Education.

Illich, I. (1971). *Deschooling society*. London: Calder and Boyars.

Inglis, T. (1997). Empowerment and emancipation. *Adult Education Quarterly, 48*(1), 2-17.

Institute of Public Administration. (2011). *Administration yearbook and diary*. Dublin: IPA.

Irish Managment Institute. (1956). *Education and training for managment*. Dublin : Irish Managment Institute.

James, D., & Biesta, G. (2007). *Improving learning cultures in further education*. London: Routledge.

Jeffers, W. (2012). *Childcare tutors: Profiles, perspectives and professional development needs*. Maynooth: Unpublished M.Litt Thesis. Retrieved December 10, 2013, from http://eprints.nuim.ie/4480/1/W_Jeffers_Thesis_final_200813.pdf

Jephcote, M., Salisbury, J., & Rees, G. (2008). Being a teacher in further education in changing times. *Research in Post-Compulsory Education, 13*(2), 163-173.

Joyce, J. (1968). *Ulysses*. London: Penguin.

Kabbani, R. (1988). *Imperial fictions: Europe's myths of Orient*. London : Pandora.

Kelleher, P., & Whelan, M. (1992). *Dublin communities in action: A study of six projects*. Dublin: CAN and Combat Poverty Agency.

Kenny, I. (1983). *Report of the Commission on Adult Education*. Stationery Office: Dublin.

Keogh, H. (2003). Learning for citizenship in Ireland: The role of adult education. In C. Medel-Anonuevo, & G. Mitchell (Eds.), *Citizenship, democracy and lifelong learning*. Hamburg: UNESCO.

Kincheloe, J. L. (2008). *Knowledge and critical pedagogy: An introduction*. London: Springer.

Kingston, P. (2008, January 8th). Lose the Label. *The Guardian*.

KLEAR. (2014). Retrieved January 15, 2014, from http://kleared.ie/

Klein, N. (2007). *The shock doctrine: The rise of disaster capitalism*. New York: Macmillan.

Knowles, M. S. (1977). *The adult education movement in the United States*. Malabar, FL: Krieger.

Knowles, M. S. (1980). *The modern practice of adult education* (Revised and updated ed.). Chicago: Follett Publishing Company, Association Press.

Knowles, M. S. (1988). *The modern practice of adult education: From pedagogy to andragogy*. Cambridge: Cambridge Book Company.

Kolb, D. A. (1984). *Experiential learning: Experience as the source of learning and development*. Englewood Cliffs, NJ: Prentice Hall.

Kristeva, J. (1986). *The Kristeva reader*. (T. Moi, Ed.) Oxford: Blackwell.

Laffan, B., & Tonra, B. (2005). Europe and the international dimension. In J. Coakley, & M. Gallagher (Eds.), *Politics in the Republic of Ireland* (4th ed., pp. 171-188). London: Routledge.

Lindeman, E. (1926). *The meaning of adult education*. New York: New Republic, Inc.

Longford Women's Link. (2014). Retrieved January 15, 2014, from http://longfordwomenslink.org/about/php

Lynch, K. (1999). *Equality in education*. Dublin : Gill and Macmillan.

Lynch, K. (2010). Carelessness: A hidden doxa of higher education, Arts and Humanities. *Higher Education: An International Journal of Theory, Research and Practice, 9*(1), 54-67.

Lynch, K., & Moran, M. (2006). Markets, schools and the convertibility of economic capital: The complex dynamics of class. *British Journal of Sociology, 27*(2), 221-235.

Lynch, K., Grummell, B., & Devine, D. (2012). *New managerialism in education: Commercialism, carelessness and gender*. Basingstoke: Palgrave Macmillan.

Mager, R. F. (1961). *Preparing Objectives for Programmed Instruction*. California: Fearon Publishers.

Mayo, M. (2012). Learning and education for a bettwer world: The role of social movements. In B. Hall, D. E. Clover, J. Crowther, & E. Scandrett (Eds.), *Learning and education for a bettwer world: The role of social movements*. Rotterdam: Sense Publishers.

McCartney, D. (1999). *UCD : A national idea: The history of University College, Dublin*. Dublin: Gill & Macmillan.

McCormack, D. (2013). *Windows don't happen: An inquiry into writing as reflexive practice in transformative adult learning*. Bristol: Unpublished EdD Thesis.

McDonnell, F. (2003). Adult education in the Republic of Ireland. *Die Magazin Thema Forum, 3*, 48-49.

McGrath, J., & Coles, A. (2011). *Your teacher training handbook*. Harlow: Longman.

Mezirow, J. (1997). Transformative learning: Theory to practice. In P. Cranton (Ed.), *New directions for adult and continuing education: No 74. Transformative learning in action. Insights from practice*. San Francisco: Jossey-Bass.

Mills, C. W. (1959). *The sociological imagination*. Oxford, New York: Oxford University Press.

Moi, T. (1985). *Sexual/textual politics: Feminist literary theory*. London: Routledge.

Moon, J. (1999). *Reflection in learning and professional development*. London: Kogann Page.

Murphy, C. (1983). *Adult Education in Ireland: A Report of a Committee appointed by the Minister for Education*. Dublin: Stationery Office.

Murphy-Lawless, J. (2002). *Fighting back: Women and the impact of drug abuse on families and communities*. Dublin: The Liffey Press.

Murtagh, L. (2009). *The Irish adult education policy process since 1997: Some lessons for the future*. Unpublished doctoral dissertation: Maynooth University. Retrieved June 10, 2013, from http://eprints.nuim.ie/1488

Murtagh, L. (2012). *Response to the SOLAS consultation paper*. Dublin: Unpublished.

National Adult Literacy Agency. (2013). *Annual report: Our year, our work*. Dublin: NALA.

National Adult Literacy Agency. (2014). *Guidelines for good adult literacy*. Retrieved January 15, 2014, from http://www.nala.ie/tutors/top-tips/guidelines/principles

National Council for Educational Awards. (1995). *Towards facilitating awards for adult and continuing education: Discussion document*. Dublin: NCEA.

National Women's Council of Ireland. (1999). *Women: Knowlege is power*. Retrieved January 15, 2014, from http://www.nwci.ie/download/pdf/education.pdf

Nic Ghiolla Phádraig, M. (1995). The power of the Catholic church in the Republic of Ireland. In P. Clancy, S. Drudy, S. Lynch, & L. O'Dowd (Eds.), *Irish society: Sociological perspectives*. Dublin: IPA.

NRDC. (2010). *Study on European terminology in adult learning for a common language and common understanding and monitoring of the sector*. Brussels: European Commission.

O Murchú, M. (1984). *Adult education in Europe: Ireland*. Prague: European Centre for Leisure and Education.

O'Connell, P. J., Clancy, D., & McCoy, S. (2006). *Who went to college in 2004? A national survey of new entrants to higher education*. Dublin: HEA.

O'Connor, T. (1998). The impact of the European Social Fund on the development of initial vocational education and training in Ireland. In A. Trant, D. O'Donnabhain, D. Lawton, & T. O'Connor (Eds.), *The future of the curriculum*. Dublin: CDVEC Curriculum Unit.

OECD. (1997). *Literacy skills for the knowledge society: Further results from the international adult literacy survery*. Paris: OECD.

OECD. (2003). *Beyond rhetoric: Adult learning policies and practices*. Paris: OECD.

OECD. (2006). *Promoting adult learning*. Paris: OECD.

OECD. (2007). *Policy brief: Lifelong learning and human capital*. Paris: OECD.

OECD. (2010). *OECD reviews of vocational education and training leadership for jobs in Ireland*. Paris: OECD.

O'Grady, M. (2012). Other-wise: Researching the habitus changes in women who participate in women's community education in Ireland. In J. Ostrouch-Kaminska, C. Fontanini,

& S. Gaynard (Eds.), *Considering gender in adult learning and academia: (In) Visable act*. Wroclaw: ESREA. Retrieved January 15, 2014, from http://www.waterfordwomenscentre.com/sites/default/files/%27Other%27-%20wise.pdf

Olssen, M. (2008). Understanding the mechanisms of neoliberal control. In A. Fejes, & K. Nicoll (Eds.), *Foucault and lifelong learning*. London: Routledge.

O'Neill, C. (2014). Interview. (M. Thompson, Interviewer) Tall Girl Shorts Film. Retrieved January 15, 2014, from http://www.tallgirlshorts.net/marymary/cathleentext.html

O'Reilly, N. (2013). *AONTAS community education network facilitator's guide*. Dublin: AONTAS. Retrieved January 15, 2014, from http://www.aontas.com/download/pdf/aontas_community_education_networkfacilitator_s_guide.pdf

O'Sullivan, D. (2005). *Cultural politics and Irish education since the 1950's: Policy, paradigms and power*. Dublin: IPA.

Penlington, C. (2008). Dialogue as catalyst for teacher change: A conceptual analysis. *Teaching and Teacher Education, 24*, 1304-1316.

Polkinghorne, D. (1988). *Narrative knowing and the human sciences*. Albany, NY: SUNY Press.

Powell, F., & Geoghegan, M. (2004). *The politics of community development: Reclaiming civil society or reinventing governance?* Dublin: A & A Farmar.

Power, M. J., O'Flynn, M., Courtois, A., & Kennedy, M. (2013). *Neoliberal Capitalism and Education in Ireland*. University of Limerick Department of Sociology Working Paper Series WP2013-03. Limerick: University of Limerick.

Quality & Qualifications Ireland. (2013). Retrieved August 2013, 31, from www.qqi.ie

Richardson, L. (1994). Writing: A method of inquiry. In N. Denzin (Ed.), *Handbook of qualitative research*. Thousand Oaks, CA: Sage.

Roberts, R. (1986). *The story of the people's college*. Dublin: O'Brien Press.

Ross, S., & Webb, N. (2011). *Wasters: The people who squander your taxes on white-elephant projects: International junkets and favours for their mates and how they get away with it*. Dublin: Penguin Ireland.

Ryan, A. (2011). Conscientisation: The art of learning. In A. O'Shea, & M. O'Brien (Eds.), *Pedagogy, oppression and transformation in a 'post-critical' climate*. London: Continuum.

Ryan, A. B. (2001). *Feminist ways of knowing: Towards theorising the person for radical adult education*. Leicester: NIACE.

Ryan, A. B. (2009). *Enough is plenty: Public and private policies for the 21st century.* Winchester: O Books.

Ryan, A., & Walsh, T. (2004). Creating new knowledge. In A. Ryan, & T. Walsh (Eds.), *Unsettling the horses: Interrogating adult education perspectives.* Maynooth: MACE.

Said, E. W. (1995). *Orientalism.* Harmondsworth: Penguin.

Scales, P., Pickering, J., Senior, L., Headley, K., Garner, P., & Boulton, H. (2011). *Continuing professional development in the lifelong learning sector.* Maidenhead: Open University Press.

Schön, D. A. (1996). From technical rationality to reflection in action. In R. Edwards, A. Hanson, & P. Raggett (Eds.), *Adult learners, education and traning1: Boundaries of adult learning.* London: Routledge/Open University.

Schön, D. A. (2003). *The reflective practitioner: How professionals think in action.* Aldershot: Ashgate Publishing.

Schultz, T. (1961). Investment in human capital. *The American Economic Review, 51*(1), 1-17.

Shamir, R. (2008). The age of responsibilitization: On market-embedded morality. *Economy and Society, 37*(1), 1-19.

Shor, I., & Freire, P. (1987). *A pedagogy for liberation, dialogues on transforming education.* Westport: Bergin & Garvey Publishers.

Skillnets. (2014). Retrieved August 31, 2013, from www.skillsnets.ie

Smith, E. (2011). Teaching critical reflection. *Teaching in Higher Education, 16*(2), 211-223.

Smith, J. (2011). Agency and female teachers' career decisions: A life history study of forty women. *Educational Management Administration and Leadership, 39*(1), 7-24.

Snow-Gerono, J. (2005). Professional development in a culture of inquiry: PDS teachers identify the benefits of professional learning communities. *Teaching and Teacher Education, 21*, 241-256.

Somers, J., & Bradford, S. (2006). Discourses of partnership in the community and voluntary sectors in Ireland. *Irish Journal of Sociology, 15*(2), 67-85.

Steinklammer, E. (2012). Learning to resist. In B. Hall, D. E. Clover, J. Crowther, & E. Scandrett (Eds.), *Learning and education for a better world: The role of social movements* (pp. 23-40). Rotterdam: Sense Publishers.

Stokes, D., & Watters, E. (1997). *Ireland vocational education and training: A guide.* Dublin: Leonardo da Vinci.

Sugrue, C., & Gleeson, J. (2004). Signposts and silences: Situating the local within the global. In C. Sugrue (Ed.), *Curriculum and ideology: Irish experiences, international perspectives*. Dublin: Liffey Press.

Teaching Council. (2011). *Further education: General and programme requirements for the accreditation of teacher education qualifications*. Naas, Co Kildare: Teaching Council.

Tett, L. (2006). *Community education, lifelong learning and social inclusion*. Edinburgh: Dunedin Academic Press.

Thomson, J. (2007). Really useful knowlege: Linking theory and practice. In B. Connolly, T. Fleming, D. McCormack, & A. Ryan (Eds.), *Radical learning for liberation 2*. Maynooth: MACE.

Tierney, L., & Clarke, M. (2007). The European qualifications framework: Challenges and implications in the Irish further education and training sector. *European Journal of Vocational Training, 42*(3), 130-142.

Tuschling, A., & Engermann, C. (2006). From education to lifelong learning: The emerging regime of learning in the European Union. *Education Philosophy and Theory, 38*(4), 451-469.

United Nations. (2014). *Short history on the Commission on the Status of Women*. Retrieved January 15, 2014, from http://www.un.org/womenwatch/daw/CSW60YRS/CSWbriefhistory.pdf

Van Woerkom, M. (2010). Critical reflection as rationalistic ideal. *Adult Education Quarterly, 60*(4), 339-356.

Vescio, V., Ross, D., & Adams, A. (2008). A review of research on the impact of professional learning communties on teaching practice and student learning. *Teaching and Teacher Education, 24*, 80-91.

Walters, S., Borg, C., Mayo, P., & Foley, G. (2004). Economics, politics and adult education. In G. Foley (Ed.), *Dimensions of adult learning: Adult education and training in a global era*. Maidenhead: Open University Press.

Waterford Institute of Technology. (2014). Retrieved August 31, 2013, from www.wit.ie

Watson, D., McCoy, S., & Gorby, S. (2006). *The post leaving certificate sector in Ireland: A multivariate analysis of educational and employment outcomes*. Dublin: ESRI and Department of Education and Science.

Wenger, E. (1998). *Communties of practice: Learning, meaning and identity*. Cambridge: Cambridge University Press.

Wheelehan, L. (2009). The limits of competency-based training and the implications for work. In J. Field, J. Gallagher, & R. Ingram (Eds.), *Researching transitions in lifelong learning*. London: Routledge.

White, T. (2001). *Investing in people: Higher education in Ireland from 1960 to 2000*. Dublin : IPA.

Wilson, A. (2010). *Knowledge power: Interdisciplinary education for a complex world*. London: Routledge.

World Bank. (2003). *Lifelong learning in the global knowledge economy*. Washington: The World Bank.

Young, I. M. (2000). *Inclusion and democracy*. Oxford: Oxford University Press.

Youth Forum Jeunesse. (2008). *Annexes to the draft policy paper on early school leaving*. Rotterdam: General Assembly.

Zappone, K. (1991). *The hope for wholeness: A spirituality for feminists*. Mystic, CT: Twenty-third Publications.